When we listen to music, what exactly ⟨ hear? How do we come to hear in new ⟨ In *The Mind behind the Musical Ear,* Jeanne Bamberger focuses on the earliest stages in the development of musical cognition. Beginning with children's invention of original rhythm notations, she follows eight-year-old Jeff as he reconstructs and invents descriptions of simple melodies such as "Hot Cross Buns" and "Twinkle, Twinkle, Little Star." In a running commentary on Jeff's discoveries and a series of dialogues between herself and two imaginary college students who take different approaches to music, Bamberger reflects on the thinking strategies that guide Jeff at various moments in his musical development. This novel approach allows the reader to experience the discovery process along with Jeff and the two students as they sort out fundamental and commonly held assumptions about music.

By emphasizing the idea that each "hearing" of musical composition is a "performance," one among many possible hearings, Bamberger suggests that there are different ways of constructing meaning and that the processes of perception and conceptualization are reciprocal. Over time, Jeff gains the capacity to make multiple hearings and descriptions of the same piece, each of which reflects his cumulating understanding of its musical structure and meaning. One of the book's central themes, played out in the student dialogues, is that knowing *how*—to sing a melody, for example, or clap a rhythm, or recognize a tune—may be quite different from knowing *about*, being able to state what it is that one knows. Both are powerful kinds of knowledge-in-action, and deep learning involves the development of a close, meaningful relationship between them. As Bamberger shows, this meaning-making as one learns to move between doing and description is a critical factor for learning in other cognitive domains as well.

For educators and cognitive scientists this book has broad implications. It will inspire teachers and researchers to think about the conventions they use in making sense of everyday materials —to become aware of the "windows" that shape their world—and to develop a corresponding sensitivity to the various ways in which children may see these materials. Recognizing the potential in what and how children already know may be critical in helping them succeed in school.

Jeanne Bamberger is Professor of Music at the Massachusetts Institute of Technology.

The Mind behind the
Musical Ear

JEANNE BAMBERGER

The Mind behind the Musical Ear

HOW CHILDREN DEVELOP
MUSICAL INTELLIGENCE

HARVARD UNIVERSITY PRESS

CAMBRIDGE, MASSACHUSETTS

LONDON, ENGLAND

1991

The poem "Simples" from *Collected Poems* by James Joyce, coypright 1918 by
B. W. Huebsch, Inc.; 1927, 1936 by James Joyce; 1946 by Nora Joyce, is reprinted
by permission of the publisher, Viking Penguin, a division of Penguin Books U.S.A.
Inc., and by permission of The Society of Authors as the literary representative of
the Estate of James Joyce.

This book is printed on acid-free paper, and its binding materials have been chosen
for strength and durability.

LIBRARY OF CONGRESS CATALOGING-IN-PUBLICATION DATA
Bamberger, Jeanne Shapiro.
  The mind behind the musical ear : how children develop musical
  intelligence / Jeanne Bamberger.
      p. cm.
  Includes bibliographical references (p.) and index.
  ISBN 0-674-57607-1 (acid-free paper)
    1. Music—Psychology. 2. Musical ability. I. Title.
ML3838.B35 1991
780'.1'9—dc20
                                                    90-24749
                                                       CIP
                                                       MN

For Chip and Josh

CONTENTS

Conclusion: Educational Implications   269

ACKNOWLEDGMENTS

SINCE THE beginnings of this book date back some twenty years, I can only mention here a few of the many people who have contributed to its long evolution. I am grateful to Don Schön for his tough but appreciative readings of many versions of the manuscript, for continuing to believe that there was a large design somewhere in the midst of all the detail, and for helping me to find it. Mimi Sinclair's careful readings were unique and indispensable; her gentle expertise as Piagetian and musician helped me to keep the relationships between those two domains both clear and honest. And I am grateful to Howard Gardner for his continuing belief in my ideas despite our friendly disagreements about what they are. Lucy Horwitz buoyed me up with her excitement over some of the ideas that I was afraid no one but I could believe in.

Among others who read versions of the manuscript, I am grateful to Martin Brody and Howard Gruber for their detailed and very useful criticism, and to Dan Bar-On, who suggested that the book was really about how Met and Mot learned. Eleanor Duckworth, who made sure I always stayed close to the phenomena, helped me especially to appreciate the importance of "giving a kid reason."

I also wish to thank the cadre of students whose contributions have made their way into nearly every corner of the book: Carolyn Hildebrandt, who helped me understand the children's drawings of rhythms;

Eugene Buder, who collected the rhythm drawings of the four-year-olds; Gary Greenberg, who provided a careful analysis of children building tunes with the Montessori bells; and especially the late Don Johnstone, who taught me, in his wisdom, to see and to pay attention to the expressive relations between rhythmic grouping and accent. Rodrigo Madanes, almost at the last minute, took a hard look at Jeff's work and helped me to see it in a new way; and Armando Hernandez continues to make the Logo Music System responsive to even my most outrageous demands.

But the list of contributors would hardly be complete without mentioning all the children who have been participants over the years in experimental music classes and in individual or group experimental task situations, along with the teachers of these children, without whose cooperation the whole enterprise would have quickly faltered. And I must especially thank Jeff, who put up with me over all those months and from whom I learned much more than he could possibly have learned from me.

Finally, I am grateful to the Spencer Foundation, and to Tom James in particular, for supporting me in the early phases of my work, and to the John Simon Guggenheim Foundation for supporting me during the year in which I was able actually to bring it all together.

The Mind behind the
Musical Ear

Introduction: The Players

THIS BOOK is the result of my continuing efforts to understand the everyday knowledge with which we make sense of the common music of our culture and how this knowledge develops in both ordinary and extraordinary ways. The themes that run through the book knit together concerns that are often associated with self-contained disciplines: musical performance, music theory, cognitive development, philosophy, and education. If they have become a single network for me, it is probably because the questions that I have found the most compelling characteristically emerge (unlike more traditional research questions) in the course of my everyday work with students in the classroom, or in working on a composition in preparation for teaching or performing it. Once I recognize an issue, and when I find it impossible to turn a question or puzzle aside, it is then that I am led to the design of more formal experimental situations. But saying that suggests other puzzles as well: for instance, what attracts my attention to these "happenings" in the first place? How do they evolve into an experimental design? What is the character of these designs? In turn, what do I take as evidence for a resolution of these puzzles or answers to my compelling questions?

Perhaps the simplest but most correct answer to the first of these questions is to be found in my eclectic background and experience: I am a performing musician with a penchant for (and some training in) philosophy and psychology, and I have had formal training in music theory together with many years of teaching it. These activities have been accompanied by a collection of questions that have haunted me from childhood (Why do people listen to music, anyway? Why do people *not* listen to the music I care most about? What is it that I *know* when I have learned how to play a Beethoven piano sonata or a Chopin ballade?). This eclectic mix of interests has resulted in my attraction to moments in which they all converge. More specifically, when the qualities of an ordinary event intersect this network of interests in an unexpected way, often creating conflict or tension, these moments are somehow marked for attention.

As a result, the design of experiments as well as the research questions that motivate them have taken on particular characteristics. In contrast to more traditional methodology associated with objective, controlled, often artificially contrived experimental situations, my experimental designs include rather open-ended task situations that are often closely related to the musical activities that generated the puzzles in the first place. Further, the tasks are rich in possibilities for the active participation of subjects and sensitive interventions by the researchers. The carefully recorded ongoing work of subjects becomes, then, the material for study and analysis. Interestingly, there is rarely a question of whether a subject can succeed in completing a certain task, because almost all can; what is important, rather, are the particular characteristics of a participant's work. For instance, in observing an individual constructing or reconstructing a melody, I am concerned with the decisions made along the way, the strategies used, the shifts in focus, including shifts in what the participant may be seeing as the problem to be solved, as well as the final product. In turn, although analysis of a subject's work often leads to insight, it just as often spawns new surprises and new questions.

Throughout my work, teaching, learning, and research are closely intertwined: research questions arise in the course of teaching; subjects are learning as they participate in the experimental task situations; and in noticing a puzzling response, I will often make an on-the-spot miniexperiment to test a hunch about how the participant may be representing the situation to herself. And the results of experiments are taken back into the classroom to inform, perhaps transform, how and what I am teaching there.

Finally, in working with participants in task situations I make a critical beginning assumption, namely that the participant in these tasks is somehow making sense in his or her actions, decisions, or descriptions, and it is my job to probe for and find the sense made. This is particularly important when a participant's observed behavior seems most anomalous with respect to my own deeply embedded assumptions. Barbara McClintock, a biologist, puts it this way in describing her observations of cells: "Anything . . . even if it doesn't make much sense, it'll be there . . . So if the material tells you, 'It may be this,' allow that. Don't turn it aside and call it an exception, an aberration, a contaminant . . . That's what's happened all the way along the line with so many good clues" (quoted in Keller 1983, p. 179).

The book is divided into three parts. Preceding these is a Prologue in which I suggest that knowing *how* may be different from knowing *about*. I ask the reader to ponder what might contribute to differing "hearings" of the same piece, and in doing so, I illustrate what will be a central theme of the book, namely, the notion that a "hearing" is itself a performance, an active process of making meaning.

In Part I my concern with different hearings focuses on rhythm, as seen through children's drawings of simple rhythms. From the differences found in the drawings, I derive a general distinction between figural and metric/formal hearings of rhythms. Interestingly, those whose drawings focus on one aspect of a rhythm find it difficult if not impossible to make sense of drawings that focus on a different aspect of the same rhythm. It is this finding that leads me to argue for the importance of *multiple hearings*.

Parts II and III are concerned with melody and specifically with tune-building. These studies focus on the development of one eight-year-old child, Jeff, with whom I worked on tune-building tasks over a period of six months. I begin with Jeff's initial project, in which he uses a computer as the medium for constructing tunes, and move on to his initial constructions and notations of tunes using the Montessori bells. Part III traces Jeff's learning and development as his construction strategies change and with them his invention of a whole series of evolving notations. Through Jeff's work I am able to see aspects of development that usually remain hidden in one-time experimental situations—for example, to observe in detail and *in situ* the disequilibrium of transition and the nature of subsequent transformations. As a result I am also able to account for what otherwise might appear to be abrupt changes from one developmental stage to another. And most important, I argue that the changing mental organizing structures that guide hearings, constructions, and descriptions at various ages and stages of musical development do not constitute a unidirectional progression in which earlier mental structures are replaced by later ones. Rather, foci of attention among relevant aspects of musical structure shift but also cumulatively build on one another. I conclude that the goal of musical development is to have access to multiple dimensions of musical structure, to be able to coordinate these dimensions, and most important, to be able to choose selectively among them, to change focus at will.

Central to Jeff's development are our mutual efforts to make sense of and to make explicit what he knows how to do already. Using this knowledge, I help Jeff confront confusions associated with changes in his inner understanding so that he can expand and elaborate his initial intuitions. Because I feel that this process is fundamental to significant learning, I return in the final chapter to the classroom: looking back and drawing on the implications of the rhythm studies and Jeff's work, I make some proposals for teaching and learning that apply not only to music but to education in other domains as well.

The book proceeds in four different modes. The first is largely descriptive: I describe the setting in which one or more children worked, what motivated the task, and the problem as it was set; I then provide a fine-grained narrative account of the children's actions, decisions, confusions, and productions—a drawing, the construction of a tune, or instructions for playing the tune. Second, analysis and discussion of these events take the form of a dialogue between two imaginary college students and myself. Third, looking back at the dialogue, I often make comments on it. And fourth, I pause from time to time to make a didactic digression about specific musical aspects of the material the children are working with. These didactic interludes may clarify work the children have already done, or they may prepare the reader for what is to come. Each of these formats contributes another layer of interpretation, all of them together making up a cumulatively developing picture of the data.

Since I see the dialogues as a central part of the book, a word about why I have chosen this format is in order. I initially adopted the dialogue format to address a difficult problem to which I could find no other solution. It is this: a hearing, like a momentary "seeing," is most often experienced all-at-once and as something immutable. How, then, could I help listeners/readers become aware that their hearing of even a simple rhythm might be only one *possible* way of organizing the material; and how could I help them to participate in, to experience, a hearing that differed from their own? Moreover, to make a hearing different from one's own often requires a fundamental restructuring of the material—

for example, regrouping, making new boundaries, giving priority to different features, perhaps even liberating features that were previously left unnoticed, even inaccessible. And to tell a reader about the possibilities of such restructuring by, for instance, naming features or relations that are not yet included in his or her hearing of a piece almost necessarily fails because these names will refer to entities that have no referents within the music as perceived. Finally, I was also aware that restructuring one's hearing is risky—it is disorienting, queasy, confusing; it attacks the very roots of previous coherence.

It seemed, then, that the only way to help readers with what was to be a crucial aspect in understanding developmental changes among my subjects was to help them live through these developmental processes themselves. To do so, I created two imaginary college students whom I thought of as typical of those students in my classes at MIT who make specifically contrasting hearings of simple rhythms. One, whom I call Met, was so named because he heard rhythms *met*rically; the other, whom I call Mot, gained her name because she heard rhythms *mot*ivically (or what I call more generally a figural hearing). In the first dialogue I ask the reader to follow as I encourage Mot and Met to confront the differences in their respective hearings. Through this process, the two students eventually succeed in making sense of each other's hearings, but only after struggling with and revealing some of the fundamental assumptions that each of them holds. And since my experience strongly suggests that one or the other of these hearings is that of the reader as well, it is my hope that in following these conversations, the reader too will come to hear in a new way. However, I am also quite aware that to do so may require just as much work on the part of the reader as it does for Met and Mot. For, while a hearing may seem instantaneous, ineluctable, it is, in fact, a construction—an active play between the tacit, often unintended mental activities that we bring to bear, and the *yet to be organized stuff out there*. What we hear depends on what we are able to think of to hear—even though we are quite unaware that thinking is going on at all.

In writing the dialogues I suspect I have been influenced by my reading of Galileo's *Dialogues on Two New Sciences*. Quite aware that his "new sciences" were in serious conflict with the beliefs of the time, Galileo created the dialogues with his two students to help readers live through the messy, groping evolution of these new ideas. In contrast to most publications of new discoveries, where the reader is presented only with clean, elegant results, as if they arrived full-blown from the head of their maker, Galileo does not obscure the work, the confusions, the roads taken that seemed to lead nowhere; and most of all he engages his students' participation (and through them, the reader's) in the design of questions, problems, and experimental situations. By letting readers in on the process, Galileo also helps them through the disequilibrium that often accompanies such fundamental conceptual restructuring. While the dialogues with my two imaginary students are hardly of the same scope or significance, I, like Galileo, reenact through these conversations the rocky routes that we traveled and that the reader is asked to travel along with us.

The dialogues serve one more function: through the evolving course of Met and Mot's conversations and their confrontations with each other, they also learn, and as they do so, they gradually become participants in helping me understand the surprises and puzzles in the work of others. Thus, as readers follow the dialogues, they are also following the development of a research methodology as it is embodied by the two students in learning how to practice it. As a result, I am also able to use the conversations with Met and Mot as a vehicle for working out some of the more difficult questions raised by the data, for making proposals concerning answers, and for speculating on their broader implications. Of these questions, the most central is: What are the circumstances that generate fundamental ontological shifts associated with perceptual/conceptual restructuring—how do we ever come to see/hear in a new way? This is the question that remains the unifying thread throughout the book.

Prologue: The Themes

I BEGIN with a conversation that will most likely sound familiar to many readers, and yet its very familiarity continues to puzzle me. It starts with a person's casual remark that, like most people, she enjoys listening to music and can make sense of most of what she hears. Upon questioning, she agrees that she can clap simple rhythms, recognize tunes she has heard before, even sing or whistle at least some of them. But then, in quick response to the other's quizzical glance, she hastens to add: "But of course, I don't know anything about music."

These remarks are so familiar that, like much that is commonplace, the puzzles in them pass by unnoticed. But if for some reason they catch our attention and we turn back to look at them, we may be surprised by what we see. Wittgenstein puts it like this: "The aspects of things that are most important for us are hidden because of their simplicity and familiarity. (One is unable to notice something—because it is always before one's eyes.) The real foundations of his enquiry do not strike a man at all. Unless *that* fact has at some time struck him.—And this means: we fail to be struck by what, once seen, is most striking and most powerful" (Wittgenstein 1953, p. 50).

The puzzle that catches my attention in the conversation is this: How can a person say that she can remember, enjoy, sing, and understand the music she hears every day and still say that she "doesn't know anything about music"? Is it the difference between knowing *how* to do something

7

in contrast to knowing *about* it? Or perhaps the distinction isn't in the "knowing" at all, but in the "it"—the music itself. Could "music" stand for two different kinds of things—one kind that you sing, dance to, recognize, and enjoy; and another kind that you "know about"? Or could it be both: when you "know about music," the music itself changes?

The conversation is important because it raises in a quite natural way some of the fundamental questions of the book: What do we mean by "knowledge"? Or, more specifically, what does it mean to know, to have, or to use musical knowledge? And even if we could come to some agreement about that, we are quickly led on to other questions. How does musical knowledge develop? What, for instance, is the difference between what you and I hear in listening to the same piece of music? Why do even professional musicians so often disagree in their "interpretations" of the same piece of music? Or, as just suggested, can we even talk about the "same piece of music"?

Musicians are more apt to talk to one another about their "hearings" of a piece rather than about knowledge. In rehearsing a string quartet, for instance, the violist might say to the cellist, "How do you hear that last passage?" And the cellist might answer, "Well, the second phrase begins on the downbeat of bar 19." To which the violist might answer, "No wonder we aren't together; I hear it beginning with an upbeat starting in the middle of the previous bar." Or among music theorists you might hear one saying of another's analysis of a piece, "Your hearing just doesn't make sense to me." What, then, is meant by a "hearing," and how can we characterize the differences among them? Or, even better, how can we try to elicit and account for the usually tacit underlying assumptions that give rise to these differences?

In what follows, I shall try to do just that. However, my evidence for such hearings consists of descriptions of them. And this raises a very knotty problem: since a hearing is by its nature a necessarily private, internal experience, an out-loud description can provide only impoverished clues to it. Further, as we shall see, descriptions are influenced in interesting and often very specific ways by the terms—the "units of description"—that the hearer has available. We need to ask, then, what the relations are—often reciprocal relations since terms also influence hearings—between these units of description and what I will call the hearer's "units of perception." And since a hearing is, perhaps paradoxically, a silent affair, how can anyone know? In any case, I shall argue that a hearing is a performance; that is, what the hearer seems simply to find in the music is actually a process of perceptual problem solving—an active process of sense-making something like that evoked by the comments of the painter Ben Shahn: "So one must say that painting is both creative and responsive. It is an intimately communicative affair between the painter and his painting, a conversation back and forth, the painting telling the painter even as it receives its shape and form" (1957, p. 49). Like a painting, a hearing, too, is both creative and responsive—a conversation back and forth between the music, as material, and the hearer as he or she shapes its meaning and form in some particular way.

MULTIPLE HEARINGS, ORGANIZING CONSTRAINTS, AND "SIMPLES"

Accounting for the similarities as well as the differences among the hearings we make is a central focus of this book. For example, if a hearing is indeed a process of instant perceptual problem solving, we need to ask, what are the sorts of processes that variously guide this perceptual problem solving? Putting the question this way, I obviously intend to suggest that what we casually call "the mind" is always actively engaged in *organizing* incoming sensory material. And I want also to suggest that this is a generative process—that we are actively doing this organizing in real time as the sound/time phenomena are occurring "out there."

But in saying that, I do not at all want to suggest that by "organizing" I mean some kind of "decoding" process, as if the incoming material has already been segmented, and these entities labeled or otherwise symbolically "encoded." Indeed, I will emphasize throughout the book that it is exactly because sound/time phenomena do not come already structured, but rather hold the *potential* for being structured, that different hearings are possible. As Isaac Rosenfield says, "We perceive the world without labels, and we can label it only when we have decided how its features should be organized" (1989, p. 187). However, I find the word "decided" somewhat problematic here, since even that suggests a more overtly intentional action than I mean to imply with the notion of instant perceptual problem solving. In fact, I suspect that the processes through which we actively organize incoming pitch-time phenomena are closely linked with the very basic, sentient organizing of our bodies as we move through space and time—gestural direction (up-down; right-left), stance, sequences of periodic movements (breathing, sucking, walking), equilibrium, as well as vectors of tension and relaxation. (For an intriguing discussion of these bodily modes and vectors and their role in artistic activity, see Gardner 1973, pp. 98–119; for more on gesture, posture, and changes of position as they play a role in memory, see Bartlett 1932 and Lashley 1951.) Indeed, I will argue that the *sequences of motions* that we practice and internalize in the process of carrying out familiar activities—most particularly sequences of actions that we internalize in learning to perform a piece on an instrument, sequences that we both *make and follow* with each new performance—that these action-paths become our most intimate ways of knowing that piece. I call these internalized action-paths "felt paths," and I will have much more to say about them.

Having proposed this rather general scenario, I have prepared the way for the following question: If we are always actively organizing incoming phenomena as they occur in time, what might be the immediately functioning *constraints* on these generative organizing processes; and how might they evolve, develop, and change? Or putting it another way, in our creative and responsive "conversations back and forth"* with phenomena out there, what are the momentary constraints that shape our instant perceptual problem solving and thus our momentary potential for making coherence and meaning in particular ways?

It seems fairly obvious that the development of constraints on the organizing of incoming musical phenomena must be strongly influenced by our experience with the common music all around us. In particular, I suggest that the evolution of those generative processes that result in the hearings we make is in some fundamental way influenced by our exposure to a relatively small set of musical relationships shared by much of the ordinary music of our culture. That is, the organizing constraints that guide our hearings develop quite naturally through the recurring experience of pitch-time relations that are common to and instantiated in much of the music that is around us every day. Thus, in constructing a hearing, we actively *seek out these relations, constructing them anew as features that we expect to find in our shaping of musical coherence.* I propose, moreover, that our active and generative organizing constraints initially limit us to seeking out just these familiar pitch-time relations. But through learning and experience, these organizing constraints are gradually elaborated and developed, and the particular course and scope of that development help to account for the differences in the hearings that individuals choose to or are able to make.

---

* Although I borrow the term "conversation" from Shahn's remarks, and have used it in a similar way elsewhere (see Bamberger and Schön 1990), I do so now with some hesitation because I feel that the term may be understood more literally than I (or I think Shahn) intended. That is, readers may too easily, and without consciously intending to do so, take these "conversations" to be mediated by language, "inner language," or at least already fixed in some symbolic form. I believe that this is exactly *not* the case.

I call these common pitch-time relations "simples," and I use the term in two senses:

1. To refer to simple tunes and rhythms—those that we all sang or clapped as children. Of these, "Twinkle Twinkle Little Star" will be the prototypical example. These actual tunes and rhythms that most of us learned in the natural course of growing up I will call the *Simples* of our culture.

2. To refer to the small set of recurring pitch-time relations that, through cultural evolution, have come to be shared by all of our common folk and pop tunes, and by and large by all of the art music from at least Bach to Brahms. These I will call *structural simples*.

The two come together in that structural simples are expressed in the most clear and unadorned fashion by our familiar Simples. Thus I argue that structural simples, as they are embodied by and most directly experienced in the Simples of our culture, form the generative scaffolding for making meaning and for instant perceptual problem solving as we construct coherence in the common music around us. But, what may be more surprising, I will argue that these same structural simples form the generative basis for our understanding of large, complex compositions as well; moreover, they have also formed an underlying base for the creative work of composers who have designed these large, complex pieces.

For those readers with little or no formal musical training, I can at this point only hint at what these structural simples might be, since much of the work of the book lies in giving them experiential and functional meaning. Consider, for example, the regular marking off of time that is generated by the temporal relations among events in all of these common tunes—the underlying pulse that you tap your foot to, "keep time to," in singing or listening to them. And consider the grouping together of these regularly recurring "beats" to form slower beats and their proportional divisions as these form faster beats. This hierarchy of periodicities, which we all experience even if we cannot say so, is an instance of a structural simple that we take for granted as a basis for coherence because it is shared by all the common music of our culture. I distinguish this *metric simple* from what I call *figural simples*. Figural simples are those shared pitch-time relations that serve to group together rhythmic and melodic events so as to form what we call phrases or figures. Within our familiar Simples, phrases are characterized by their *temporal symmetry or "balance."* Moreover, in the progression from one phrase to the next, there is usually a continuing swing between *stability and tension*—one phrase moving toward tension, the next moving toward the resolution of this tension. And this alternation between stability and tension is also generated within metric simples—this is heard as the regular alternation between strong and weak beats. It is interesting to note that all of these structural simples have direct analogues with the sentient organizing of body feelings and movements to which I referred earlier—for instance, periodicities, equilibrium, vectors of tension and relaxation.

Because we have learned to seek out and reconstruct these structural simples as basic features, even as norms, in making the sense we seem just to find in "sensible tunes," composers for the last two hundred years or so have been able to assume these simples as culturally shared norms. And as such, composers generate them in new guise over and over again, but they also use them as a common base from which to deviate. When they do, they can assume that these "anomalies"—for instance, a disruption of the metric hierarchy, or asymmetrical phrase structure and often with it a prolongation of tension—will be noticed, heard as interesting, complex. And just for that reason, toying with these simples as composers do in developing a motive or elaborating a phrase is a way of creating those special affective moments in the unfolding of a piece.

Thus structural simples serve two functions for both the listener and the composer in their work of making meaning through the unfolding of complex works: on one hand, structural simples serve to establish a familiar musical universe—they are "norms" generated in and shared by the music that pervades our musical culture; on the other, structural simples provide the constraints, the limits, within which composers develop the unique complexity of a particular work. Composers such as Beethoven, then, do not discard familiar structural simples, replacing them with other components. Rather, complexity, as I am using the term, is created as a *function* of these structural simples: they serve as a basis for elaboration, and their implications, what we expect to happen, may be extended, delayed, or led astray.* (For more on the role of these structural norms, see Meyer 1973; Narmour 1977; Lerdahl and Jackendoff 1983; Gjerdingen 1988.)

---

* To characterize these structural simples is also to characterize a "style," here the style often referred to as that of the "common practice period." As we move beyond Brahms to the music of the twentieth century, we find that composers are indeed *replacing* many, but not all, of the structural simples to which I am referring. Although some may view the result as the development of greater musical complexity, this is not necessarily so. Moreover, I am certainly not speaking here of complexity in this sense of stylistic change. It is probably the case, however, that as composers generate complexity still within the norms of a particular style, they may also contribute to the erosion of the norms themselves.

This book and the work of those who participate in the experimental tasks are focused almost entirely on Simples and on the structural simples that are embodied by them. I have limited my focus in this way because I believe that gaining insight into the nature of the pitch-time relations that generate structural simples, together with gaining insight into the surprisingly complex mental organizing through which we learn to make sense of these structures, are critical steps in understanding how we come to make sense of musical complexity as well. There is, then, a potentially interesting relationship between the development and elaboration of our mental organizing constraints on one hand, and on the other, the development and elaboration of structural simples as these occur within complex compositions. The relationship suggests that the degree to which we are able to make sense of and appreciate the unfolding of complex works may be intimately intertwined with the development of our active organizing constraints as these guide the construction of our seemingly spontaneous hearings. Indeed, these processes of developing and elaborating our networks of organizing constraints may be a significant factor in helping to account for differences in the hearings we make and also for our momentary value judgments about the music we hear. And at least in some cases, we may be able to characterize the bases for these differences as learning to go beyond structural simples.

MUSICAL DEVELOPMENT

This brings me to a theme that is, of course, central to the working out of this book, namely the evolving course of musical development. But I must again alert the reader to my focus on Simples, and with it a concern only for the development of organizing constraints that might be at work in making hearings of these Simples. I will have very little to say about the musical development that occurs within the unfolding of complex compositions, or the going beyond structural simples that its appreciation entails; that must be the story of another book.

In the chapters that follow, I will argue and show evidence to suggest that specific changes in subjects' organizing constraints occur even in the earliest phases of musical development. Moreover, in some ways these changes follow closely what Piaget, Vygotsky, and others describe as conceptual change in their characterization of "stages of development." However, unlike most of Piaget's interpreters (but perhaps more like Piaget himself), I argue that while the sense of movement from one "stage" to another is certainly important, the sense of "progress" in this movement may be less so. That is, I will argue that the characteristics of stages that typically develop later are not unequivocally better: we must ask, "better for what?" This is a question that Piaget answers only implicitly. Deriving his criteria primarily from capacities he associates with scientific inquiry, he unequivocally equates a later stage of development with more fully elaborated capacities for *symbolic abstraction*. These include, for example, the mental construction and internalization of fixed reference structures in relation to which particular properties of phenomena can be differentiated, measured, and classified, these classifications, in turn, remaining stable in the face of changing context, or, as Piaget says, "in spite of the route traveled."

In contrast to this focus and its prevailing view of development, I argue that, at least with respect to musical development, active organizing constraints associated with an earlier stage of development need not be simply *discarded,* to be replaced by or even absorbed into a later one. If we look on development as a *cumulative* process rather than one of displacement, this cumulative process can be a source for developing our capacities to make multiple hearings of the "same" musical material as we shift our focus from one kind of relationship to another. Indeed, I will show that if we are able to give equal importance both to organizing constraints that are typical of those that shape hearings during the earliest stages of development and to those constraints that seem to develop later, we are then able to shift our focus of attention among different but still legitimate, specifiable, and potentially significant features of musical phenomena. Moreover, at best this capacity to shift focus can be coupled with the freedom to choose among these various aspects through selective attention, to coordinate them, and to know when and why to choose one over another.

In following Jeff's work, for instance, we will see him developing the capacity to make multiple views and multiple hearings. He initially organizes incoming sensory phenomena around the changing musical situations or contexts in which these momentary experiences occur (what I call his figural strategies for representing* a rhythm or tune to himself). Later on, these figural constraints as well as the subsequent development

---

*The term "representation" has many of the same entangling alliances that give me pause in using the term "conversation." That is, both seem to imply something that is external, mutually shared, and scrutinizable, and particularly something that is already encoded in some symbolic form. I have used "representation" throughout the book; I hope the reader will understand that I mean by such locutions as "strategies of representing a rhythm or tune to himself" the invisible, inner, active processes that guide the ongoing making of meaning—what I have come to call an individual's current network of organizing constraints.

of less context-dependent formal constraints are both available to him for organizing material, depending on what he wants to do and on the task at hand. Indeed, I have argued elsewhere that creative expertise in a domain may, to an important extent, derive from the continuing development of, and the continuing tensions between, figural and formal modes of organizing present phenomena—what Don Schön and I have called the "figural/formal transaction" (1979).

SYMBOLIC CONVENTIONS

There is yet another theme that will run throughout the book: I will propose that symbolic conventions associated with a domain may strongly influence the course of learning and development. I will show, for example, that in the long history through which standard music notation (SMN) developed, as in all efforts to externalize knowledge in some publicly accessible form, the end result succeeds in implicitly selecting for attention, and implicitly bounding by naming, particular elements and relations while ignoring others. And while the aspects of musical relations captured by SMN certainly include information that is *necessary* as minimal instructions for performing a piece, as well as information necessary to richer descriptions and to the development of more complete and complex theoretical frameworks, SMN is not *sufficient* to either performance or theory-making.

This raises a critical question concerning the relations between the descriptive conventions that are taught and learned primarily through formal instruction, and the development of organizing constraints initially associated with structural simples—those that seem to be achieved, like language, without any formal instruction. These differences become important because notations-in-use by a community of professionals tend to gain a privileged status. I will argue that as units of description, the notations help to shape their users' internalized, active organizing constraints—their ways of segmenting a given universe even in what seems to be immediate apprehension, carving out just which kinds of objects and relations are given legitimacy, even credence. Thus, units of description as embodied by notations-in-use strongly influence units of perception, the ontology as well as the epistemology associated with expertise in a domain—the "things" or even the "natural kinds" that are taken to exist.

Along with this go our received notions of "knowledge" in a domain. Indeed, it is the influence of our learned notations-in-use on what we take to be "knowledge" that may help to account for the conversation with which I began these comments: knowing how is often differentiated from knowing about to the extent that we can *talk about* what it is we know how to do. And knowing how to talk about what we know how to do in the privileged terms of a domain is often equated with "knowledge" in that domain.

But what may be at least equally important are the correspondences and the lack of correspondences between the theory of a domain as expressed in its privileged languages and the actual operative know-how, the *practice,* of experts—what they know how to *do,* in contrast to what they know how to *say.* This will be a recurring issue throughout the book, raising the question I asked at the outset: Is it possible that "music" can stand for two different kinds of things—one kind that you sing, dance to, play, recognize, and enjoy; and another kind that you "know about"? Or could it be both: when you "know about music," the music itself changes?

But we have spent enough time in the world of high abstraction. If the reader is, like me, a practical person, he or she will agree with William James (1956, p. 69) when he says: "When weary of the concrete clash and dust and pettiness, [the practical man] will refresh himself by a bath in the eternal springs, or fortify himself by a look at the immutable natures. But he will only be a visitor, not a dweller in the region; when tired of the gray monotony of her problems and insipid spaciousness of her results, he will always escape gleefully into the teeming and dramatic richness of the concrete world."

PART I

Rhythm

CHAPTER 1

Children's Drawings of
Simple Rhythms

I BEGIN these studies of rhythm with a description of a fourth grade music class at the Happy Hollow School in Wayland, Massachusetts. The participants are a group of 25 eight- and nine-year-olds, and the material with which they are engaged is a very simple rhythm that one of the children has invented. The rhythm is sparse, indeed, appearing at first to be of little musical interest. And yet the drawings the children make of their rhythm reveal issues that are strikingly similar to those that emerge when I ask students in my college classes to describe their hearings of a complex work such as a movement from a Beethoven piano sonata (see Bamberger 1978).

In both situations, for example, we find that participants focus on different but *possible* and legitimate features of the material—those that contribute to the coherence that each student has made. Interestingly, in both situations participants initially defend their hearings as if defending an underlying "belief system." But as each description reveals multiple possible faces of the music itself, students in both college and elementary school classes are encouraged to shift their focus to differing features and relations—those which, at least in verbal or graphic translation, capture students' differing experiences of the musical material.

Moreover, there are important similarities among the specific kinds of differences that occur among hearings despite the two seemingly quite different situations. For example, there is the issue of boundaries—

19

where do "parts" begin and end? In listening to a Beethoven sonata movement, for instance, several students in one college class agreed that the piece had three parts; but when they were asked to show where the three parts were, it turned out that the boundaries they heard, and thus the three parts themselves, were entirely different. Similarly, in making their drawings of the rhythm, the children also describe different boundaries. Although the scope of "parts" in the rhythm is obviously much smaller than in the Beethoven movement, still the children segment the flow of events differently from one another, just as the college students do. So in both situations we need to ask, what are the differences in feature focus that contribute to these differences in boundary-making?

Closely related to boundary-making is the issue of which elements or events are heard as the same and which as different. For example, in listening to the Beethoven movement, several students typically fail to hear that the opening passage is immediately repeated. This failure might seem puzzling if you are following the printed score—you are obviously "going back" over the same page of music again. But although we can readily "go backwards" in the paper-space of a printed score, we cannot "go backwards" in time. And if you are not following the spatial succession of marks on a score, but rather following a succession of events as they occur in real time, the "same thing" when heard in a different context can sound very different. On the most extreme view, there is no "again"; the meaning of events depends on where they happen, and what happens later is never the same as what happened before. Indeed, as we shall see in the rhythm examples, comparing moments that are distanced from each other in time in order to recognize them as either the same or different requires a particular kind of selective attention. And in listening to a simple rhythm just as in listening to a work of Beethoven, selectively listening for "the same thing again," we may sometimes lose our sensitivity to the immediate moment, and to meanings that change in response to situational context where the "same thing" can always be different.

The children's rhythm, in clear contrast to the complexity of a Beethoven movement, is an instance of what I have called a Simple. Though "invented" by one of the children in the class, it is familiar because it matches the rhythm of several familiar nursery tunes. For instance, the children's rhythm matches the rhythm of "three, four, shut-the-door; five, six, pick-up-sticks"; it also matches the rhythm of the chant, "Rah, rah, siss-boom-bah; rah, rah, siss-boom-bah." Indeed, when children are asked to make up a rhythm, it is very often the case that this is the one they clap. And the rhythm also embodies in bare form some of the characteristic structural simples that form the scaffold upon which musical complexity is built. Thus in studying the children's drawings, we are also implicitly studying the "means of comprehensibility" (as Schoenberg calls them) from which musical complexity grows.

INVENTING THE CLASS PIECE

The work I report on here resulted from my participation in an experimental music program at the Happy Hollow School; the drawings as well as the children's comments about them were made by individual children who were participants in one of the music classes that I helped to design and teach. I begin with these drawings not only for the reasons suggested earlier, but also because they were made quite spontaneously in the course of the children's classroom work. Thus they help to make my point that the most interesting questions and puzzles concerning musical development often arise in the context of working with children in actual classroom settings. Indeed, it was the puzzles and questions raised by the disagreements I found among these first drawings of a rhythm that later led to the design of more focused experimental situations. These subsequent experiments included subjects from ages four to twelve, and later included adults as well. The experiments, derived from the initial spontaneous drawings, generated a much wider range of drawings, and these in turn served to test, confirm, and expand the distinctions that first emerged in the classroom. I will turn to these experimental results in Chapters 3 and 4.

The children's interest in drawing rhythms arose initially in the midst of their work on an extended composition project. Over a period of several days they had listened closely to a work by Paul Hindemith and discussed it at length. The piece was the fourth movement of Hindemith's Kleine Kammermusik (op. 24 no. 6), composed for wind quintet. The children's task was to design their own composition modeled after the Hindemith piece. During their work, the children noticed that the most important contrasts occurred between solos played by the various wind instruments and the recurring "chorus" played by the instruments in unison. The changes from solos, where each player seemed to be improvising new material on his instrument, to the chorus, where the music was always much the same, created boundaries or "edges" that outlined the large structural elements of the piece.

To help the children in designing their own piece, I had asked them to

Figure 1–1

improvisatory solos and the "chorus"

make drawings that showed the general plan of the model piece—the two kinds of structural elements, improvisatory solos and the "chorus," along with their order of occurrence. Once made, the drawings also functioned as a kind of score for the basic design of their new piece. Figure 1–1 shows an example of one of these drawings. (For more on the drawings, see Bamberger and Watt 1979.) With their drawings as a guide, the children agreed that their piece, like the model, should include a number of solos, and alternating with them, the "chorus" would be played by the whole class in unison. The solos could be improvised by the "soloists," but the chorus needed to be composed since "everyone had to play the same thing, together."

On the fourth day of the project, the session with which we are concerned here, the children had set to work on the details of actually making their piece. One child, I'll call him Henry, played a rhythm on his drum that he proposed should function as the "chorus." Others felt it was "too short," and it was agreed that the same rhythm should be "played twice." All the children learned to play Henry's repeated rhythm in unison on the percussion instruments that formed their "orchestra." They called their rhythm the "Class Piece." (Recall that the rhythm of the Class Piece matches the rhythm of the familiar nursery rhyme, "Five, six, pick up sticks; seven, eight, shut the gate.")

At this point a fortuitous situation occurred: with much work still to be done on the project, someone noticed that the music period was nearly over. Although the regular music teacher, Lucy Sperber, assured the class that they could go on with their work the next day, one of the children quite wisely said, "But how will we be able to go on if we've forgotten the Class Piece by tomorrow?" Someone else suggested a creative solution to this problem (perhaps inspired by the group's earlier work with the Hindemith piece): "We could write it down and then we'd have something to remember it by." It was this suggestion that led to the intriguing and puzzling drawings. With only a few minutes left, paper and crayons were quickly handed out, everyone clapped the Class Piece once more, and then all the children were encouraged to "put down on paper whatever you think will help you remember the Class Piece tomorrow or help someone else play it who isn't here today." In the ten minutes or so before the bell rang, all the children finished their drawings. In doing so, the children invented a way to translate their actions—their experience in playing the rhythm—into graphic descriptions of it, and these descriptions were, indeed, still there the next day.

The drawings not only served the functional need that had inspired them—the children did use them the next day to remember the Class Piece—but, as is often the case with invention, there was an unexpected spin-off: a close look at the drawings (which I collected before the children left) suggested that among them there were two distinctly different types, and that the disagreements between them seemed to reflect, or better, to enact different possible "hearings" of even this rudimentary rhythm. As in my college students' accounts of the Beethoven movement, the questions raised by the rhythm drawings were compelling; but in contrast to the Beethoven piece, the Class Piece was sufficiently limited in scope so that specific questions could be formulated and detailed analysis in search of answers would be quite possible.

THE FIGURAL/FORMAL DISTINCTION

I tentatively organized the 25 original drawings of the Class Piece into the two types, which I labeled "figural" and "formal," respectively. Characteristic examples of each type are shown in Figure 1–2. What features distinguish the two types of drawings from each other, and what features do they share? Note first that both types of drawings share the following features: each drawing includes the same total number of shapes (10), representing the 10 claps in the Class Piece. Further, within each drawing, the first five events are drawn in the same way as the second five events—that is, events 1–5 are repeated exactly by events 6–10. But already we see a difference: in comparing the two drawings, note that it is only in the figural drawing that the repeated figures are graphically or visually clear. In contrast, the graphics of the formal drawing visually obscure the repetition. In this regard, it is important to recall that in creating the Class Piece the children had made this repetition quite explicit: Henry had initially clapped just the first half, but the children subsequently agreed that "it should be played twice." The piece was

Figure 1–2

Figural

Formal

Figure 1–3

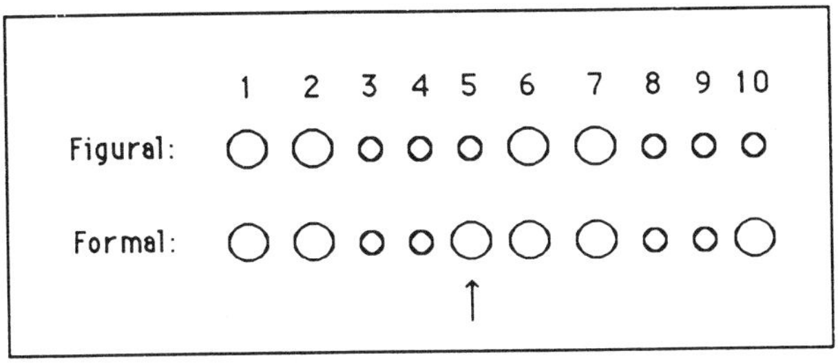

event 5 is the critical element

thus composed and also described as being in two parts, the second an exact repetition of the first. It should be obvious, then, that the figural drawing is so named because, unlike the formal drawing, the graphics clearly show the figures the children intended.

But what about the name I have given the second type of drawing—why have I called it "formal" when the form of the rhythm is graphically obscured? To approach this question we need to move in on the details of the drawings. Specifically, we need to look at the kinds of shapes that represent each clapped event. At this level of detail, it becomes clear that the two types of drawings differ most noticeably with respect to which of these events (claps) are drawn the same and which are drawn differently. For example, in both of these prototypical figural and formal drawings we see only two kinds of shapes—big and small; however, the clustering of alike shapes differs: in figural drawings events 3–4–5 form a run of alike shapes (small), and these shapes differ from those representing claps 1, 2, and 6 (big). In contrast, in the drawing labeled "formal" events 5–6–7 form a run of alike shapes, and these differ from events 3 and 4. Event 5, then, is the critical element—it is drawn the same as events 3 and 4 in the figural drawing but the same as events 6 and 7 in the formal drawing (see Figure 1–3).

These differences in the clustering of similar shapes help to account for why the repeated figures are so clearly visible in the figural drawings but obscured in the formal ones: as the Gestalt psychologists (Köhler, Koffka, Wertheimer) have shown, we tend to see shapes that look similar as clustering together or "going together" so as to form bounded figures; these figures, in turn, are seen as visually separated from the differing shapes around them (see Figure 1–4). In the same way, the runs of similar shapes in the children's drawings cluster together to form bounded visual

Figure 1–4

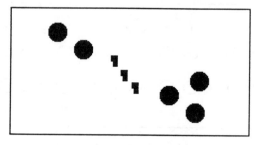

shapes that look similar cluster together

figures as well. But if we focus on the differences in the visual figures that emerge in these two types of drawings, it becomes quite clear that they are significantly different from each other with respect to the rhythm as composed and performed. As pointed out earlier, the visual figures that emerge in the drawing I have labeled figural correspond with the apprehended figures of the rhythm—that is, to the repetitions that the children intended for their Class Piece. In contrast, the groupings we see in the formal drawing conflict with the figures the children described in composing their piece. In particular, the run of similar shapes in the formal drawing (5–6–7) runs right across the boundary between the two repeated figures they clapped. And in doing so, this run of larger shapes obscures the structure that the children had made quite explicit in composing their piece.

So once again, as in the Beethoven sonata movement, the significant disagreements that emerge in these graphic descriptions (albeit on a much more detailed level here) concern which events are described as the same or different and where boundaries occur. Although it was not surprising, given the complexity of the Beethoven example, that students disagreed about boundaries (where did parts begin and end?) or that they disagreed about what was the same and what was different, it may seem surprising to find that it is similar disputes that most vividly characterize the disagreements among the children's drawings of their rather musically impoverished Class Piece.

ACCOUNTING FOR THE DIFFERENCES

To account for the differences between figural and formal drawings, we now need to ask: to what features of the clapped rhythm could the drawn shapes and their relations of similarity and difference refer? And more specifically, in what respect could events 3–4–5 be alike; and in what respect could events 5–6–7 also be alike? What possible features of the rhythm could give rise to these different expressions of similarity and difference?

The accounts the children gave of their own drawings provide some important clues. For example, when I asked Roger, who made the figural drawing, "How does your drawing work?" he said: "Well, you can see that there are two claps and then three. The three little circles go together and they get faster." He gestured with his arm to show that "go together" meant somehow bound together as in one gesture. Roger's comments were challenged by Jessica, who made the formal drawing. She said: "But that clap (pointing to clap 5 in Roger's drawing) is a long one; it's the same as the first two. It's hard to play it with a short clap there." Roger countered with: "No, there's a gap there, a space. It doesn't matter how long that one is (clap 5); you just stop and start again."

The children's comments are revealing. First of all they make quite clear that bigger circles stand for "longer" events while smaller circles stand for "shorter" events. And in these terms, it seems that the disagreement over clap 5 has to do with whether it is a long or a short—Roger draws clap 5 with a small circle; Jessica draws clap 5 with a larger circle. Further, Jessica seems more concerned with classifying and measuring, comparing events (claps) in terms of her measuring—even claps that are not adjacent to each other in the rhythm: "(clap 5) is a long one; it's the same as the first two." Roger seems to pay more attention to the succession of adjacent events and how they group together: "two claps and then three." In doing so, he focuses on the boundaries of these small figures as these boundaries form landmarks along the path of his actions. And for Roger, measuring is of little concern: "There's a gap . . . It doesn't matter how long that one is; you just stop and start again." Notice, too, that Roger uses a kind of action-language: "get faster," "go together," "and then." Jessica uses more static language in her account: "is a long one," "it's the same."

Returning now to my earlier question—what possible features of the rhythm could give rise to these different expressions of similarity and difference?—the answer seems to be simple enough: in the figural drawing clap 5 is drawn with the same shape as the previous two claps because all three belong to the same faster figure. In turn, clap 5 is drawn the same as claps 6 and 7 in the formal drawing because they all have the same longer "duration." Or to put it more precisely, claps are drawn the same when the time between one clap and the next is the same. Thus, a figural drawer like Roger draws claps 3–4–5 the same because his focus of attention is on the way claps group together to form figures. In contrast, a formal drawer like Jessica draws claps 5–6–7 the same because her focus of attention is on measuring and classifying—all longs are drawn with big circles, all shorts are consistently drawn with small circles. Expressions of similarity and difference among events result, then, from the specific kinds of possible features of the rhythm that each drawer chooses (or is able) to give precedence to: grouping of adjacent events into figures on one hand, and on the other, comparing, measuring, and classifying of events according to their duration.

The answer to my earlier question, why have I called these latter drawings "formal" when the form of the rhythm is graphically obscured, should now be clear. I do not intend the term "formal" to refer to the "form" of the rhythm—the structure that the children described in creating the Class Piece. Rather, I use the term to refer to formal properties. And in this case I use the term "formal" to refer to a drawer's explicit or implicit classification of events according to the formal durational or metric properties they share.

But unfortunately, things are not so simple. As the reader must already be aware, this account leaves a number of unanswered questions and includes certain ambiguous statements. For example, what is meant by "belongs to the same figure" when we don't yet know what generates a figure? And what is meant by "measuring" when we don't know what the unit of measure is or how it is derived? But dealing with these issues presents another: as the conversation between Roger and Jessica already suggests, those who make figural drawings and accept the figural drawings of others as "right" have great difficulties accepting or even understanding formal drawings. For example, figural drawers on looking at a formal drawing will typically say, "That drawing is wrong, or else it must be a different rhythm." And formal drawers have just as much difficulty with figural drawings—focusing their attention on different kinds of features, formal drawers see the figural drawings as simply "wrong." In another situation, we asked adults to draw the Class Piece and then showed them typical drawings of the rhythm that included instances of the two types, followed by a careful account of the differences. But when asked to draw a figural and a formal drawing of a new rhythm, they borrowed the shapes from the sample drawings of each type but continued to make the type of drawing they had made in the first place (Hildebrandt and

Bamberger 1979). Nor does it help to resolve the problem when I propose that both types of drawings are "right" but that they capture different aspects of a rhythm.

It would seem that the difficulty does not just rest on the fact that each
person focuses on different features; in its strongest version, this is what
I have called an ontological problem: on the view that the sense made of
phenomena is always a construction—a conversation back and forth between the material and its viewer/hearer—each of the individuals finds
in the material and thereby gives existence to aspects that simply do not
exist for the other. For the person who attends to the metric aspects of
the rhythm, figures remain unrecognized; for the person who attends to
figures, the classification of events according to their shared duration remains inscrutable. As a result, for one person to see/hear as another does,
he must quite literally come to hear in a new way. And doing so entails
risking the queasy discomfort of cognitive and perceptual disorientation—the very means that have served each person so well in making
sense of familiar phenomena are pulled right out from under him.

Thus, in addition to their intrinsic interest, the rhythm drawings are
significant because they present us with a rare instance in which we find
among both children and adults a robust example of conflict with respect
to explicit feature focus. It is this issue of irreconcilable conflict that presents me with an immediate problem: my experience strongly suggests
that precisely because individuals hold so tenaciously to their figural or
their formal hearings, an accounting of the drawings such as the one I
have just given remains unconvincing, even incomprehensible, to both—
and this, along with possible answers to my unanswered questions, most
likely applies to the reader as well.

To deal with this problem I shall take a route that I have found effective when discussing the rhythm drawings with my students at MIT. The
class, like most, usually includes students with varied backgrounds in
music and thus also includes both figural and formal rhythm drawers.
My tactic is to bring them into direct confrontation with one another,
the challenge being that each should try to "put on another's head"—
that is, each should try to hear the rhythm in the way his or her counter-
part does. What follows in the next chapter is an imaginary dialogue
modeled after many I have heard in these classes. There are three participants: Mot, who like Roger is a figural or MOTivic person; Met, who
like Jessica is a METric person; and myself. This is the first of my conversations with Met and Mot, who will continue to join me in later chapters

as we discuss the often puzzling results of subsequent experiments. And as they do so, Met and Mot will also learn. Through their learning I will illustrate developing musical intelligence in action, and at the same time suggest a model of research practice in which research, learning, and teaching are all closely intertwined.

CHAPTER 2

Conflicting Hearings of Rhythms: Introducing Met and Mot

THE IMAGINARY dialogue begins after I have asked each of the students to clap and draw the Class Piece. They have already looked at one another's drawings and are now in the midst of arguing about them. (As shown in Figure 2–1, Mot, like Roger, makes a proto-typical figural drawing, while Met, like Jessica, makes a prototypical for-mal drawing.) Met is a computer science major who is very forthright in his opinions. He took clarinet lessons in elementary school and currently plays the guitar. Mot is a humanities major who has had no formal music training; she is rather easily intimidated by Met.*

MOT (TO MET): I don't see how you can say that my third little circle should be a big one or a long. With a big circle there it just doesn't look the way it feels when you clap it.

JEANNE: Well, let me assure you, to begin with, Mot, that your picture is perfectly reasonable . . .

MET: Wait a minute. It just seems obvious that Mot's third little circle has to be a big one—at least if the circles are supposed to stand for longs and shorts.

MOT: Of course they are . . .

*In order to get the most from this dialogue, the reader should try to enter into the discussion and especially into the activities that stimulate the students' sometimes conten-tious disagreements. This might mean, for instance, clapping the rhythms, drawing them, and even participating in the arguments by taking sides along with the participants.

Figure 2–1

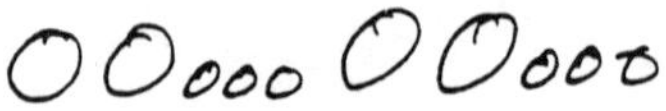

$O\ O_{ooo}\ O\ O_{ooo}$

Mot's drawing

$O\ O_{oo}\ OO\ O_{oo}\ O$

Met's drawing

JEANNE: Just be quiet for a little, Met, while I talk to Mot, OK?

MET: OK. But it's going to be very difficult for me to understand the rhythm the way Mot has drawn it.

JEANNE: We can try to help you with that, Met. For instance, what I think Mot is paying attention to, and what I see in her drawing, are the little motives or groups of claps inside each of the larger repeated rhythms.

MOT: Yes, that's right. Inside of each larger repeated pattern there are two *groups* of claps—you can see them quite clearly with my two big circles and then three little ones. And in between the two larger patterns I sort of take a breath and start again. I could make the grouping even more clear with a drawing like this (Figure 2–2).

JEANNE: That's good. Now could you clap the Class Piece again, and while you're clapping say some numbers that seem to go along with your clapping?

MOT: Sure. It would be (clapping the Class Piece): 1 2 1–2–3, 1 2 1–2–3.

MET: But that's wrong again!

JEANNE: Please try to be a little patient, Met. Now would you put the numbers you just said under the circles in your drawing so that we can see just what you mean? (Mot adds numbers to her drawing; see Figure 2–3.)

JEANNE: OK, now try something else. Think of the tune "Twinkle twinkle little star" and see if you can clap *just the rhythm* of the first two phrases.

Figure 2–2

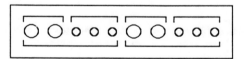

Figure 2–3

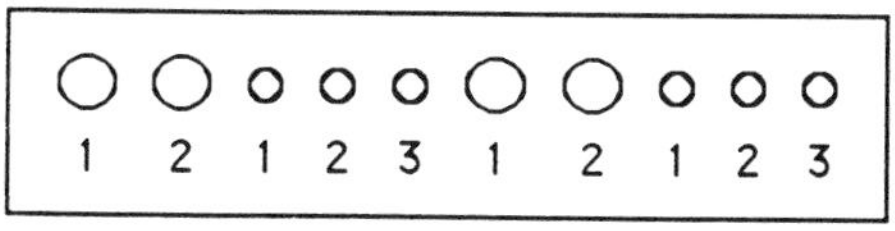

MOT: (claps the rhythm of "Twinkle twinkle little star; How I wonder what you are.")

JEANNE: Can you clap that rhythm again, Mot, and this time say some numbers that seem to go along with your clapping?

MOT: Sure. (clapping and counting):

```
   1   2   3   4 5 6   7   1   2   3   4   5   6   7
 Twin-kle twin-kle lit-tle star, How I won-der what you are.
```

MET: Oh my!

JEANNE: All right, Met, how would you count it?

MET: It's obvious. (Met claps and counts):

```
   1   2   3   4 1 2   3   4   1   2   3   4   1   2   3   4
 Twin-kle twin-kle lit-tle star,    How I won-der what you are.
```

JEANNE: Does that make any sense to you, Mot?

MOT: Not really. I especially don't understand why Met keeps counting up to 4 and then starting over again with 1.

JEANNE: Well, let's leave that problem for the moment. Could you draw a picture of the rhythm of Twinkle as you did for the Class Piece, Mot, and then put in numbers just as you said them when you were clapping?

MOT: I think so. (She draws and numbers her graphics; see Figure 2–4.)

MET: Now you're getting someplace! Did you notice that you left a space between the two phrases, I mean between the words "star" and "How I"?

MOT: Of course. That's where you sort of inhale, take a breath. As I said about the Class Piece, you take a breath and then start again.

MET: Exactly. But you have to *count that breath, too*—that stop before you start again.

Figure 2–4

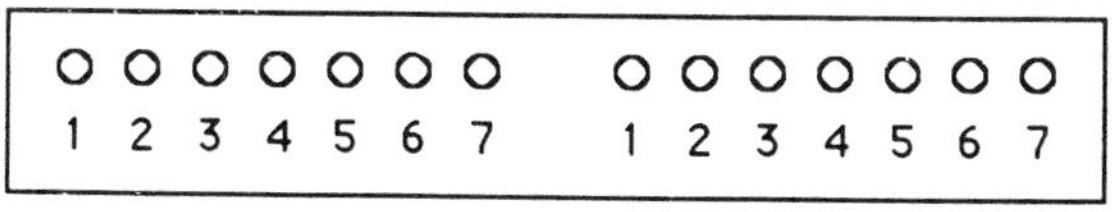

Figure 2–5

```
1  2  3  4  5  6  7  8  1  2  3  4  5  6  7  8
O  O  O  O  O  O  O     O  O  O  O  O  O  O
1  2  3  4  5  6  7     1  2  3  4  5  6  7
```

MOT: What do you mean?

MET: Well, if I count up like you did, then it would be like this. (Met writes his numbers above Mot's drawing; see Figure 2–5.)

MOT: That's interesting! You mean it's as if there's a *ghost beat* there (she points to the space where Met has written an "8"). You don't actually sing or clap the ghost beat, but it's there anyhow.

MET: A ghost beat; I really like that. You see, time, or the beats, keep right on going and you have to keep right on counting, too, right through the breath, even though you're not making any clap there.

MOT: Why don't we actually put the ghost beat in—the one you call "8." (Mot draws her ghost beat; see Figure 2–6.)

MET: You got it.

MOT: And now I see how you got your "8." Where I counted up to 7 and stopped, you counted up to 8 because you counted the ghost beat, too. So the ghost beat is the stop which sort of isn't a stop after all. That was very helpful, Met.

MET: It's just that I liked that ghost beat idea; it made me think about the rhythm differently.

MOT: But still, it *is* a stop, you know. I'm getting confused again.

MET: I guess we still have a way to go if we're going to help Mot out of her confusion.

JEANNE: Yes, but confusions need to be nurtured, too; they are often the necessary first step to learning anything new. And we're asking poor Mot to really turn her head around—to see and hear rhythms in a whole new way.

Figure 2–6

```
1  2  3  4  5  6  7  8  1  2  3  4  5  6  7  8
O  O  O  O  O  O  O  ⊙  O  O  O  O  O  O  O
1  2  3  4  5  6  7     1  2  3  4  5  6  7
```

Mot's ghost beat

MET: I'm beginning to believe that.

JEANNE: Maybe you'll find your head turning around too, Met, before we're finished. But let's go back to the Class Piece. Mot, would you mind clapping it again? And this time pay attention especially to the breath you talked about between the two larger figures.

MOT (clapping the Class Piece again): Yes, it seems like there's a space there, too; I mean between the two larger figures. Or I guess you could call it a space-of-time.

MET: You really have got a way with words, Mot.

MOT: How come I didn't notice that space before?

JEANNE: Well, what do you think?

MOT: Mostly I didn't think you could think so much about a silly rhythm that anyone can clap. Anyhow, I seem to come to a boundary. I mean, when I clap the rhythm it's as if I'm going along heading for a goal. For instance, I'm going along the path inside the inner fast figure till I come to the goal; and then I'm just inside the next figure, going along that one. I never paid attention to what was going on *in be-tween* the two larger figures. In fact, there really wasn't any in between; I was simply in one figure and then I was in the other. The Twinkle rhythm made me realize there *is* an in between. I sort of get it, but I don't.

JEANNE: That's quite understandable; it's hard to pay attention to all the different things that are going on: the claps you're making as you move along anticipating the goal or boundary; then arriving but also going across the boundary crossing. I think the way you talked about being inside one figure moving along the path to the goal and then inside the next one really captures what it feels like to be clapping a rhythm.

MET: Sounds pretty strange to me. The rhythm is just there.

MOT: Wait, I just realized something else.

MET: What's that?

MOT: I could put a ghost beat into my picture of the Class Piece, too. (She draws the Class Piece, adding a "ghost beat" between the two larger figures; see Figure 2–7.)

MET: That's great!

Figure 2–7

JEANNE: Do you think you could clap the Class Piece and actually clap the ghost beat, too, Mot?

MOT: I can try. (She claps the Class Piece and includes the "ghost beat" as in Figure 2–7.) It seems like you almost expect that ghost beat to be there but instead there's nothing.

MET: There isn't *nothing*. If there were nothing, you would clap it wrong. In fact, that's interesting—you clap it right, but you draw it wrong. Think about it this way: the breath you were talking about exactly takes up the space, I mean time, of your ghost beat.

JEANNE: Good point, Met. And that suggests another question: Mot, how many faster claps would you say there are for each slower one?

MOT: Well, I think the little ones go twice as fast as the big ones. So I guess there are two for one. In fact, you could say there is a ghost beat inside of every big circle, too.

JEANNE: Could you explain that a little more?

MOT: It's hard to explain . . . It seems like there's always a silence, a space, between every clap-sound, and I think the actual clap-sounds are always the same. So it must be the space-of-time *between* clap-sounds that makes the difference between longs and shorts. Gosh, this is getting so detailed!

JEANNE: But getting down into the details is useful, provided you can integrate what you've learned down there into the larger design when you climb back up again.

MET: That's a good description of the problems we have in computer programming, too. Anyhow, what we are calling the *length* of a clap is really the clap-sound *and* the gap before the next clap-sound.

MOT: Yes, a package that includes both. But when you're actually clapping, you don't think about that at all. With the first two claps you set a natural pace, and then you double it . . . or halve it . . . Which is it, anyhow?

MET: When you start the faster claps, you double the speed but halve the time from one clap to the next.

MOT: This is beginning to sound like physics, not music.

MET: Not really. But now it should be obvious that if there is a clap and a ghost beat inside of every big circle as you said, then your fifth clap, plus the ghost beat, will make up a slow one. So the fifth clap that you've drawn as a little circle together with the gap is just the same as the slow sixth clap (he draws; see Figure 2–8).

MOT: But now that just doesn't look right. I can't see the larger repeated

Figure 2–8

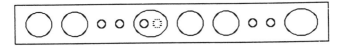

the fifth clap together with the gap is the same as the sixth clap

patterns any more. And besides, the fifth clap isn't just like the sixth clap. The fifth clap is an *ending;* the sixth clap is a *beginning*—it starts the repetition, and that's not the same at all!

MET: Well, that's all beside the point.

JEANNE: No, Met, that *is* the point! You see, Mot is saying something very important. It's true that both the fifth clap and the sixth clap are the same if what you're paying attention to is simply measuring the time from one clap to the next. But that's not all there is to rhythms. Did you notice, for instance, that Mot talked about "beginnings" and "endings"?

MET: I did, but . . .

JEANNE: What do you make of that?

MET: Well, I guess you can't have a beginning and an ending without something happening that makes a start and stop. For instance, the drip of a dripping faucet doesn't have any beginning or ending—unless you fix it and then you want to forget the beginning.

JEANNE: Good point, but go on.

MET: I have a feeling you're putting words in my mouth.

JEANNE: I'd prefer to think of it as ideas in your head.

MET: So I guess Mot's first little circle or faster clap *starts off* a new thing—what you would call a new figure; and the last of her little circles (that fifth clap, again) ends the figure, or more like stops it.

MOT: Yes, and that's exactly why your big circle for the fifth clap gets me so upset. If you draw the fifth clap as a big circle, it makes the fifth clap look like the beginning of a three-clap slower figure when really the fifth clap is the ending of the previous faster figure.

MET: But we're not talking about how things *look.* I think we're getting off the track; we're supposed to be talking about time and motion, not about how things look standing still in space. Now I'm getting confused.

JEANNE: That's a beginning, too, Met. In fact, what you just said is the beginning of a real philosophical insight, so just hang onto your confusion for a bit. What do you think makes an event function as the beginning or the ending of a figure?

MOT: I've been wondering that, too. It seems like the *function* of a clap, whether you hear it as beginning or ending a motive, depends on where it happens—what comes before and after it. For instance, when I start clapping the rhythm, I sort of set the normal pace with the first two claps. So when I start going faster with the third clap, or really when I go *from* the third *to* the fourth clap, it feels like the beginning of something new. That new pace sets off the new figure.

MET: And I suppose the next one, the fifth clap that we keep arguing about, stops that run of claps. You get going at this new faster pace and when you get to the fifth clap it's longer than you expect.

MOT: Well, I'd say it's because what you expect doesn't happen.

MET: I don't get it.

MOT: I mean, you're going along faster, and then you're stopped short because nothing happens. All right, I know, Met, we've been through this before; it's the gap, the ghost beat that's there but you don't actually play it. But that silent ghost beat is more like a comma at the end of a clause. So I guess another reason I made a small circle for the fifth clap is because I was *drawing the claps I actually made* and not the silent punctuation mark. After all, when we're reading out loud we don't *say* commas either; we just make a little pause and that helps us to group the words so they make sense. Anyhow, just because the fifth clap has the same event-time as the sixth clap that comes next, that doesn't mean that they're just the same.

JEANNE: Great! Now, let's see if I've got it straight. What I hear you saying, Mot, is that even if two events have the same time value, they can still be different depending on where they happen. To use your example, if there's a change to a faster pace, that will set off a new little figure. Then you are moving along inside the new figure at that faster pace, expecting that pace to keep going. But when that pace changes because there is a silence where you might expect another event to occur if the faster pace continued, the new figure is brought to a halt. And that's what makes the boundary.

MOT: That's right.

JEANNE: But Met wants to make things simpler.

MET: Exactly. Since the fifth clap and the gap after it together make a long, it's a long event. What's the problem?

MOT: But if you only pay attention to how *long* an event lasts, never mind *where or when,* then you'll miss the boundaries altogether. And you will also miss the functional differences between beginning and ending events.

MET: That's funny. I never thought of it before: in a rhythm "where" and "when" are the same thing.

MOT: Yes, I guess that's true. Anyhow, a long after a run of shorts just isn't the same as a long after a long.

MET: Wait a minute, are you trying to tell me that the same two claps can be both the same and different at the same time?

MOT: Yes, depending on where they happen and what you're paying attention to.

JEANNE: Well put, Mot. And that turns out to be very important when you're performing a real piece of music. For instance, even though two notes have the same time value—let's say they both look like this in standard music notation (she draws ♩♩)—you might very well play them differently exactly in order to express a beginning in contrast to an ending of a motive or a phrase. And the difference might involve, among other things, just how long you sustain a note; that is, the relation between sound and silence inside the same package or the same event-time as Mot just called it. But when you're really playing a piece, you don't think about it at that level of detail; if you did, you'd feel paralyzed. It all becomes part of expressing the meaning of the piece, including its motives and phrases. But the funny thing is, even though conventional music notation in its barest form is very good at showing you the time value of events in relation to one another, it really doesn't tell you anything about beginnings and endings of phrases or figures. That's why violinists, for instance, spend so much time and thought experimenting with bowings and fingerings, and clarinetists worry so much about where to take a breath—they're trying to find the best way to project these important differences between notes that look the same on the page. Sometimes, for instance in some of Bach's suites for solo violin, practically all the note values are the same. Can you imagine what that would sound like if the violinist weren't paying attention to the differences in the *functions* of events that otherwise look the same time-wise? It's true that composers, or sometimes editors in the case of Bach, try to help by adding various kinds of so-called expressive markings—slurs, or staccato marks like these (she draws; see Figure 2–9). But still, if you strictly follow the rule, what you see is what you get, you'll hear a pretty boring and very unmusical performance. I remember Louis Krasner, the violinist who commissioned the Berg Violin Concerto, saying to a

Figure 2–9

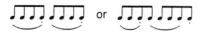

expressive markings: slurs or staccato marks

student, "Just forget the score and play the music." But to get back to where we were, yes, two events can be both the same and different depending on the context and on what you're paying attention to.

MET: That reminds me of a picture I saw once in a book on vision. When you look at it, you see this same shape in two different ways depending on what's next to it (see Figure 2–10). At first it seems like you have no choice—you see two different shapes, a diamond and a square. But if you really pay attention to the *geometric properties*— just stare at the angles and the sides of one shape at a time—of course you can see that they're the same. So, yes, you could say that they're both the same and different depending on what you're paying attention to.

MOT: That's a great example, Met.

MET: But you know, we keep shifting back and forth between time and space, and that makes me think of something else. Talking about performers and experimenting, let's try one. You, Mot, pull this piece of paper slowly across the table. While you're doing that, I'll move my pencil up and down in one place, tapping out the rhythm over your moving paper. (Mot and Met make the experiment. It leaves the trace shown in Figure 2–11.)

MOT: That looks fine. You can see the repeated big patterns and the little inner figures, too. How come that works?

MET: It works because we really made time become space. The trace left behind shows how continuous time or motion—the paper moving across the table—was marked off by my taps. That's the way the old

Figure 2–10

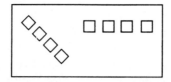

the same shape in two different ways

Figure 2–11

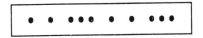

the trace left from Met's experiment

piano rolls worked, and the first mechanized looms, too. First the paper was punched out as someone played—much like the way we just
marked off the moving paper. Then whenever the sensing mechanism
moved across a hole in the paper piano roll, a piano key would be
activated. So spatial relations turn into time relations or rhythms.

MOT: I guess I understand, but I keep getting confused about the dots
and the spaces between the dots.

MET: Well, just reverse the process. Run your hand at a steady pace over
the dots we made, and every time you come to a dot make a click or
something. (Mot tries it.)

MOT: It works, all right. And I can really see the faster inner figures, too;
the run of three faster claps stands out because there's a bigger space
on either side of it—that's really a space-of-time, of course. In fact,
what you see is the change of pace that actually *generates* the boundaries of figures.

MET: And putting it that way helps me to understand your drawing better, Mot, and to hear what you mean by figures, too.

MOT: Well, I'm glad of that. But what about the last clap? You could
just go on forever.

MET: As a matter of fact, that's been bothering me all along. You can't
know how long the last clap is because it always takes two to tango. I
mean, seriously, you always need two claps to mark a time interval.
It's your beginning and ending problem, in a way, but on a smaller
scale: a beginning by itself, one mark or one clap, as you said, can go
on forever; you need another one to stop it. But then, of course, you
wouldn't know how long that one was.

JEANNE: This is getting pretty metaphysical. I really liked your experiment, Met, and I especially like the trace it left behind. It's a new notation that I think might have real possibilities. But we should stop—
I'm worn out.

MET: OK, but you said I'd had some kind of philosophical insight back
there. Aren't you going to tell me what it was?

JEANNE: Actually, the two of you sort of acted it all out just now. It was
about the problems we make for ourselves when we try to describe

actions moving through time. We make descriptions of moving things on paper in order to make them stand still, but then we end up with all these issues and confusions about time and space—like the ones that you've both noticed as we've been going along. When you learn how to make motion stand still as you've just been doing through your drawings of rhythms, you gain real power because then you can see, all at one time, what we necessarily experience as fleeting, evanescent, gone. For instance, it was only after Mot had made her drawing of Twinkle that she was able to invent her ghost beat. Once the rhythm was held still in paper-space, then she could *see* the bigger space between the two phrases. And once seen, she could also recognize it as really a space-of-time. Only then could she catch on to what Met was saying, even if she didn't totally agree with him. Making these static, spatial descriptions solves the problems of time and motion that Heraclitus might have put this way: "You can never put your foot in the same river once." The trouble is, we are able to find ways of making actions and motion stand still on paper through the invention of a notation system, and that is very useful, sometimes even profound. But once such a system is made and deeply internalized through continuous use, we come to believe in the notation so thoroughly that we actually experience whatever it is—clapping, wheels turning, drummers drumming—through the lens of the notation itself. So we go from Heraclitus's problem to taking literally, what-you-see-is-what-you-get.

MET: If that was my philosophical insight, I guess you're right, Jeanne, it is profound. In fact, this has all been really interesting, even though I didn't think it was going to be at the beginning. And I think I do understand, now, what you were showing in your drawing, Mot.

MOT: Thank goodness. Things got better once you calmed down, Met. And I have to say I learned a lot, too. In spite of your unpleasantness at the beginning, and in spite of feeling like my head was swirling around some of the time, you helped me get at things I probably would never have gotten to by myself. Are we going to go on with this discussion?

JEANNE: Absolutely.

COMMENTS ON OUR CONVERSATION

While Met and Mot begin their conversation in what seems like irreconcilable conflict, by the end of their sometimes contentious discussion they have clearly come to a resolution of their disputes. But interestingly, they have done so without either of them giving up the hearings expressed in their initial drawings. Instead, by actively confronting each other, each helped the other to notice features and relations of the rhythm that had been essentially inaccessible at the outset.

In the course of this ecumenical resolution of their figural/formal disputes, Met and Mot also clarify an issue that remained ambiguous in my earlier account of the children's prototypical drawings of the Class Piece. Through Met's experiment—Mot pulling the paper while he taps out the rhythm with his pencil—Mot can see that it is a *change of pace* that generates the boundaries of figures. As she puts it, "The run of three faster claps stands out because there's a bigger space on either side of it—that's really a space-of-time, of course." And in summarizing her comments, I point out that if there is a change from a slower pace to a faster pace, that will set off a new little figure; and within that faster pace if there is an event of longer duration, that will bring the new figure to a halt, thus creating a boundary.

Such contrasts in the prevailing rate of events can suffice in accounting for figural boundary-making within these musically minimal examples—in particular, where events differ only with respect to their time values. But an account that may suffice for brief rhythms played on a non-pitch instrument (claps), where there is not even any change in loudness, will hardly be sufficient when we consider "real compositions" such as the Beethoven movement with its much richer network of intersecting dimensions. Indeed, the issue of what generates grouping boundaries and how hearings may differ with respect to the groupings heard is a vexing and fascinating topic to which a number of music theorists have given their attention in recent years (see, for example, Cooper and Meyer 1960; Lerdahl and Jackendoff 1983; Lewin 1986). And yet, as I have suggested earlier, musically impoverished examples like the Class Piece can help to make clear just what kinds of questions we need to ask, what kinds of clues we need to look for, and how seemingly irreconcilable conflicts among disparate hearings might be resolved.

In the dialogue between Met, Mot, and myself, I have shown a first instance of just how such clues can emerge, and how, through their recognition, hearings can develop and change as each participant brings into existence features and relations that were inaccessible to him or her at the outset. For example, Mot's initial drawing provides clues that her attention is focused on the grouping of adjacent events as these form figures. And despite Met's objections, she seems unable to recognize, or is at least inattentive to, the shared proportional time values of some events. Met, recognizing these clues, helps Mot to hear that "time keeps on going" and that she needs to count the time "in between" clapped events, as well. This leads Mot to invent her "ghost beat" which, in turn, helps her to bring into existence, so to speak, an entity that had simply not existed for her before. And once seen, this new entity also helps Mot to understand why Met insists that the disputed fifth clap in the Class Piece should be a big circle instead of a small—albeit she doesn't like "the way it looks."

Met's initial drawing shows us clues to his singular focus on the measured time properties of events—all events that share the same event-time are, for him, simply the same. Despite Mot's repeated attempts, she is at first unable to help Met shift his focus so as to hear her figures. But as she recognizes a critical aspect of her own hearing, Mot is able finally to help Met, too. When Mot points out that even though two events may share the same time value, their *function* can change depending on the context in which they are embedded, Met is finally able to hear and appreciate the significance of the figural groupings within the rhythm. And in doing so, he too brings into existence an element that had not existed for him before.

Through this process of reflective confrontation, then, new features emerge, making it possible for both students to include new aspects of even these trivial rhythms in their hearings. And it is also this "liberation" of new features that eventually enables Met and Mot to resolve their disputes. With each having access to the preferred features of the other's hearing, they are able to agree that two events can be both the same and different *depending on what you are paying attention to*. Specifically, even though two events may be the same in that they *share the same event-time* (for example, claps 5 and 6), they can still be different with respect to their *figural function*—"where and when they happen." Thus claps 5 and 6 are indeed the same with respect to their time values, but they still differ in their functions—one an ending, the other a beginning. This is, then, a first instance of what I mean by the capacity to hold multiple mental representations and thus to make multiple *possible* hearings of the same phenomena.

I turn in the next chapter to the data from the larger experiment. In this context, it will be important for the reader to bear in mind that Met and Mot's initial drawings and the conflicting features that they capture are critical clues in differentiating between figural and formal hearings, and, most important, that the respective foci of attention that each drawing suggests also point to legitimate if contrasting aspects inherent in the structural relations of rhythms themselves.

CHAPTER 3

A Typology of Rhythm Drawings: Musical and Developmental Implications

IN AN EFFORT to test the significance and robustness of the figural/formal distinction that emerged in the first, spontaneous drawings of the Class Piece, I designed an experiment that enlisted the participation of 186 children between the ages of six and twelve. During their regular music classes in the Happy Hollow School, the music teacher, Lucy Sperber, and I asked children in the first through sixth grades to clap back and then draw six simple rhythms. In addition, children between the ages of four and five were subsequently interviewed individually. These younger children were asked to clap only two rhythms (including the Class Piece). Instructions to all the children were much the same as those the fourth grade children had given to themselves in drawing their Class Piece: "Put something on paper so that you can remember what you clapped, or so someone else who isn't here today could clap it." After they had made drawings of the six rhythms, all but the youngest children were asked to clap each rhythm once more and then, for each one, to "put in some numbers that seem to fit."

With the 186 drawings in hand, it was clear that the figural/formal distinction was a robust one, indeed. But what I had not anticipated was the emergence of a developmental progression within the more general distinction between figural and formal drawings. Using only the drawings of the Class Piece (not the numberings) as the example, I developed a first typology that showed both musical and developmental implications. Prototypical drawings of each type are shown in Figure 3–1.

Figure 3–1

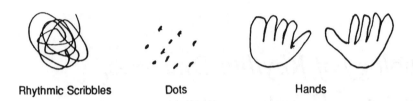

the typology of rhythm drawings

The reader will notice that Roger's figural drawing and Jessica's formal drawing (or figural and metric as I shall now call them) are shown in the typology as F.2 and M.2, respectively. These were the most common types I found; one type or the other is made by most children from age eight or nine up. As such, they are embedded in the middle of the typology. The drawings marked 0, F.1, and M.1 are typical of those made by younger children—those labeled 0 only by children between ages four and five, those marked F.1 and M.1 primarily (but not exclusively) by children between five and seven. The remaining drawing, M.3, was made by a child in the original fourth grade music class but is more typical of older children, especially those with some formal music training.

The typology, then, has two global dimensions reflected in the labels I have assigned to them: one is the figural-metric distinction (F.1–F.2; M.1–M.2–M.3), and within this, differences related to age, development, and/or learning (0, F.1–M.1; F.2–M.2; M.3). It is important to notice that both figural and formal/metric tendencies emerge in the drawings at all ages (even among the youngest children) and in all periods of development. I take this as strong evidence for my contention that both figural and formal characteristics are inherent in rhythmic structure itself. Indeed, this is precisely what is behind the statement that "a clap can be heard as both the same and different depending on where they happen and what you are paying attention to." At the same time, by looking at the drawings along both of these global dimensions, distinct features of rhythmic structure emerge that otherwise tend to be blurred or overlooked entirely.

DRAWINGS OF FOUR- AND FIVE-YEAR-OLDS: SCRIBBLES, DOTS, AND HANDS

The three kinds of drawings made by the youngest children (Figure 3–2) are particularly interesting as a case in point: they reveal aspects of performed rhythms that are essentially buried by the conventions of standard rhythm notation (SRN). I shall spend time on them because it was in the process of coming to understand these drawings that I discovered how important it is to take Socrates' advice seriously when he says, "We will be better and braver if we believe it right to look for what we don't know than if we believe there is no point in looking" (Plato [*Meno*] 1956, p. 130).

Look first at the drawing labeled "rhythmic scribbles." If, following Socrates' advice, we make an initial assumption that the drawing pictures some aspect of the performed rhythm, what could that aspect be? Of course, we could conclude that the children were simply at a loss and thus "scribbled." But the persistence of these drawings and the manner in which the children drew them, along with the characteristics they share with the other drawings made by children of this age (dots and hands), make a strong argument that the scribbles should be taken as the children's serious attempt to picture what for them was "memorable."

Figure 3–2

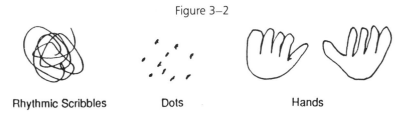

Rhythmic Scribbles   Dots   Hands

drawings made by the youngest children

If you try clapping the rhythm, paying particular attention to your movements as you clap, you may discover for yourself what these scribbles could represent. Notice that in clapping the rhythm, your movements are actually *continuous;* that is, your arms move back and forth or in and out in a continuous swinging motion, even though the span of the swings changes. However, as adults influenced by the conventions of music notation and other external descriptions of events in time and motion, we have become entirely inattentive to our own continuous body motions in *making* the rhythm. Focusing only on the results, the discrete "attacks," the individual clap-sounds, we fail to notice the means by which we make these sounds. We thus represent to ourselves as "the rhythm" only the separate sounds that result from our continuous actions, no longer noticing the continuousness of our performance.

Thus, through considering (in my conversation back and forth with the material) that the children's focus might be different from mine, and in searching for what it might be, an aspect of rhythms was "liberated" that previously escaped my attention: the continuousness of actions in actually performing rhythms, which also mirrors the rhythm's continuous unfolding in time. In turn, I had found an aspect of performed rhythms that would give meaning to what at first seemed meaningless scribbles: the children in scribbling could be putting on paper, imitating, the feel of their own continuous body motions in clapping the rhythm. This is in contrast to the discrete sounds—the external, public, acoustic results of these motions—that are represented by SRN and that constitute what we usually think of as simply "the rhythm" itself.

But there is more—not to be seen in the trace left behind on paper, but in the children's actions as they drew. Watching them, I saw the children moving their hands continuously but also with a regular *pulsing* motion—each circular scribble "keeping a steady beat." That is, as the children moved their hands, they did not copy the rhythm of the Class Piece—the longs and shorts that they had previously clapped; instead they seemed to be responding to the pulse that was also going on in the background. Indeed, the possible ways of structuring as well as the tensions between these two faces of any common rhythm—the temporal variety that we clap, and the temporal constancy that lies behind but is not actually performed—emerge as critical in making sense of and differentiating among the children's drawings.

But having recognized what *possible* aspects of the rhythm the children are attending to, it also becomes clear what it is the children are *not* attending to in their scribbling: they do not differentiate or separate out ("extract") the discrete sounds or the variations in time among them from the swinging, continuous motions of their own bodies in producing these acoustic events. As a result the trace may show the process of "clapping," but it shows nothing that would help either the player/drawer or another to recognize the features of *this* clapped rhythm.

When we compare the rhythmic scribble with the dot drawing (see Figure 3–2), this distinction between continuous and discrete aspects of clapping becomes very clear even in these drawings by children of about the same age. While the scribbles show a continuous, essentially undifferentiated swirling line, the dots are clearly discrete—that is, separate and distinct. Moreover, although the dots appear to be randomly arranged on the paper, the way the children made them points up another important difference between these dot drawings and the scribbles. Watching the children, I saw that, unlike the scribblers, these children did actually tap out the rhythm of the Class Piece on the paper. In doing so, they gave the pencil two functions: it was a percussion instrument used to play the rhythm, and at the same time it was a graphics instrument used as a means to carry out the task they were asked to perform—to put on paper something that would help them remember what they had clapped. As a result of this dual function, the children's performance left a graphic trace of the sounds they actually made but no trace of the temporal relations among them. Focusing on the longs and shorts they had just clapped, they transported these discrete and temporally varied actions onto paper. However, the trace left, a jumble of dots, shows neither the process by which it was created nor any recognizable features of the rhythm itself—characteristics the dot drawing shares with the rhythmic scribble.

It is interesting to note that although the dot drawing does show quite literally the separate events the children played, it would hardly be correct to say that the dots *refer* to these events; rather, the dots are simply the *result* of the performed events themselves. And it is exactly in this respect that we cannot see the rhythm in the picture. That is, in transporting actions directly to paper, the children are not concerned with following some orderly transformation rule whereby actions in "performance time/space" become recognizable in static, two-dimensional "paper-space."

This, then, is another instance of how, in trying to make sense of what at first seemed senseless material, the jumble of dots, I became aware of conventions so thoroughly internalized that I had forgotten I ever learned them—that is, the rules for transforming actions/events moving through time into static paper-space. It is easy to forget that we have learned a set of conventions when we have learned how to make time and actions stand still to be seen all at once (wheels turning or drummers drumming). For once these conventions are internalized, their influence becomes, so to speak, invisible: we hardly notice that in using them, we transform actions and their temporal relations into various signs or symbols and arrange them spatially in paths or "line-ups," with time always going from left to right on the paper. Indeed, this was the gist of Met's "philosophical insight" in the conversation with Mot and me, when he spoke of "the problems we make for ourselves when we try to put moving things on paper in order to make them stand still." The powerful influence of the conventions for doing so, which Met took as simply common sense, became clear in the dialogue and will emerge again when we compare the drawings of these youngest children with the older children's lined-up rhythm drawings.

Finally, I saw some children actually tracing their own hands, leaving behind pictures something like the one marked "Hands" in the typology (see Figure 3–2). When I watched the first child tracing her hands, I assumed that this must be a unique phenomenon. But when this was repeated by a number of other children, I had to take it as the children's serious effort to carry out the task. Again the other drawings were helpful. It seems that in responding to the instruction to make a drawing "so you can remember what you clapped," those who traced their hands did not distinguish between the objects that made the claps, their hands, from the "objects" that are made by them, namely the sounds. And once I "let the material tell me," the hand drawings also helped to make sense of the scribbles and dots. That is, although these drawings of hands are totally different from the scribbles or dots as pictures, all of them show the children putting on paper in various ways their own bodily experience: they transport to paper either their motions in making the rhythm (scribbles, dots) or a picture of what did the job (hands).

DEVELOPMENT WITHIN THE FIGURAL DIMENSION

Looking first at the drawings marked F.1 and M.1 (Figure 3–3) within the framework of the two global dimensions of the typology, we see the following: along the developmental dimension, the distinguishing features of scribbles and dot drawings seem to have crystallized in these drawings of slightly older children. That is, the drawing labeled F.1, with its two continuous undulating lines, can be seen as a more articulated

Figure 3–3

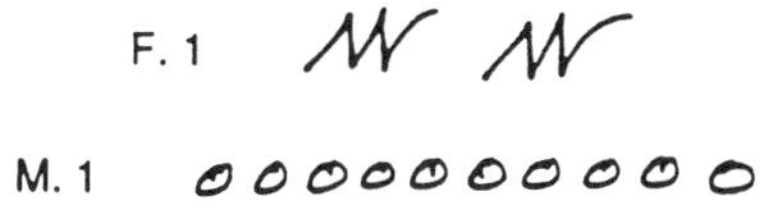

F. 1   ⋀⋁ ⋀⋁⟋

M. 1   ⌀ ⌀ ⌀⌀⌀⌀⌀ ⌀ ⌀ ⌀

scribble. In turn, the M.1 drawing, with its discrete and alike shapes, can be seen as a more fully articulated dot drawing. And now in both we see line-ups: instead of swirling, undifferentiated lines or a jumble of dots, both the lines and the discrete shapes line up, with time moving "straight ahead" from left to right across the page.

Moving in, now, to consider development along the figural dimension, we can see, albeit still dimly, familiar features that characterize prototypical figural drawings. For example, the undulating lines of F.1 are interrupted by a space, a "gap" forming two graphic figures, the second an exact repetition of the first. In turn, the ups and downs within the boundaries of each figure articulate the continuous line into exactly five events. The children who made F.1 drawings, like those who made dot drawings, actually *played the rhythm on the paper*, but the process was quite different. Instead of using the pencil as a percussion instrument to tap out the rhythm on the paper, these children moved their pencils continuously across the paper: first slowly (⋀), then proportionately faster (⋀), then a pause, with the pencil suspended in the air; and then an exact repetition of their previous actions. The trace left behind almost magically reflects back the figural structure of the rhythm: two alike figures with their boundaries marked by the pause, which is transformed, like Mot's drawing of "Twinkle," into a space, an "in between." But within these figural boundaries, the trace left by their playing/drawing remains continuous—we see the correct number of events (since they played the rhythm correctly) but no trace of the changes in pace, no differentiation among them save succession. Still, in carefully interrupting their continuous actions at the larger figural boundary, these children quite clearly demonstrate their attention to the grouping of their claps into two large gestures. But unlike the fully developed figural drawings of Roger or Mot, the trace left by their playing/drawing does not capture the inner groupings formed by the changes of pace along the way.

Compared with the uninterrupted, pulsing, swirling scribbles made by the four- and five-year-olds, however, these drawings by slightly older children who have already been in school show significant development within a basically figural approach:

- The correct number of events.
- The conventional line-up going left to right across the page.
- The two clearly articulated graphic figures corresponding to the repeated figures the fourth grade composers had originally designed into their Class Piece.

Finally, it is important to note that because the children's playing/drawing leaves a trace that in many of its aspects is recognizable as what they clapped—a reflection *of* it as if in a blurry mirror—it also provides material that holds still so that the children can reflect *on* it. In a conversation back and forth between playing on the paper and looking back at the trace left behind, the children can learn about their own knowledge, *functioning knowledge,* which ordinarily escapes scrutiny as it passes by in action and through time.

Looking now at the fully developed figural drawing, F.2 (Figure 3–4), and comparing it with the earlier F.1 drawings, we see in the F.2 drawing the results of a growing ability for reflection among these somewhat older children (between the ages of eight and twelve)—particularly an ability to reflect *on* their own actions. As evidence, notice that these drawings include more information—the continuous undulating lines of F.1 drawings are differentiated into big and small shapes that show both changes in pace and also inner groupings. And most important, in making these shapes, the children are no longer simply transporting their actions directly onto the paper (playing/drawing); what we see instead are "thought actions"—discrete graphic shapes that *refer* to actions rather than being the direct *result* of the actions themselves. Just as the F.1 drawings are more distanced from the immediate experience of actually clapping the rhythm as compared with the swinging scribbles of the youngest children, so the F.2 drawings are more distanced from immediate experience as compared with the F.1 drawings. It would seem, then, that a critical aspect of development is the moves back and forth between reflections *of* experience and reflection *on* experience.

Figure 3–4

comparing F.1 and F.2 drawings

Figure 3–5

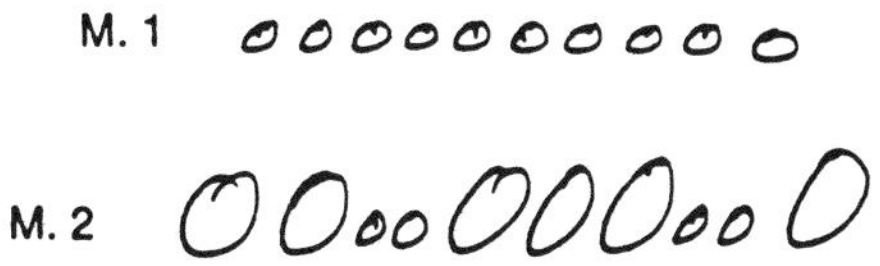

M. 1　𝒐 𝒐 𝒐 𝒐 𝒐 𝒐 𝒐 𝒐 𝒐 𝒐

M. 2　𝒪 𝒪𝒐𝒐 𝒪𝒪𝒪𝒐𝒐 𝒪

DEVELOPMENT WITHIN THE METRIC DIMENSION

Going on to the metric dimension of the typology, in what sense can the drawing marked M.1 (Figure 3–5) in fact be considered metric? Just looking at it will not, by itself, help. As with other drawings made by the younger children, one needs to have been there while they were making their drawings in order to make sense of what they leave behind as a product. Indeed, as I watched the children making their drawings, I saw them also watching themselves: as they clapped the rhythm back to themselves, I saw them at the same time slowly and laboriously "grabbing" and counting up each clap as it went by, 10 claps in all. Then, with the result of their count-up clearly in mind, they carefully put down on their papers a row of 10 discrete shapes, ungrouped and undifferentiated with respect to shape or size—a count-up.

I have called the M.1 drawings at least nascently metric in contrast to the F.1 drawings, first because the children focus on discrete events in contrast to continuous motions, and especially because they focus on *counting* in contrast to the construction of *figures*. That is, the children who made M.1 drawings are selecting out or "extracting" as a memorable property from their continuous actions a single property, namely, just *how many* discrete sounds they made. But still, like the children who made F.1 drawings, these children do not attend to differences in the pace of their actions. Each clap is drawn the same except for its position in the series—simply next-next-next. Thus, even though the children's interest is in counting each event—each clap is a "unit" to be counted—their counts do not stand for units as in a "metric unit"—something that stays the same in its value so that it can be used to measure, as in counting along a number line or counting inches along a ruler. Interestingly, as we move on to the M.3 drawing, it is exactly the sense of what constitutes a "unit" in these drawings—that is, what is a thing to count on and to count up—that will distinguish them from all the others.

But still, the M.1 drawings, like the F.1 drawings, show evidence of a growing capacity for reflection on, and distancing from, immediate experience as compared with the earlier dot drawings. For in order to make these drawings, the children had quite literally to look at themselves clapping: first translating their continuous actions into a count-up, then translating the count into a line-up of all-alike shapes going from left to right across the page. And finally, the shapes, unlike the continuous lines in the F.1 drawing, *stand for* claps rather than being the direct result of making them.

If we now look at the prototypical M.2 drawing and compare it with these M.1 drawings within the metric dimension of the typology (see Figure 3–5), it should be clear that the same aspects of development— reflection *on* actions and distancing from immediate experience—have once more come into play. Like the F.2 drawings in comparison with the F.1 drawings, M.2 drawings include more information than M.1 drawings. The all-alike shapes of M.1 are differentiated in M.2 drawings: we see large and small shapes that stand for long and short claps rather than standing for an indiscriminate count-up of them all. But along the figural-metric dimension, it is exactly with respect to what the shapes refer to in these prototypical M.2 drawings that I have called them metric rather than figural. As I emphasized earlier, children who made M.2 drawings, unlike those of about the same age who made F.2 drawings, focus their attention on the *time value* of events, consistently *classifying* each as either a long or a short. And in order to do so, the children must distance themselves not only from their immediate experience, but also from the given sequence of their performed actions. Rather than going along the path of the rhythm, next-next-next (or as Mot put it, "simply in one figure and then in the other"), they must remove themselves from this path so as to compare events that may be distanced from each other in their order of occurrence. And most important, they must compare events that belong to different figural groups. That is, in order to recognize that clap 5 is the same as claps 1 and 2, they must, in their imagination, compare events that are contained within the slower and faster inner figures, respectively; and they must also cross the boundary between the two larger figures to compare and identify clap 5 as the same as clap 6. But notice, too, that as in all metric drawings, the figural groups that are so clear in both F.1 and F.2 have once again disappeared entirely.

A FULLY METRIC DRAWING

What about the drawing I have labeled M.3 (Figure 3–6)? When Susan, the child who made the M.3 drawing, was asked how her drawing

Figure 3–6

M. 3

worked, she said, pointing to the ⊙, "Well, you can see that there are two for one, there." This is a sure clue: the "two" she refers to would be the two small circles inside the bigger circle, and these would represent the two faster claps; the "one" she refers to is the big, outer circle, and this would represent one beat. Reading the whole drawing back confirms the hunch. The large circles always stand for the *background beat*— eight beats in all. And when performed events are equal in time to the background beat, coinciding with it as in events 1 and 2, Susan draws only an empty circle. But when performed events go twice as fast as the background beat, as in events 3 and 4, she draws her large circle for the background beat and inside it puts two little circles that stand for the two faster claps which together equal the time of one background beat— a proportional relation of 2 : 1. So Susan's M.3 drawing shows not only long and short events, like the big and small circles in the M.2 drawing, but also *how much* longer or shorter they are—the two little ones go twice as fast as the background beat, or, as she said, "two for one." In fact, Susan has invented a notation for a real metric unit, the background beat, which is always the same. And in relation to this unchanging unit of time, she can also show the relative time value of each of the clapped events in the rhythm.

From the viewpoint of development *within the metric dimension* of the typology, the M.3 drawing is clearly the most mature. And once again, development suggests a greater capacity for reflection and distancing. For in order to invent her notation, Susan had to reflect on her actions so as to differentiate and "extract" the underlying beat from the varied durations of the events she was actually performing. There is an interesting comparison here between this more mature capacity to extract the *underlying beat* and the younger M.1 children, who had to "extract" *each clap* from their continuous motions of clapping. But in addition, Susan had to coordinate the 8 unchanging background beats, which are not always being performed, with the variations in pace among the 10 events of the rhythm itself—that is, to map one onto the other. In all these ways, then, it seems fair to say that the M.3 drawing shows real development as compared with the nascent metric drawing, M.1, and the emergent metric drawing, M.2.

Interestingly, the units of description used in M.3, as I will show in the chapter that follows, are much the same as those used in SRN. But it is again important to emphasize that in the M.3 drawing, as in SRN as well as in the other metric drawings, *the figural units of the rhythm are not represented at all*. Indeed, one adult whose hearing focused on figural elements rather than metric units of the Class Piece found Susan's drawing very confusing. Assuming that each circle represented a clap, he saw her ⊚ as three events which together formed the faster inner figure rather than, as Susan intended, two faster events against the background beat. Not surprisingly, then, in trying to clap the rhythm from Susan's drawing, this player made three faster claps when he arrived at Susan's ⊚, and then concluded that in her drawing "there are too many claps in all."

In the following chapter I will return to the question of what is a "thing" to count up and to count on. And I will also consider in some detail how Susan's metric unit lends itself to a kind of counting that is quite different in kind from the count-up the children used in making their earlier M.1 drawing. But before going on, I would like to sympathize with readers who may feel, by this time, a little as if they are in Alice's Wonderland where the most ordinary things seem to come to life in confusing ways. And the situation will get even worse when we come to naming things—what do we give names to and what do the names mean? Or as Humpty Dumpty and Alice put it in *Through the Looking Glass* (Carroll 1960, p. 263):

> "Don't stand there chattering to yourself like that," Humpty Dumpty said, looking at her for the first time, "but tell me your name and business."
>
> "My name is Alice, but . . ."
>
> "It's a stupid name enough!" Humpty Dumpty interrupted impatiently. "What does it mean?"
>
> "Must a name mean something?" Alice asked doubtfully.
>
> "Of course it must," Humpty Dumpty said with a short laugh: "my name means the shape I am—and a good handsome shape it is, too. With a name like yours, you might be any shape, almost."

CHAPTER 4

Counting and the Metric Hierarchy

IN THIS chapter I will make a didactic pause to consider the role of counting and the conventional uses of numbers as units of description in invented notations and in traditional musical practice. I will organize the discussion around the following questions:

- What is an element or a thing to count up ON?
- How far do you count UP, or when do you start again with 1?
- What is a "unit"?

The questions point to issues that have come up in various forms in previous chapters, but they are of more general interest, too. It is often just such issues that confound children in the early years of school, leading to problems in mathematics but in other subjects as well. The problems are doubly confounding because the answers to these questions tend to remain tacit, quietly embedded in just those notational conventions that we have forgotten we ever learned.

Recall first the disagreements among my college students to which I alluded earlier. In their descriptions of the Beethoven sonata movement, several students agreed that the movement included "three parts"; however, it turned out that the three parts they counted were almost entirely different. Thus, although they all arrived at the same count-*up* (there were three parts), what they each took as a thing to count *on*—the passages they used as an element in counting—were quite different. And these differences eventually provided clues to the kinds of features that each was giving importance to. Counting, then, is not as objective, as neutral, as it may sometimes seem; it is closely intertwined with an individual's hearing of a piece, how her past learning and experience guides her hearing, and with this, what is heard as the same and different. Indeed, if I as the teacher had simply stopped with the question, "How many parts do you hear?" I would have supposed wrongly that the students were in agreement.

To take another example, consider the disagreements between Mot and Met concerning how to count the rhythm of "Twinkle Twinkle":

	1	2	3	4	5	6	7			1	2	3	4	5	6	7
Mot:	Twin-	kle	twin-	kle	lit-	tle	star,		How	I	won-	der	what	you	are.

	1	2	3	4	1	2	3	4		1	2	3	4	1	2	3	4
Met:	Twin-	kle	twin-	kle	lit-	tle	star,			How	I	won-	der	what	you	are.

What is in contention here, as in the disagreements among the students about the Beethoven movement (although at a quite different level of detail), is the elements that each of the participants takes to be a *thing to count*. Notice, first, that the grouping of their count-ups differs—Mot twice counts up to 7, while Met repeatedly counts up to 4; and second, they arrive at different totals—2 × 7 or 14 for Mot, and 4 × 4 or 16 for Met. What, then, are the "things" each student uses to count *on*, and what are the differing strategies each student uses to count *up?* What, in short, do their numbers refer to?

As the conversation evolved, it became clear that each of Mot's numbers refers to a *performed event* in Twinkle; she gives each of her claps one count. In turn, she counts up within each figure separately. That is, she starts counting at the beginning of a figure, continues until she comes to its boundary, and then starts over again with 1 at the beginning of the next figure. The grouping of numbers, then, 7 + 7, is a clue to her focus on the figural grouping of performed events in the tune.

From Mot's view, Met's counting seemed strange indeed; and for Met, Mot's counting was simply wrong. To probe these differences and to help the students "get into each other's heads," I asked Mot to make a drawing of the first two phrases of Twinkle. The drawing helped Met to see that he had made a count where Mot did not, namely on the "space" between the two figures where there was no clap. It was this that led Mot to invent her "ghost beat." And in recognition of this new element, Mot changed her count-up to 8, including, now, a count on the "space" between the two figures (see Figure 4–1).

Figure 4–1

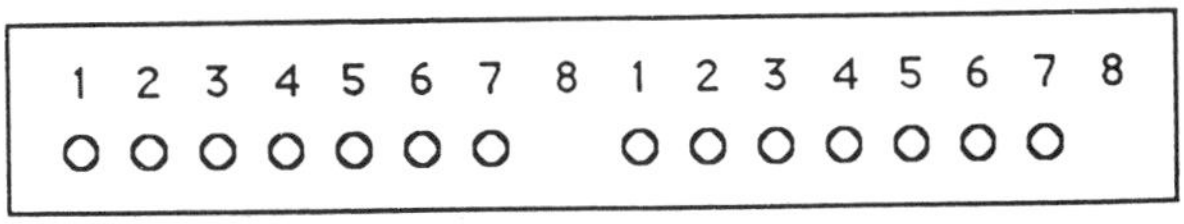

1	2	3	4	5	6	7	8	1	2	3	4	5	6	7	8
O	O	O	O	O	O	O		O	O	O	O	O	O	O	

a count on the space between the figures

Figure 4–2

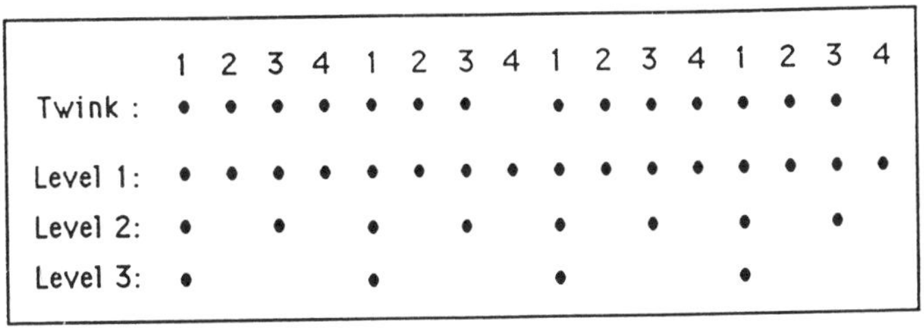

	1	2	3	4	1	2	3	4	1	2	3	4	1	2	3	4
Twink :	•	•	•	•	•	•	•		•	•	•	•	•	•	•	•
Level 1:	•	•	•	•	•	•	•	•	•	•	•	•	•	•	•	•
Level 2:	•		•		•		•		•		•		•		•	
Level 3:	•				•				•				•			

the metric hierarchy of Twinkle

But what about Met's count-up, which was so clearly different from Mot's? As Mot said at the time, "I especially don't understand why Met keeps counting up to 4 and starting over again with 1." I finessed this question at the time, going on instead to Met's problems with figures. But if we had pursued Mot's confusion, the best way would have been to use the experiment Met invented, with Mot pulling the paper across the table while he tapped out the rhythm. If this experiment is carried out with the rhythm of Twinkle, the trace left would look like the top line-up of dots in Figure 4–2. The line-up of dots beneath the rhythm of Twinkle is a rather different elaboration of this rhythm, which, as we shall see, Met's invention makes possible.

THE METRIC HIERARCHY*

The top line-up of dots in Figure 4–2 shows the rhythm of Twinkle with time relations transformed into spatial relations—the trace that Met's experiment would have left behind. Above it you see Met's counting. In the line-up labeled Level 1, you see the underlying or *background beat*

---

* The discussion in this section is intended primarily for readers who have little formal background in music; it covers material that may seem obvious to readers who are experienced musicians. However, even these more experienced readers may find the discussion useful, since the approach I take to the material is directly influenced by results from the experimental situations. The discussion both reflects these findings and suggests new ways of thinking about rhythm structure.

that is generated by the varied durations of Twinkle. This "beat" is what you "keep time" to, tap your foot to, when casually listening to a piece. Using Met's experiment, for instance, if you just kept a steady beat, the trace left behind as you tapped your pencil would look like what you see in Level 1. A beat, then, is the marking off of time into *regular or equal units*. Level 2 shows a slower beat that you might also use to keep time, and Level 3 is a still slower beat. These three levels of beats together form what is called the *metric hierarchy* for Twinkle. And since in every line-up time relations are transformed into analogous spatial relations, you can also see when (where) beats at the three levels coincide with one another and with the rhythm of the tune.

If we look again at Met's counts, it should be clear that he is counting *beats*. In contrast to Mot, who gives each performed event one count, Met gives a count to each of the underlying beats at Level 1. As he explained it to Mot: "time, or the beats, keep right on going and you have to keep right on counting, too." Thus, the kind of element that Met counts on is significantly different from the kind of element that Mot counts on. Specifically, Met's counts mark off time into *regularly recurring units,* the same for each count, while Mot's counts vary along with the *varied durations* of the tune. And this difference also helps to make clear why I called M.1 drawings of the Class Piece only nascently metric: like Mot, these young children count on and count up along each of their performed events, and these events, unlike the background beat, vary in their time values. As I said earlier, even though in the children's counting each clap is a "unit" to be counted, their counts do not stand for units as in a "metric unit"—something that stays the same in its value and thus can be used to measure.

As for Met's count-up in groupings of 4, we can see by looking at the diagram of the metric hierarchy that he starts over again with 1 *each time the fastest beats at Level 1 coincide with the slowest beats at Level 3.* Thus, as Met goes along counting on the beat at Level 1, he counts up in groups of 4 because this is the cycle at which Level 1 beats and Level 3 beats coincide. Or to put it another way, there is a 4:1 relationship between the rates of the fastest and slowest beats generated by the structure of the tune. Met is responding to this relationship by grouping his counts in 4's.

Now, more conventional music terminology would describe Met's counting as responsive to "accents" that occur every four beats. And since Met's counting is consistent with convention, it was very easy for him to say that Mot's counting was simply wrong. But received tradition has little to say about what *generates* such accents, let alone what generates figures. With respect to what generates accents, given only non-pitch events like claps or drum sounds, I propose the following: if we look at the diagram of the metric hierarchy, it seems that the regularly recurring accents we call *metric* accents (in contrast to other kinds of accents, such as those made by playing some events louder) are generated whenever beats at two or more levels coincide. And if we assume that this underlying metric structure is in some sense actively going along in our hearing of the tune, it would seem also that when beat levels meet in the continuous flow of time, these moments are as if reinforced (louder?) or at least somehow marked for attention and thus "accented." (Of course, this proposal is at best only a partial explanation; it begs the question of what, for instance, generates a beat, which I will have much more to say about later.)

To get a feel for this metric hierarchy, the reader might make a little experiment: sing Twinkle and keep time with it, switching from one beat level, one rate of beat, to the other. It should be clear from this that the beats you clapped *followed* your singing. Thus beats at all levels of the hierarchy are actually generated by the tune, that is, by the particular temporal and pitch relations that give the tune its structure and coherence. As one child said in trying to make a picture of the tune and how it coincided with the beats, "You can't put the piece *on* the beat, you have to find the beat *in* the piece." This is a critically important point, and I will return to it in the discussion of the children's drawings of the more complex rhythm in the following chapter. (For a more complete discussion of the metric hierarchy, see Bamberger and Brofsky 1988, chap. 2; Lerdahl and Jackendoff 1983.)

THE CLASS PIECE AND THE METRIC HIERARCHY

In light of the foregoing discussion, it will be useful to look again at Met and Mot's countings for the Class Piece. In Figure 4–3 I show a spatial drawing of the Class Piece and below it the metric hierarchy generated by these varied durations. Looking at Mot's counting, 1 2 123, it is clear that, consistent with her counting of Twinkle, she gives a count to each of her performed events and counts up within each of her "little inner figures." Although I did not give Met a chance to count the Class Piece during our discussion, I can presume that he would have used the same principle as in his counting of Twinkle. Thus, in Figure 4–3 I show him giving a count to every beat at Level 1 and grouping his counts in 4's—1 2 3 4 1 2 3 4. Indeed, his counting looks exactly the same as for Twinkle, and the reason is that the metric hierarchy generated by the

Figure 4–3

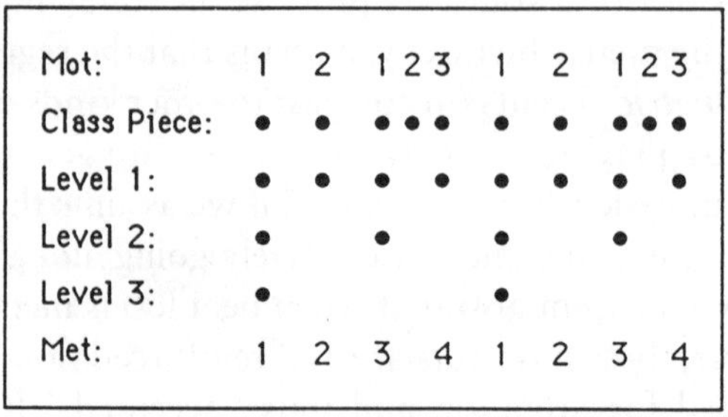

Mot:	1	2	1	2	3	1	2	1	2	3
Class Piece:	•	•	•	• •		•	•	•	• •	
Level 1:	•	•	•	•		•	•	•	•	
Level 2:	•		•			•		•		
Level 3:	•					•				
Met:	1	2	3	4		1	2	3	4	

the metric hierarchy of the Class Piece

two rhythms is also the same—Level 1 beats coincide with Level 3 beats in a cycle of 4:1. This, then, is another instance of how the formal properties of musical structure tend to obscure unique particulars, and also an instance of the ways in which "same and different" depend on what you are paying attention to.

But this very sameness can be quite useful. Looking at the rhythm of the Class Piece embedded within its metric hierarchy, it is easy to see, for example, that the equal units marked off by the Level 1 beat measure, like a ruler, the time values of the varied durations of clapped events. And once we have seen this, it is also quite clear that, as Mot guessed, her "little ones go twice as fast as the big ones." The diagram of the metric hierarchy also makes it eminently clear that Met and Jessica, who made the original formal drawing of the Class Piece, were implicitly using the beat as a unit of measure when they insisted that clap 5 in the Class Piece was the same as claps 1, 2, and 6.

It should also be apparent by now that Susan's M.3 drawing is another notation for representing this same metric information about the rhythm. That is, Susan's row of large circles serves the same function as the line-up of equidistant dots at Level 1 in the metric hierarchy: each represents the unchanging background beat in relation to which the varied durations of clapped events can be measured. But Susan's notation has a nice advantage in that you can see in one line-up instead of two the background beat, performed events, and the proportional relation between them.

But how is a unit of measure like the background beat different, for example, from other units such as performed events or even a figure? And most important, when these various kinds of units of description are given names, such as number names, what kinds of entities or relationships do these names name; what does each kind of unit of description tell you about the rhythm? For instance, when Mot names performed events (each of her claps) and groups them—1 2 123—the numbers tell us how many events she clapped (5) and how they group into figures (2 + 3). But the numbers are not names for a unit to measure with. For if a unit is to be used to measure with, it must remain constant—that is, whatever its value, in time or space, it must be repeated the same each time it is used, like a minute or a second on a clock face. In contrast to Mot's numbers or the M.1 children's count-up, which name events that vary in their time value, Met's numbers name units that keep their time value. Like Susan's larger circles, they serve very well for measuring because they mark off the continuous flow of time into equal bits—the same each time they are used.

TRANSFORMING MET'S NOTATION INTO STANDARD RHYTHM NOTATION

Interestingly, Met's space-time notation easily transforms into standard rhythm notation (SRN). And Susan's would as well, but Met's graphics make the transformation clearly visible. That is why I said to Met at the time that his new notation had real possibilities. The procedure is quite simple: first, substitute a stroke for each dot in Met's notation. Thus, still keeping the space-time relations as before, Figure 4–4 shows a line-up of strokes for the performed rhythm and below it another line-up of strokes for the Level 1 beat. Now, to transform this spatial notation into SRN, take the Level 1 beat as the unit of measure. Leave alone each event in the performed rhythm that coincides with the Level 1 beat and is thus equal in time to this background beat; but when there is more than one performed event for a Level 1 beat, connect these events together with a cross beam. The result is shown in Figure 4–5.

Magically, Met's space-time notation becomes standard rhythm notation, and it works because the principle is the same for both: with the background beat as a *metric unit,* varied durations of the performed rhythm can be measured in relation to it. In this example the symbol | is used to represent the background beat, while ⊓ represents events where,

Figure 4–4

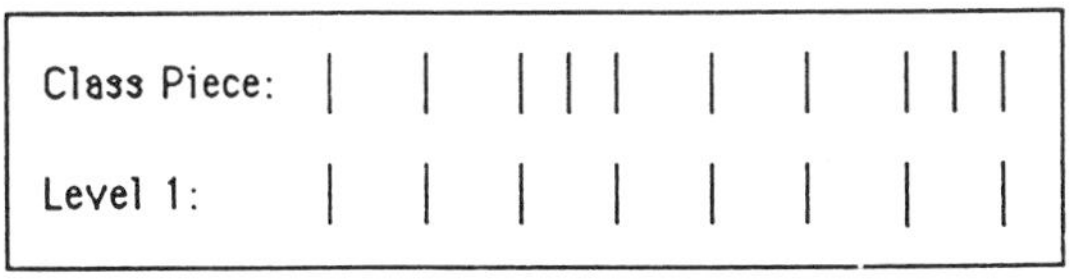

| Class Piece: | | | | | | | | | | | | | | |
| Level 1: | | | | | | | | | | | | |

Figure 4–5

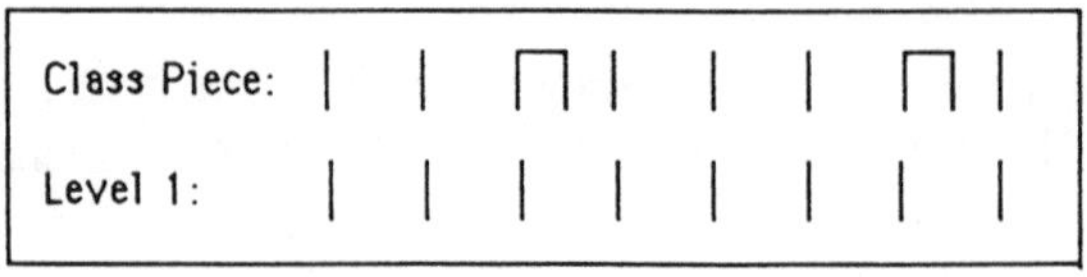

Met's space-time notation becomes standard rhythm notation

as Susan said, "you can see there are two for one there." Of course, SRN as it appears in a printed score may not always keep the space-time relations as constant as I have in my examples. And SRN also includes a number of other conventional symbols for showing the proportional time relations among events. But once you understand the underlying principle of measuring proportional time values in relation to an underlying unit of time (a beat), the whole set of conventions becomes quite clear. It is a little like catching onto the principle of the decimal system: once understood, the whole network of conventional symbols for representing numeric values also becomes quite clear. And when it does, it is just as easy to add 2,000 + 2,000 as to add 2 + 2. Similarly, once the principle of SRN is understood, it is just as easy to understand ♫♫♫ as to understand ♫ : if the beat is represented as ♩, then ♫♫♫ means that there are four-for-one instead of two-for-one as in ♫ .

But notice that, as Met's notation magically transforms into SRN, just as magically Mot's original problem is suddenly resurrected: the Class Piece doesn't *look* right—you can no longer "see the repeated big patterns and the little inner figures, too." So the essential tension between figural and metric hearings appears once again. And seeing the transformation happen before your very eyes also makes quite clear just what the symbols of SRN do and do not represent: in the service of measuring, figural groups have been broken up, obscured, lost. And this is exactly what I was talking about when I said to Mot and Met that although conventional notation is very good at showing you how long and short events are in relation to one another, it really doesn't tell you anything about beginnings and endings of phrases or figures.

This also explains why SRN is so often confusing for beginning music readers: as the conversation between Met and Mot illustrated, and as the typology of rhythm drawings strongly suggests, for people who have not yet learned to read music, units of perception are figures. However, the information encoded by SRN is only metric. There is, then, a serious mismatch between the *hearings* of these novice readers, for whom figures

Figure 4–6

the Class Piece

are the *units of perception,* and the metric *units of description* used in SRN, which readers *see* in the printed score. And since novice readers quite naturally hear events/actions grouping together to form figures, it is not surprising that they expect to find these figural groups somehow represented in music notation, too.

Once this is recognized, it becomes clear that there is good reason for the common mistakes made by beginning readers. For example, consider Figure 4–6, in which the rhythm of the Class Piece is notated as in SRN. Novice readers will typically play the two joined notes faster than the two preceding notes, but they will also add a little time, a "gap," on either side of the joined pair (Figure 4–7). How can we account for these performances, which are very familiar to all those who teach music? Consider the following: by making a little space-of-time on either side of the joined notes, these novice readers actually turn the notated *metric unit* into a performed *figural unit.* The reasoning behind this proposal becomes clear if you look once again at the spatial drawings of Twinkle and the Class Piece. Recall that it is a change in pace, a longer space-of-time, that effectively generates the boundary between the two repeated larger figures in the rhythm of the Class Piece and also a temporal "gap" that generates the boundary between the two phrases of Twinkle. Just so, by adding a little temporal "gap" on either side of the two-note metric unit in playing from SRN, novice readers effectively succeed in turning the notated metric unit into a performed figural unit. The result, of course, is something less than satisfactory; beginning readers are left puzzled because what they hear in listening back to their own perform-ance "just doesn't sound right."

Figure 4–7

novice readers add gaps

The example is an important one because it so clearly illustrates two points that are critical to the basic arguments of this book: first, the importance of conversations back and forth with material where "the material" is puzzling behavior—and this includes especially recurring mistakes that happen spontaneously in the classroom or the studio—and second, the importance of distinguishing between knowing *how* and knowing *about*. With respect to the first, if we assume that a student's mistakes somehow have good reason and we search for what that reason might be, then an apparent mistake can reveal, on the one hand, crucial information about what the student knows how to do already and, on the other, how this knowledge may be specifically different from what we are expecting of him. In the case of the novice reader, it is the clear conflict between the student's *internalized units of perception* and the meanings implicit in our *conventional units of description*. And with respect to the second point, this example demonstrates that even if an individual does not know about the conventions of SRN, she does, rather remarkably, know how to create, to make on the spot, a perfect little rhythmic figure.* That is, the reader sees graphics that are meant to stand for metric units as standing instead for familiar figural units, and in doing so she is able, instantly, to play the metric unit as a figural one. And this evident know-how suggests another intriguing puzzle that needs to be pursued: How is it that we have all learned how to do that? How have we learned that a little extra time around a group of notes puts a boundary around them, joining the notes together to form a figure?

The example, then, is particularly important in its educational implications, and I will come back to these in more detail later. For now I will simply suggest that when a commonly occurring mistake can be traced to a mismatch between internal mental representation and conventional descriptions, it is useful to help students confront these differences. In this instance, that would mean helping students to move back and forth between metric and figural hearings and between metric and figural descriptions of a rhythm or melody, much as I helped Met and Mot to do in my conversation with them. The problem lies in learning both to differentiate and to coordinate these different kinds of entities—clapped

---

* Although I have made a strong case for figural aspects of rhythms being "natural," I would be remiss in not mentioning the naturalness, even the inborn capacity, for what we might call "pulsing," as in sucking, breathing, rocking, or, indeed, "rhythmic scribbling." In fact it might well be that with this innate ability to "keep a beat" we have a kind of nascent metric unit, the bodily beginnings of the capacity to measure.

events, figures, and metric units—with their different meanings, different functions, and different levels of aggregation. Learning to do so exemplifies in a very specific way what I mean by the capacity to make multiple mental representations, and with this the capacity to make multiple hearings. These capacities play an important role in musical development, and I will return to this critical point in the discussion of the children's drawings of the more complex rhythm and also in the discussion of melody in Part II.

CHAPTER 5

Convention, Innovation, and Multiple Hearings

IN MAKING the original typology of rhythm draw-ings, my conversations with the material had focused on a search for common strategies. In an effort to reduce complexity, I had necessarily collapsed observed differences among the drawings, organizing diversity into a few general types. But in doing so, I had also put aside drawings that did not seem to fit—or as Barbara McClintock put it, drawings that seemed like "an exception, an aberration, a contaminant." The typology was, in fact, a set of focused "snapshots" amidst the blur of a dynamic, varied, and mobile field. But once the typology was in hand, I turned my attention to making sense of these errant drawings. Against the stable background of the prototypes, I could recognize among these initial "throw-aways" examples that I now saw as richly provocative: mixed strategies, conflicts, multiple hearings that were strongly evocative of real-world musical experience.

Recall, for a moment, the situation of the experiment: 186 children in grades two through six were asked during their regular music classes to clap and then draw six different rhythms, then to go back, clap each again, and "put in some numbers that seem to fit." Going back to put in numbers gave the children a chance to make a "second pass" through the rhythms. In asking them to do so, I had several hunches in mind: the conventions associated with numbers in contrast with graphics might trigger a shift in a child's focus; this, in turn, might "liberate" new and different features; and finally, the result of juxtaposing the two modes of description might reveal conflicts between them and even, within one child's work, the potential for multiple hearings.

Prototypes were easily found among the drawings and analogous types within the numberings as well. But when I revisited the whole collection of drawings with a view toward differences rather than patterns of similarities, it was clear that the use of two modes of description had paid off. One of the rhythms, I called it the Target Rhythm, stood out as particularly interesting. The children's work with this rhythm resulted in a remarkable diversity of drawings and numberings. Although differences could be subsumed under features that characterized prototypes, still there were not more than five or six examples that were literally identical in both graphics and numberings. In turn, the data as a whole showed that children attended to differing features of the rhythm, resulting in multiple hearings; even within single examples, there was evidence for multiple and sometimes conflicting hearings. In short, the very simplicity of the task and of the rhythm revealed, as if in magnified microcosm, the potential for complexity inherent in musical structure itself, and certainly in our intelligent capacities for making sense of it.

The complexity was made even more manifest through the moves across performance media—clapping, hearing, describing—that were built in to the task. As the children moved from one medium to another, each mode of description became a reflection *of* the other and at the same time a reflection *on* the differing and particular qualities of each medium—graphics, "numbers that seemed to fit," describing the structured coherence of body-actions and sounds moving through time. The process had an unexpected effect: the assumed meanings of notational conventions—names, numerals, graphics, line-ups, use of paper-space—came apart as they were bent to comply with phenomena that were intimately familiar in sound and in action but not yet held still in description.

But there is a serious problem here: to simply *tell* the reader doesn't *make* it so. Understanding the substance of the children's work, its significance in illuminating the multiple dimensions of musical structure, along with understanding the intelligence that is involved, requires actually living through the children's work oneself. The reasons are expressed most saliently in Wittgenstein's comments which I quoted in the Prologue: "The aspects of things that are most important for us are hidden because of their simplicity and familiarity . . . And this means: we fail to be struck by what, once seen, is most striking and most powerful" (1953,

p. 50). How, then, do we come to notice these unnoticed, familiar aspects of music—those I have previously called "structural simples"; how can we be struck by that which is so common that we take it for granted? Probably only when we are confronted with an experience that is so anomalous that it forces us to look at what usually can remain buried in its everyday use and meaning. Just as the college students in my classes eventually came to hear what seemed initially to be a simple, unproblematic motive in a Beethoven movement in all its potentially multiple ways through Beethoven's transformations of it, so the reader can come to hear this apparently simple, unproblematic Target Rhythm in all its potentially multiple ways through the children's varied expressions of it. To move you to do just that, I will ask you to participate actively in the puzzles and confusions presented by a few examples from the children's work.

The first step is to become intimate with the Target Rhythm. This rhythm embodies some of our structural simples but not all, and this is interesting in itself. However, the rhythm does almost match the rhythm of a composed piece that will be familiar to most readers as the Lone Ranger theme. If you think of that rhythm as beginning on the longer note *after the first two notes,* you will have the Target Rhythm. With that rhythm in mind, begin by making the experiment that I asked the children to make: first clap it and then make a drawing of it, or perhaps several drawings mimicking the several strategies found in the original typology. Then go back, as I asked the children to do, and put in some numbers that seem to fit.

Now consider how the rhythm would look if you made Met's space-time experiment (Figure 5–1). Next, picture the rhythm embedded in its metric hierarchy (Figure 5–2). Finally, use the hierarchy to translate the Target Rhythm into SRN (Figure 5–3). As might be expected, the complexity of the rhythm is largely hidden by these last metric drawings, including SRN. Still, a clear description of the metric structure of the rhythm is useful as a backdrop, a limiting point of departure. Against this backdrop, the children's drawings will show that the complexity of the rhythm and its potential for multiple hearings lie in the intersections

Figure 5–1

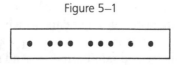

Met's space-time experiment: the Target Rhythm

Figure 5–2

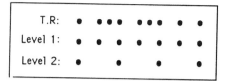

embedded in its metric hierarchy

Figure 5–3

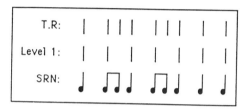

translated into SRN

between its metric and figural structures. Although the metric structure of the rhythm is expressed and encased by the conventional units of description given by SRN, description of its figural structure must be an invention—a reflection of and on our learned strategies for boundary-making. And to these multiply intersecting dimensions we must add a new one, the possibility for contention over boundary lines: "hearings" can differ most dramatically when boundaries conflict.

MET AND MOT PUZZLE OVER DRAWINGS OF THE TARGET RHYTHM

To help readers make their way through the multiple aspects of the material, I will again engage in a dialogue with Met and Mot. As they try to make sense of a few examples chosen from the children's work with the Target Rhythm, they will once more confront puzzling situations and also some surprises. The process itself is at least as important as the sense they eventually make of the children's work. The ten examples that we discuss are shown in Figure 5–4; the reader should refer to the drawings while following the discussion.

JEANNE: Now that you've gotten inside each other's heads a little, I'm curious to see what you'll make of some children's drawings of an-

Figure 5–4

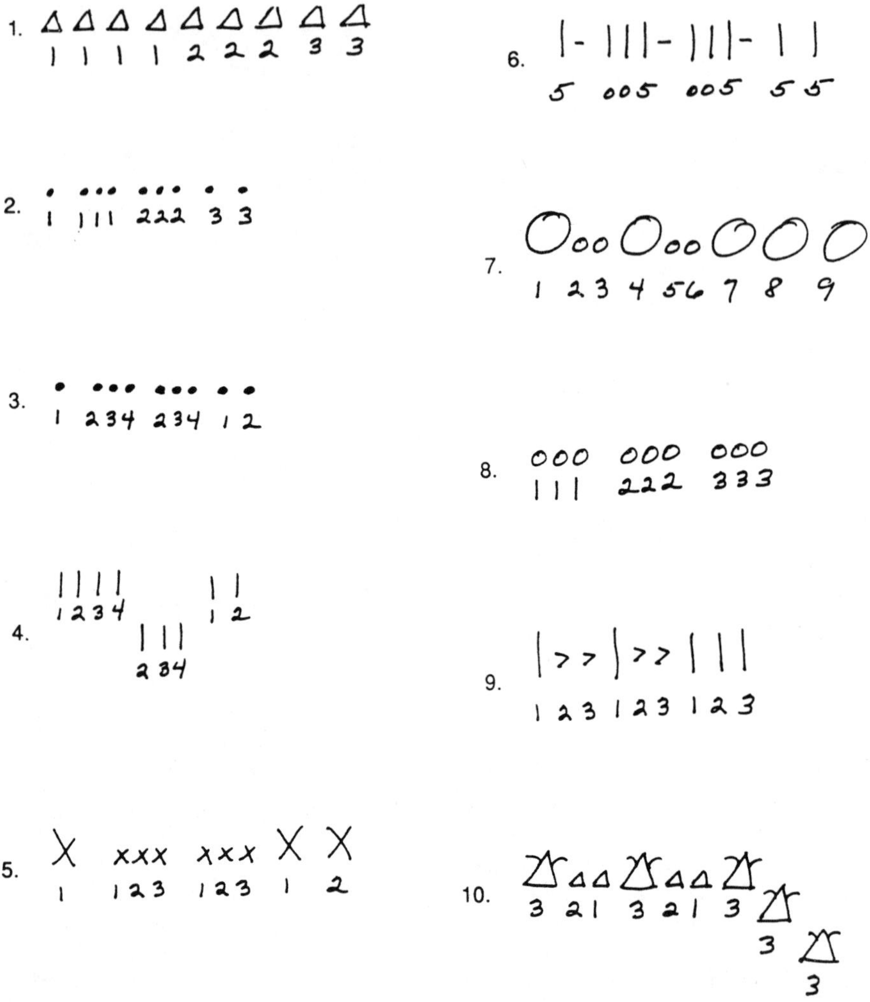

1. △△△△△△△△△
   l l l l 2 2 2 3 3

6. |- ||| - ||| - | |
   5 oo5 oo5 5 5

2. • ••• ••• • •
   i ¡|| 2л2 3 3

7. O₀₀ O₀₀ O O O
   1 23 4 56 7 8 9

3. • ••• ••• • •
   l 234 234 l 2

8. ooo ooo ooo
   ||| 222 333

4. ||||
   l234 | |
        ||| | 2
        2 34

9. | >> | >> | | |
   l 23 l 23 l 23

5. X xxx xxx X X
   l l 23 l 23 l 2

10. ⅄△△⅄△△⅄
    3 2l 3 2l 3 ⅄
            3 ⅄
              3

ten drawings of the Target Rhythm

other rhythm. (I show them the ten examples.) First of all, you'll notice that I asked the children to put in some numbers after they had
drawn the rhythm. Can you guess what the rhythm was?

MET: I can hardly believe they are all drawing the same rhythm. For
instance, look at Example 2 and then at Example 8. I would clap Example 2 like this (he claps):

and Example 8 like this (he claps):

MOT: Yes, me too. But how come?

MET: It's obvious. We're both reading space as time; I mean where there is a bigger space, we're leaving more time between claps, and that makes two very different patterns.

MOT: But we're doing something else, too.

MET: What's that?

MOT: I don't know quite how to say it . . . I guess we're just assuming that the space has a ghost beat in it.

MET: Oh, you mean we're making all the claps proportional to one another.

MOT: Well, maybe, but I certainly don't think "proportional" when I'm doing it—looking at the drawing and clapping it, I mean. It's more like I get going along this path . . .

MET: But it's *you* who are making this path of yours.

MOT: I'm making it and following it at the same time . . . Anyhow, it's sort of amazing that we can just do all that. By the way, did we get the rhythm right, Jeanne?

JEANNE: Yes, the one you clapped for Example 2 is what we gave the children; and yes, it really is quite remarkable. After all, the children's drawings don't tell you anything about how long or short, fast or slow, the claps are meant to be. You know, we seem to have a natural need to seek, or maybe to make, coherence in whatever it is we're paying attention to.

MET: What do you mean by "coherence"? I thought that what we take to be "coherence" was sort of the whole point.

JEANNE: You're absolutely right, Met, and it obviously depends on a whole collection of things, including a person's particular past experience.

MOT: This begins to sound like psychoanalysis, not musical analysis.

JEANNE: Well, it is in a way. For instance, in "reading" the children's drawings you are, without even thinking about it, seeing them through your own absorbed experience and learning: conventions for putting time into paper-space, as you said, and also your long experience in listening to the music around you, including its most common rhythmic gestures. And maybe most of all, your sense of how to make groupings or figures. This last aspect of coherence-making usually includes making accents that come along regularly to form points of gravitation within these figures. These are at least some of the generative organizers without which, I think, we would be left with only some kind of inchoate mess.

MOT: But when I looked at Examples 2 and 8, for instance, it felt like I just clapped them back naturally, all at once. What you just said seemed to take it all apart.

JEANNE: Yes. The analytic stories we tell often seem far removed from that all-at-once feeling, and from those paths of yours, Mot.

MOT: That's true, but why?

JEANNE: It's partly a different sense of time. In our analytic stories we, so to speak, hop off the internal time of this path you are going along, in order to stop and look *at it* in our own time. Then we can talk about before this, after that, and compare, measure, and classify. But when you're making and following an action-path, you take on *its* time and its own directionality of movement toward goals, too. This kind of time and movement, internal to the path itself, is quite different.

MOT: Yes, for me it feels more like passing through different zones. I guess I would call them something like "not yet; here; and gone."

JEANNE: So it seems that when you're clapping the rhythm, moving along the path in *its* time, you can look ahead, anticipate, but you can't look back. And when I step off the path in order to try to account for and say what seemed to you natural and all-at-once, it must seem to you as if we're "imposing our stories and our deathly arithmetics on your coherent landscapes."

MOT: Yes, that's right, even though I never could have said it like that. For instance, if I follow Example 7, I would clap it the same way as Example 2 without even thinking about it, even though they look completely different. It just seems natural to clap the big shapes longer and the little ones faster so they fit into the slower ones, somehow.

Example 7

Actually, Example 7 works just like your drawing of the Class Piece, Met.

Met's drawing of the Class Piece

That's why I like Examples 2 and 3 better—you can see the claps that go together.

MET: Here we go again—it all depends on what you mean by "go together." For instance, in Example 7, all the little ones go together because they're all alike—shorter.

MOT: Yes, I can see that now. But I can only see it after I step off the path I'm making in clapping the rhythm and, as Jeanne said, stop and *look at* the drawing. Then if I jump around, taking claps out of the order they come in, I can compare them, measure, and count. For instance, there are 4 shorts and 5 longs. But that kind of information certainly wouldn't help anyone to play the rhythm!

JEANNE: You remind me of a conversation between the White and Red Queens and Alice. It starts with the White Queen, who says:

> "We had *such* a thunder storm last Tuesday—I mean one of the last set of Tuesdays, you know."
>
> Alice was puzzled. "In *our* country," she remarked, "there's only one day at a time."
>
> The Red Queen said, "That's a poor thin way of doing things. Now *here*, we mostly have days and nights two or three at a time, and sometimes in the winter we take as many as five nights together—for warmth, you know." (Carroll 1960, p. 324)

MOT: Are you suggesting that I'm like Alice because I like to take things one at a time, just as they come? I think the strangest part is that once you or the Queens start putting things together *out-of-time*, you can do almost anything—put things together that . . .

MET: Are *you* suggesting that I'm . . .

JEANNE: Hold on a minute, now. Let's get back to the children's drawings. "Go together" can clearly mean different things and be used for different purposes, too. You two have just noticed two meanings for "go together," both of which are, I think, useful in thinking about how we make sense of rhythms: claps can "go together" when you're going along an action-path, taking events as they come; then they seem to group together as they collectively head for the upcoming goal or boundary.

MOT: Yes, those are the kind that stand out clearly in Examples 1 and 2.

JEANNE: Or claps can "go together" because they share some common property and thus belong to the same class of things.

MET: Like all Tuesdays.

JEANNE: Or all orange things or all round things.

MOT: And I suppose, in this case, all long or short things.

JEANNE: Of course, if you're paying attention to one meaning of "go together," it's easy to forget about any others or even, as we've seen all too clearly, just call another one wrong. But I think you two have gotten beyond that kind of single-mindedness!

MET: OK. Anyhow, I've just been looking at the numbers the kids put in and they seem very confused—or should I say confusing? The numberings in Examples 2 and 3, for instance, look really different from each other even though the pictures are identical. Then look at Examples 1 and 2—they're just the opposite: the pictures are really different from each other but the numbering is exactly the same in both of them (see Figure 5–5).

MOT: Well, the differences between 1 and 2 don't bother me because they don't actually contradict each other. The pictures in Example 1 are really neutral; I mean they don't tell you much since they're all the same. Maybe that kid just didn't bother much with his drawing. But when he went back over it to put in the numbers, he used the numbers to make something of the picture. What I mean is that he grouped and separated the pictures by the places where he changes to the next

Figure 5–5

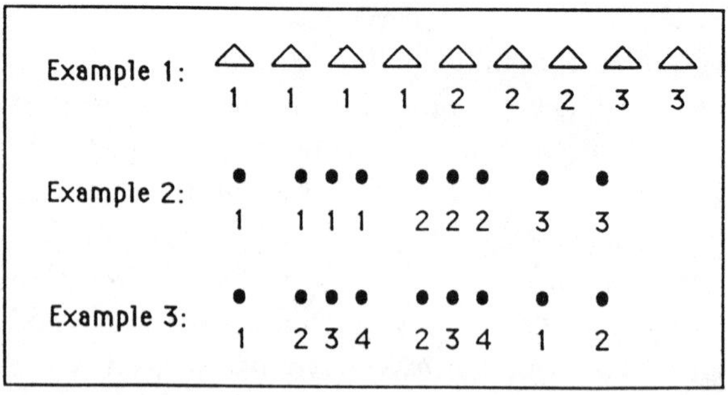

in Examples 1 and 2, the pictures are really different
but the numbering is exactly the same

Figure 5–6

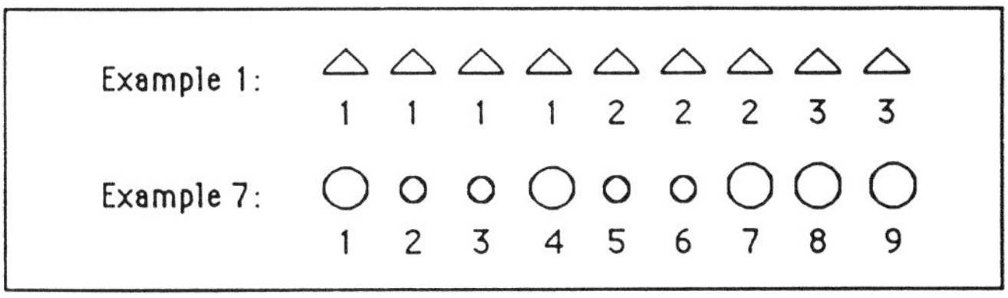

Example 1: △ △ △ △ △ △ △ △ △
            1 1 1 1 2 2 2 3 3

Example 7: ◯ ◦ ◦ ◯ ◦ ◦ ◯ ◯ ◯
            1 2 3 4 5 6 7 8 9

Example 7 is just the opposite of Example 1

number up each time. And I just noticed something else: Example 7 is just the opposite of Example 1 (see Figure 5–6). The graphics in Example 7 make the rhythm very clear—as I said before, it was really easy to clap the rhythm by looking at the graphics. But the numbering doesn't tell you anything except how many claps there are in all, and that they come one after the other. So in that sense, the numbers in Example 7 make the claps *all the same,* just as the pictures are all the same in Example 1. The kid who made Example 7 must have been more into graphics and not much into numbers; and the kid who made Example 1 was clearly not into graphics.

I just noticed something else: in Examples 3 and 4 the numbering is the same, even though the pictures are different; but that numbering seems really different from the numbering in Examples 1 and 2 (see Figure 5–7).

MET: OK, but what do the numberings mean? Wait a minute, maybe the numberings aren't so different after all. Look, in both pairs—Examples 1 and 2, and Examples 3 and 4—the kids are using numbers to group and to separate, as you said, Mot. And all four of them seem

Figure 5–7

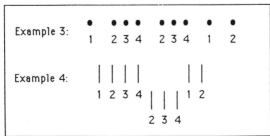

really different from the numbering in Examples 1 and 2

to be marking the same three groups or figures, but they have different ways of doing that: the two kids who made Examples 1 and 2 keep the same number *inside of a whole little group;* then they move to the next number up when they cross a grouping boundary—1 1 1 1, 2 2 2, 3 3. And the kids who made Examples 3 and 4 *number up inside of each group;* then they start numbering up over again when they cross a figure boundary—1 2 3 4, 2 3 4, 1 2. If you look at it this way, all four children are making boundaries in the same place.

MOT: That's great, and it helps me to see more, now: the children who number up when they cross a figure boundary—1's for the first group, 2's for the second group, and then 3's, as in Examples 1 and 2—show you not only where they hear *grouping boundaries* but also the *total number of figures* in all, namely, three. It's a little like the kid in Example 7 who shows you the total number of claps in all. But the children who made Examples 3 and 4, by numbering up *inside of* each group separately, show you something else, namely, how many claps there are in each group—four in the first group, four in the second . . . wait a minute, that's not right. They don't start over again with 1 each time—why do they go 2–3–4, instead of 1–2–3?

MET: Well, everything doesn't have to make sense—after all, they're just kids.

JEANNE: That won't get us very far, Met—if you'll pardon an obviously judgmental comment. What if you at least assume for the time being that the numbering *could* make sense . . .

MOT: I've got it! I just clapped the rhythm to myself again, and, do you know what . . . how shall I say it? The second little group starts in the middle of the first little group. I mean, the second group, by itself, is like a *piece* taken from the first group.

MET: Yes, you're right: the 2–3–4 of the first inner group is also the 2–3–4 of the second inner group.

JEANNE: Go on . . . and?

MET: I hear the rhythm differently, now, and I have to admit that that 2–3–4 numbering is beginning to make sense. If you clap the rhythm and say the numbers—1, 2–3–4, 2–3–4—then you *hear* repetition. I mean, you hear the part of the first group that becomes the second group. In fact, the second group, the 2–3–4, is like the first group but with its head chopped off; the 1 in the 1–2–3–4 is chopped off so it becomes just 2–3–4. And the third group at the end is a whole new thing, so you start over again with 1—so then you have 1–2. But I think *I'm* beginning to sound like someone in *Alice in Wonderland.*

JEANNE: When you put it that way, and hear it that way, the structure of the rhythm reminds me (don't worry, no more Red and White Queens) of Beethoven. What you have just noticed, Met, reminds me of the kind of thing Beethoven does with a motive when he's developing it. For instance, in developing a motive, he will sometimes fragment it, use just part of it, in order to make a varied repetition. It's an example of actually making something that's both the same and different. The kids' numbering in Examples 3 and 4 shows that process very clearly. I hadn't noticed it before.

MOT: So you're learning something from us, too. But have you looked at Example 5? Actually, the numbering in 5 does just what I expected to find in Examples 3 and 4. Look, the kid who made Example 5 *numbers up within each figure,* just like the children who did Examples 3 and 4. But because the first clap is all by itself in Example 5—like a figure with just one clap—the next two figures can both begin with 1: 1–2–3; 1–2–3.

```
Example 5:   X   XXX XXX   X   X
             1   123 123   1   2
```

can both begin with 1: 1-2-3, 1-2-3

And for that reason, you can see how many claps there are in each figure: one in the first, three in the next two, and two in the last.

MET: Now hearing the first clap as a figure all by itself makes me hear the rhythm still differently. How many ways are there to hear it, anyway? It seemed obvious to me in the beginning . . . aren't we really making too much of this?

JEANNE: Possibly so. But I'll tell you, once you start getting really involved with what the children have done, that is, taking their work seriously, even this seemingly simple rhythm seems to become endless in its multiplicity.

MOT: Speaking of multiplicity, I've just been looking at some of the other drawings again. They are really mixed up—or maybe I should say, mixtures.

MET: Very nice, Mot, but what do you mean?

MOT: Well, some of the kids seem to mix strategies. For instance, in Example 5, the graphics mix the *classification* strategy we saw in Example 7, where all the longs are bigger and the shorts are smaller, with the space-for-time strategy we saw in Examples 2 and 3. For instance, some of the longs in Example 5 are drawn with a big X, like the first clap and the last two; that's like the strategy we saw in Example 7 where bigger shapes stand for longer events. But longer events are also made by drawing a small x and leaving bigger spaces after them. That's like the longer claps in Examples 2 and 3.

```
┌─────────────────────────────────────────┐
│               X  xxx xxx  X  X          │
│  Example 5:                             │
│               1  1 23 1 23  1  2        │
└─────────────────────────────────────────┘
```

a mix of strategies

So 5 would be consistently like 7 if you made all the longs with a big X and all the shorts with a small x, like this (she draws):

```
┌─────────────────────────┐
│  X xx X xx X X X        │
└─────────────────────────┘
```

all the longs with a big X and all the shorts with a small x

Or, if you consistently use space-for-time, as in the graphics in Example 2, then you would have to make Example 5 look like this (she draws):

```
┌─────────────────────────────┐
│  x  xxx  xxx  x  x          │
└─────────────────────────────┘
```

consistently using space-for-time

But it doesn't seem right to use both strategies in the same drawing.

MET: Oh, come on, Mot, remember what Emerson said (I think): "Consistency is the hobgoblin of little minds." Leave the kids alone.

MOT: Well, that's an about-face!

MET: Besides, in your effort to make Example 5 consistently like Example 7, it doesn't *look* right. You can't see the figures anymore, as you used to say.

MOT: OK. So then tell me, what about the numbering in Example 6?

MET: It's a mixture, all right, or maybe a blend, but it's neat.

Example 6: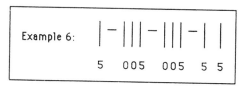

a mixture or a blend

MOT: Yes, I really like that one; I guess I would call it a *hybrid*. In fact, the child who made Example 6 is a perfect hybrid example of you and me, Met: he makes *me* happy with his graphics because the larger spaces show the claps that go together to make figures; but his numbering is for *you*: his numbers (his 0's and 5's) show your kind of "go together." See, the 0's and 5's name the claps that go together because, as Jeanne said, they share the same property—5's for all the long-types and 0's for all the short-types.

MET: Of course he might just as well have called the longs Alice and the shorts Humpty-Dumpty since, as you said, the numbers he uses are really just names. At least as far as I can see, they don't refer to any kind of quantity or any kind of measure. I think he was just having a good time with the task, making fun of it—especially using 0 for the shorts!

JEANNE: You're quite right, Met. I remember the boy who made that drawing; he was a really clever kid, and quite a joker, too.

MET: Sounds like me as a kid.

JEANNE: But back to the drawings. I like your notion of a hybrid, Mot. And the interesting thing is that you couldn't even think of a hybrid unless you already had a clear idea of what "pure types" might be. For instance, the two of you seem to be treating Examples 2 and 3 as norms to compare the other drawings with. But speaking of norms and anomalies, what do you think the kids were thinking and hearing to come up with the numbers in Examples 9 and 10? And what do you make of Example 8 now that you're catching on to all the kinds of things kids can do? (See Figure 5–8.)

MOT: Well, there's something interesting about all three. If these kids are using numbers like the kids who take-things-as-they-come, then they must be hearing the rhythm in a really strange way—I don't get it.

MET: But the graphics in Examples 9 and 10, at least, are just perfect: in Example 9 the sticks are all the longs and the > things are all the shorts.

Figure 5–8

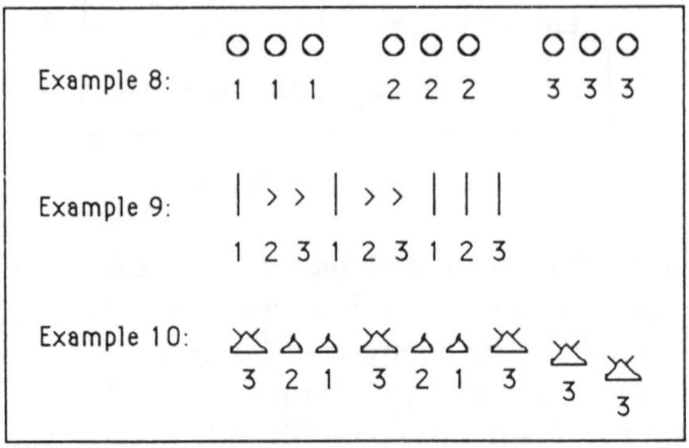

speaking of norms and anomalies

MOT: That's your sense of "perfect," anyhow.

MET: But the trouble is, the numbers don't go with the graphics. Actually, though, they sort of do in Example 10—at least all the longs are 3's. But what's this going-backward numbering—3 2 1—and then all the last ones 3's? That's got to be some kind of weird hybrid.

MOT: But look at Example 9. The child who made that one seems to be numbering up inside of figures as in Examples 3 and 4. But the runs of numbers start and stop at really different places from Examples 3 and 4. So if the Example 9 child is numbering up inside of figures, then he must be making boundaries in completely different places from those in Examples 3 and 4. Or for that matter, in different places from all the other examples we've been looking at.

MET: Let's say that you're right, Mot, that the strategy for numbering in Example 9 is like the strategy in Examples 3 and 4—numbering up inside of each little figure. And I agree, if that's true, then Example 9 must be representing different figural boundaries. But now look at Example 8. Let's say that the child who made Example 8 was using the numbering strategy we saw in Examples 1 and 2—keeping the same number inside of each figure and then changing to the next number up at boundaries. Now, if we're right about both Example 8 and Example 9, then Examples 8 and 9 *are making boundaries in the same places!* And actually, if you count counting backwards (gosh, another meaning for "count"), then Example 10 makes the same boundaries, too.

MOT: That's really amazing! And looked at that way, Example 10 is kind of intriguing: she (or he) counts *down,* taking claps as they come inside of those two figures, and then uses the other strategy for the last figure—same number for a whole group. But what's neat is that she gives you the best of both worlds: taking things as they come *and* classifying, since all the longs come out being called 3's!

MET: And there's something else: did you notice that when you group it this new way, the rhythm always ends up with *three big ones at the end;* but when you group it the other way, it always comes out with only *two big ones at the end.*

MOT: I wonder if I can clap the rhythm so that I can hear the claps grouping this new way. (Looking at Example 9, Mot claps.)

MET: Do you know what you did?

MOT: No, what?

MET: You made the first clap in every group louder.

MOT: I did? I wonder why.

MET: Well, do you know what that does? It keeps the shorter claps from running into the longer ones. In Example 9, for instance, clapping louder on the events numbered 1 in each figure made those events into beginnings. And something else: some of those same claps that we're hearing as beginnings now we heard as endings before. And that explains why you hear two big claps at the end when you group it the old way, and three big claps at the end when you group it this way. I think we can see it clearly if we put the two groupings together. (Met draws; see Figure 5–9.) I'll tell you, if I thought I was hearing the rhythm in different ways before—like Example 5 with the chopped-off head—that was nothing compared with this! It almost makes me dizzy.

Figure 5–9

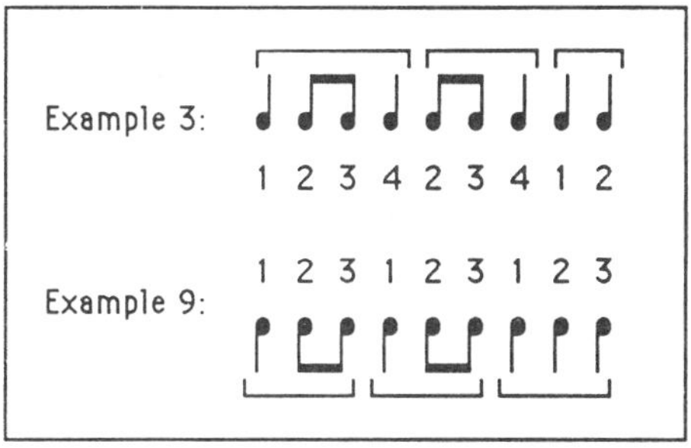

Example 3:

1 2 3 4 2 3 4 1 2

Example 9:

1 2 3 1 2 3 1 2 3

put the two groupings together

MOT: Me too. I wonder if we can get it back the way we heard it before? Met, try clapping it both ways, going back and forth between the two ways of grouping, and I'll listen.

MET: Good idea. (Looking at Examples 3 and 9, he claps first one and then the other.)

MOT: Gosh, they sound like different rhythms. Where the accent comes inside of figures seems to make a huge difference. I think you said something about "point of gravitation," Jeanne?

JEANNE: Good point, Mot. Actually, I was paraphrasing Schoenberg when he said: "The way the notes are joined is less important than where the center of gravity comes or the way the center of gravity shifts." And music-theory people sometimes talk about "beginning-accented" in contrast to "end-accented" figures. It's the issue of *function* again: the claps that just naturally sound accented (long claps after the two shorts, for instance) take on different functions in Met's two performances. As he regroups the rhythm in looking first at Example 3 and then at Example 9, the same accented clap comes out in different places within figures—sometimes the accent functions as an ending and sometimes as a beginning.

MET: So in the original grouping, the one pictured in Examples 1 and 2 for instance, the shorts went *to* the longs, with the longs making the boundaries of figures—like this (see Figure 5–10). But in the other grouping, the one we found in Examples 9 and 10, the function of the longs was just the opposite: figures took off *from* the longs, instead of going *to* the longs as in the other grouping—this way (see Figure 5–11).

MOT: And didn't Jeanne say that we hear a metric accent, a regularly recurring stronger beat in contrast to weaker beats, when beats coincide at more than one level of the hierarchy?

MET: Right; it's when faster beats at Level 1 meet up with slower beats at Level 2. You can see where the beats meet if we make a picture of it like this (see Figure 5–12).

Figure 5–10

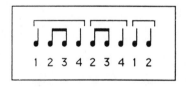

shorts went to *the longs*

Figure 5–11

figures took off from *the longs*

Figure 5–12

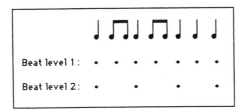

when faster beats meet up with slower beats

Figure 5–13

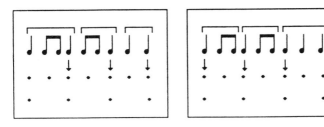

we can see exactly where the accent falls in each figure

MOT: So now if we look at the durations that we actually clapped grouped in the two different ways, together with the metric grid, we can see exactly where the accent falls inside of each figure (Figure 5–13).

MET: Yes. And in the original grouping we found, the one on the left, the figures always go *to* the accent.

MOT: Or putting it the other way, the accent always falls at the ends of figures, so these figures are "end-accented."

MET: But in the grouping we found later, in Examples 9 and 10, the one shown on the right, figures always kick off *from* the accent; so I guess they would be called "beginning-accented."

MOT: And when you clapped the rhythm as we see it in Example 9, you reinforced those beginning accents by clapping them louder. That kind of kicks off the figure. And then you have to catch your breath before you kick off the next figure.

MET: By the way, which of the groupings is the right one for this rhythm, Jeanne?

JEANNE: You two are beginning to sound like real performers. And I have to admit that was one of the things I had hoped would happen. For instance, your question, Met, about the "right grouping" is just the kind of question a performer might ask himself in the course of studying a piece; or, indeed, the kind of question that might form the basis for an argument between two performers—each defending what he or she believes to be the "right" one. For the moment let me just say, in answer, "it depends."

MET: Oh, come on, is that all there is to say?

JEANNE: OK, let's see if I can be a little more explicit. You may remember from our last conversation that I talked about how performers spend a lot of their working time experimenting with bowing and fingering if they're string players, or where to take a breath if they're wind players or singers. As I suggested before, much of that work has to do with developing a convincing hearing of the piece and then making sure that the hearing they intend is properly projected to an audience. It's what people sometimes call a convincing "interpretation" of the piece. And that process often has to do with issues of grouping, of accents, and with the possible functions of events—such as whether a note should be heard as an ending or as a beginning.

MET: How do they know how to do that?

JEANNE: For performers that process is usually a very active one that involves, among other things, experimenting with one grouping and then another. It's something like what Met just did with our rhythm, except that the performer has to be both maker and listener—both you, Met, making the music, and you, Mot, as listener. And learning to do that—to both play and listen to yourself—is no small task; in fact, it's an important part of becoming an artist.

MOT: You mean sort of performer and critic at the same time?

JEANNE: Exactly. And that's why I answered your question about right and wrong, Met, with "it depends." You see, the work that goes on in preparing a performance of a piece often involves making changes in what may seem like tiny details—something like the way you played some claps a little louder, or that sense of catching your breath. And it's just those decisions that eventually shape the meaning . . .

MOT AND MET (together): *Decisions?*

MOT: I certainly didn't consciously *decide* to play the beginnings louder. I mean, I didn't stop and think about it. In fact, I didn't even know I had done it.

JEANNE: Of course not, and neither does the experienced performer in more cases than not. It's a much more interactive process, a kind of conversation back and forth between the performer, his instrument, and the composition. As Ben Shahn said about the relationship between the painter and his painting, the sound of a passage on the instrument in the performer's hands "talks back" to him, "telling" him something about the piece even as he is shaping it. Repeating the passage in the course of this continuing conversation, the player will emphasize a note here, hesitate or urge the music on a little there; but not so much because he has stepped back, stopped, reflected *on* it and then made some decision—although that can sometimes happen, too. It's more a continuously active process of experimenting. One set of actions, one "for instance" performance of a passage, suggests the next one in response to the performer's hearing of the first. Reflection, then, is more *in* (rather than on) this chain of actions: thinking, decision-making, feeling, expression, and playing are all one closely intertwined and inseparable process of meaning-making.

So in answer to your question, Met, about right and wrong grouping, it depends on all of the above. How a performer plays a single small passage is influenced by and, in turn, can influence everything that is going on in the piece and in the performer's experience with it—even the character of the whole thing. And how well a performer learns to do all that has very much to do with his or her development as an artist.

MET: But doesn't the composer have something to say about all this? After all, I don't suppose *anything* will do; I mean the performer certainly doesn't have complete freedom. For instance, to come back to our lowly little rhythm, my two performances were triggered by what the kids had done—what they had put on paper.

JEANNE: Of course you're right. Composers have many ways of telling performers about grouping, for example. And, in fact, in many instances there is little ambiguity, especially when each of the multiple dimensions of a complex piece are, so to speak, in accord—reinforcing one another: melody, harmony, texture, instrumentation, and so forth. For instance, our rhythm is almost the same as the one Rossini uses in the William Tell Overture—the passage you may recognize as the Lone Ranger theme:

the Lone Ranger theme

Notice that in that version of the rhythm, there's a new head added to
our Target Rhythm, and that makes the grouping totally unambig-
uous.

MOT: Yes—having the extra two faster notes at the beginning sets it up
so you have to hear it as end-accented.

JEANNE: That's right, Mot. And composers also help to tell you how
they want groupings to be made by adding what are called "expressive markings" like the ones I showed you before. For instance, in our
rhythm, a composer might add markings something like this for the
groupings shown in Examples 3 and 4:

the groupings in Examples 3 and 4

Or you might see something like this for the groupings shown in Examples 9 and 10:

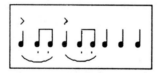

the groupings in Examples 9 and 10

The > sign means to make an accent by playing the note louder; and
the dots under notes mean to play them "short" rather than sustain-
ing them. Beethoven even added fingering here and there in the piano
sonatas explicity to tell the performer how he wanted the notes
grouped into figures. Interestingly, he used fingerings for this purpose when really no other kind of conventional expressive marking
would do.

MET: It seems like the kids have actually invented their own kinds of
expressive markings in the drawings and numberings—ways of showing the reader-performer how to group the rhythm just as composers

do when they add on these expressive markings to the bare notes. That's why, after all, I played Example 3 differently from Example 9. And you know what, I just caught on to Example 8. The spaces between circles that I thought meant longer time, before, are not time at all; they're—what should I call them—figure-dividers. I mean the spaces are like those expressive markings—they show you where to catch your breath between figures but without leaving any extra time.

Example 8:

| O O O | O O O | O O O |
| 1 1 1 | 2 2 2 | 3 3 3 |

the spaces are figure-dividers

Now I see how wrong a person can be: just because I used space for time, I assumed everyone else would too; and that's what made me think that Example 8 was a whole different rhythm. Remember, I originally clapped it like this:

originally clapped Example 8 like this

MOT: Yes, but that also shows how useful traditions and conventions can be. After all, real performers in learning to play a piece must be perfectly familiar with all those conventional expressive markings. In fact, I suppose they "read" them right along with the notes. The kids' inventions are really wonderful, but at this point I could do with a little of that conformity. My head is swimming with too many possibilities.

JEANNE: Yes, I know what you mean, and you have both been terrific—taking the children's work seriously and really sticking with it.

COMMENTS ON OUR CONVERSATION: FREEDOM AND CONSTRAINTS

Mot's last comments about conventions, the comfort of conformity, and the overabundance of possibilities suggested by the children's inventions recall an issue that has become an insistent thread in this developing web of concerns, suggesting the following paradox: on one hand, in order to become a professional in a field, it is necessary to learn the descriptive conventions associated with its practice. For in learning the notations, symbols, terms in good currency, we also learn the accepted, canonical structure of the domain itself. On the other hand, in doing so, we also "buy into" the organizing constraints, the mythology, and even the accepted ontology of that domain—that is, the tenets of current practice with respect to the "things" that are taken to exist as "occupants" of that particular world. The notations in use by a community of professionals have built into them just what the practitioners accept as "objects that work" as well as how to make them. How, then, is innovation born, and how are we to understand what a person knows how to *do* but cannot yet *say* within the limits of acceptable notational forms?

The point can be seen more clearly, perhaps, by considering the effect of such conventions in a field where the effect is grander, more palpable, and more immediately manifest. In her book *Planning: Rethinking Ciudad Guayana,* Lisa Peattie talks about the influence of representational conventions (sketches, maps, statistical projections) in the work of planners designing a new city in Venezuela. She says:

> Representations were not simply the way the planners presented a world, intimately known, in order to achieve some particular effect on an audience; the planners to a substantial degree experienced the city through their own representations of it . . . All forms of representation are abstractions from reality which bring some aspects forward to the attention and leave some in the background or eliminate them completely . . . But a description, because it selects and emphasizes, because it makes a statement about the world, to the degree that people attend to it and are influenced by it has political effects . . . Form and content are intertwined. What can be said depends on the language for saying it. (Peattie 1987, p. 112)

The children's drawings, together with Met and Mot's efforts to make sense of them, to "give them reason," demonstrate on a small scale the justice of Peattie's point and at the same time show the paradox between limits and freedom inherent in the power of descriptive conventions. The puzzles that Met and Mot encounter, and later the discoveries they make, are nearly always triggered by confrontations with representational conventions—particularly with conventions that they, albeit unknowingly, are, at the moment, taking for granted. For in reading the descriptions made by others, we quite naturally bring to them our own thoroughly internalized notational conventions; but these may well be different from the conventions assumed by those whose descriptions we are reading.

Once internalized, conventions behave like powerful reading glasses.

That is, notational conventions, like lenses to look through, are transparent—we don't notice them unless they get in the way. At the same time, they so thoroughly focus and shape our perceptions, along with the meanings we presume are there, that we can hardly escape their influence. Indeed, it is only when something goes very wrong and when we can no longer dismiss the situation as "merely an anomaly" that we are willing to confront those ingrained conventions that we depend on. For to question them can often threaten the very bases of our most ordinary ways of making sense—pulling the rug out from under us. So, in asking Met and Mot to engage the puzzles found in the children's work, I was asking them to "give the children reason," but also to do more than that: I was asking them to attend to their own, still transparent "reading glasses"—to look *at* what they were looking *through*. In this process, confrontation necessarily brought the children's notational conventions to the surface, including the various ways in which the children were understanding the descriptive conventions taught in school. Indeed, the children often found quite novel ways to use these conventions—for example, conventions associated with the use of numbers, line-ups, and space. Perhaps we can attribute their inventiveness to the fresh, still malleable ways in which they took these conventions; they were not yet fixed in their use, function, and meaning.

In fact, the situation was reciprocal in an important way. On one hand, neither the readers (Met and Mot) nor the makers (the children in carrying out the task put to them) had yet acquired or at least not yet thoroughly internalized the descriptive conventions of music notation. On the other hand, both readers and makers had know-how for making descriptions in other domains (math, space, reading/writing) and also know-how for clapping and making sense of rhythms. As a result, both were inventively borrowing from the familiar means they had for *describing* to say what they could about their familiar *actions*. This reciprocity between action, description, and invention was instrumental in triggering insights, particularly insights concerning multiple hearings of the rhythm that might have remained hidden if both readers and makers had remained within the constraints given by notational convention.

Consider some examples from the conversation. There was Met's discovery about the child's use of space in Example 8: "the larger spaces between dots that I thought meant longer time, before, are not time at all . . . just because I used space for time, I assumed everyone else would, too." Then there was the puzzling meaning of the numbering in Examples 3 and 4, where Met initially suggested that "everything doesn't have to make sense—after all, they're just kids." The presumed convention here was the use of "counting numbers" to count up the events or things included in some bounded entity—the number of eggs in a carton, the number of boys and girls in a classroom, the number of stars we see in the "figure" we call the Big Dipper, or, in this case, the number of claps in the figures we hear in a rhythm. Given the accepted conventions for counting up, why, Mot wondered, did the children number the claps 1–2–3–4, 2–3–4, 1–2, instead of 1–2–3–4, 1–2–3, 1–2? Confronting the numbering as a puzzle instead of simply some aberrant notation led to musical insight. The children, in fact, had used numbering not only to count but also to name. That is, when a segment of a series was repeated exactly, the numbers given to the elements in that segment could also be used to designate or name just that segment of the series that was repeated. And by bending the counting-up convention in this fashion, they seem to have found a way to express a particular *musical* meaning. In turn, the children's notational invention, which Met initially treated as a "throw-away," led him to a new hearing of the rhythm: "The second group, the 2–3–4, is like the first group but with its head chopped off":

But the most telling lesson that Met and Mot were learning was how to seek out and probe for the musical meanings "hiding" in a child's invented notation. The process became a kind of lively quest in which even notational "inconsistency" in a child's work could bear fruit. For instance, Examples 5 and 6 were called "hybrids": the children mixed classification with space-for-time strategies in their graphics, and Example 6 showed a mixed numbering strategy as well. Example 6 was a particularly interesting hybrid: Mot found her figural strategy (F.2) in its graphics but Met's classification strategy (M.2) in its numbering.

But it is important to note that Mot and Met could only have recognized Examples 5 and 6 as hybrids in the light of the earlier examples which they had come to think of as "normal." That is, within this small community of two students, the notational strategies used in some of the examples (particularly Examples 1–4) had acquired the status of conventions. Met and Mot were repeating in microcosm the behavior of larger communities of "experts": conventions that crystallized from within a particular practice became established as norms; and once established, examples that did not match these norms—albeit newly derived—were then seen as anomalous. But as Met and Mot learned to use the conventions as a backdrop to frame or set a problem rather than merely to exclude possibilities, they were also able to see the examples in new ways: recognizing an example as a hybrid helped to make the features of "pure types" more clear.

But conventions, once articulated, can serve as vehicles for musical insight as well. For instance, it was only by using the conventions that had crystallized through the study of Examples 1–4 (for example, numbering up inside of figural boundaries) that Met and Mot were finally able to make sense of Examples 8–10. Mot says, at first (giving a name to the relevant convention), "if these kids are using numbers like the kids who take-things-as-they-come, then they must be hearing the rhythm in a really strange way—I don't get it." But, using this notational strategy as a vehicle for finding figural boundaries, Met discovers that in all three examples the children are "making boundaries in the same places . . . but in completely different places from all the others we've been looking at." It seemed possible that it was not the notational strategy that was anomalous, but rather what the notation was expressing—the children seemed to be describing a different *hearing*. When Met and Mot tested their hunch by turning to action—playing the rhythm so as to feel and hear this new grouping—the result was dizzying. Shifting grouping boundaries and the position of accents within them was positively disorienting: "They sound like different rhythms." Once understood and accepted, notational conventions can be powerful indeed: the children were able to tell their readers how to perform the rhythm and, in turn, bring them to hear it in a whole new way.

Once Met and Mot had moved into the world of musical performance ("which is the right grouping?"), the children's graphics and numberings could be seen as expressive markings—like the ones composers add on to the bare notation of pitch and time. But interestingly, even though the children's notations did not include the information conveyed by SRN, namely, the proportional time relations among events, their "expressive notations" showing figural grouping or phrasing seemed to substitute for this missing temporal information. That is, although none of the children's representations of the rhythm told their readers exactly how long or how short events should be, Met and Mot, like most of us, were still able to find the intended rhythm in them.

Even though we are working here with minimally musical material, it still serves to illuminate the critically reciprocal relations between notations and meaning: on one hand, notational conventions carve out, give particular shape and meaning to, a world of phenomena; on the other, bending convention, once it is recognized, can liberate new meanings. It is for a similar reason that poets bend lexical and syntactic conventions; in doing so they liberate otherwise unnoticed feelings, senses, even objects, making the reader experience even what is simplest and most familiar in new ways. Here is a beautiful example by James Joyce:

Simples

Of cool sweet dew and radiance mild
The moon a web of silence weaves
In the still garden where a child
Gathers the simple salad leaves.

A moondew stars her hanging hair
And moonlight kisses her young brow
And, gathering, she sings an air:
Fair as the wave is, fair, art thou!

Be mine, I pray, a waxen ear
To shield me from her childish croon
And mine a shielded heart for her
Who gathers simples of the moon.

LOOKING BACK

Through these conversations—with the children's work and between Met, Mot, and myself—I have tried to give the reader a feeling for some of the important ideas emerging from the data:

- Possibilities for multiple hearings and multiple representations of even an apparently simple rhythm.
- The variety of ways children find to use numbers and, in turn, the variety of meanings they are able to give to them.
- The powerful reciprocal influence between representations, on the one hand, and on the other, what you see or hear or even take to exist in the phenomena before you.
- The influence of conventions—how they crystallize within a community and how they can be used and abused.
- Perhaps most important, the idea that in taking the work of children (and others) seriously and confronting the puzzles that result, one plays out a process in which teaching, learning, and research are all closely intertwined.

With these ideas in mind, it would be useful to look back for a moment to the series of questions with which I began the Prologue:

- What does it mean to have or to use musical knowledge; is there a difference between knowing *how* and knowing *about?* Could it be that when you know *about* music, the music itself changes?
- What is meant by a "hearing," and how can we characterize and account for differences among them?
- What are the relations between "units of perception" and "units of description"?

With respect to the first question, the discussions of the children's drawings of rhythms and the conversations with Met and Mot demonstrated that individuals with no formal music training certainly do know *how* (to clap, to sing, to group, to count), and that in knowing how they know well but also differently from those with formal music training—those who know *about.* In turn, the drawings and the conversations provided evidence through which to characterize how "hearings" (perhaps "the music" as well) may differ and, to some extent, how we might account for these differences. The figural/metric distinction in the typology of rhythm drawings in Chapter 3 explicitly accounted for some of these differences, but with the caveat that even though the kinds of features captured in each type of drawing differed, all are relevant aspects of rhythmic structure itself.

At the same time, the collection of experiences around the figural/ metric distinction dramatically demonstrated the extent to which differences can exist as individuals construct the coherence they seem simply to find. In constructing coherence, individuals must, for example, differentiate and aggregate, determine same and different, find and build patterns at various levels of structure. And these same mental actions that guide the constructing of coherence even in such small, musically minimal examples also help to shape the quality, value, and meaning they give to much larger and more significant phenomena in the world around them.

With respect to the third question (the relations and disjunctions between "units of perception" and "units of description"), the drawings, along with our conversations about them, made clear that as individuals make descriptions—for example, as they externalize in static paperspace that which is experienced in motion and through time—significant transformations are involved. And perhaps most important, the particular transformations implicit in our *conventional* units of description may be quite different from the transformations implicit in the units of description that people *invent*. Finally, we also saw that the results of the transformations, the external descriptions, are often too easy to believe in, even when we know that they reflect only some of the possible features and relations of the phenomena while ignoring others.

But static descriptions have power: they allow their makers as well as their readers to discover relations that might otherwise remain unnoticed, even inaccessible. For example, static descriptions in paper-space make it possible for people to notice and compare events that are distanced from one another in real time or space. In the course of making descriptions, Met and Mot were able to discover that their differences often involved contentions over what each meant by "go together." For Mot, who prefers to "take-things-as-they-come," claps go together when, as a succession, they form a little bounded entity, a "figure." Met, "jumping off" the internal time of his action-path, takes things out of order so as to select just those events that share some common property. For Met, then, to "go together" means to form a class—like the class of all longs or all shorts.

It was also pointed out in our dialogues that in the broader context of the performance and understanding of complex musical compositions, figural and metric strategies are also relevant—perhaps even helping to account for divergent "hearings" among professional musicians. In the more traditional language of performing musicians, figural grouping has to do with "phrasing," with the "shaping of a phrase." However, since figural grouping is most often not given in the printed score (because the conventional units of description for temporal relations describe only metric units), these groupings must be constructed by the performer through selective attention to particular features and relations as these occur in the flow of the piece. Performers reflect and project these figural relations and figural groupings in their decisions concerning bowing, breathing, fingering, dynamics, and the subtle give-and-take of the measured beat. Or to put it more operationally, constructing, on one hand, and projecting figures, on the other, are in practice (or in practicing) reciprocally interactive: the feel of a passage on the instrument, experimenting with these action-paths, listening to the resulting "back-talk" as the instrument responds, and the construction of figural groupings all work together in developing a performer's particular "hearing" which is realized in performance.

Further, just as in the musically sparse rhythms, two events that are the same in measured time (like two "longs" in the Class Piece) may take on quite different effect and function in the unfolding of large, complex works as well. For example, depending on their *situation* within a single composition, the function of two events, even two figures that look the same on the printed page, can change, transform, regroup in response to new proximities or to particular changes among relations in other dimensions.

All the stories thus far have carried with them another message: the urge to maintain a particular view as *the* view is pervasive and powerful. It protects all of us from the threat of upsetting the very means by which we make sense of some small part of the world around us. And yet learning to shift focus, to restructure our current "windows to the world" so as to appreciate the view of another, may be the most crucial aspect of any significant learning experience. But it always involves risk: the risk of temporary cognitive disequilibrium, which we saw so vividly in Mot's discovery of the "ghost beat" and again as both Met and Mot struggled to make sense of the children's drawings—especially the dizzying effect when they eventually discovered that some of the children were depicting a different grouping, a different hearing.

Finally, I would like to make quite explicit a message that was perhaps too hidden in my talks with Met and Mot and to which I will return in the final chapter of the book: to help children learn in ways that will make a difference, both teachers and students need to be encouraged to take just such cognitive risks. For example, instead of remaining comfortably ensconced in our descriptive conventions and always asking children to subscribe to these "privileged" descriptions of a melody or rhythm, we can ask them, instead, to make multiple descriptions of the "same" thing. And in doing so, we can recognize that each description, including the traditional one, captures different but legitimate features, these in turn suggesting different *possible* foci of attention. Like Met and Mot, both teacher and student may, in this way, discover new ideas and at the same time come to a better understanding of each other as well.

As we go on in Part II to stories about melody and tune-building, many of the same issues will recur but now in a musical environment that is enriched by pitch relations. In some ways this new dimension adds complexity, but in other ways the greater richness will lend clarity both to the distinctions and to the questions themselves.

Tune-Building

CHAPTER 6

Building "Hot Cross Buns" with Tuneblocks: Introducing Jeff

THE TUNE-BUILDING stories I will tell focus on one child, Jeff, with whom I worked over a period of about six months. Jeff was one of six children who came into the Children's Learning Lab at MIT as participants in an experimental teaching project in the fall of 1975. At that time, I and other members of Seymour Papert's research group were exploring and developing possibilities for using computers and the computer language Logo for "teaching children thinking." Jeff, like the others, was chosen by lot from a third/fourth grade class at the Cambridge Alternative Public School. The children came to the Lab twice a week for about an hour and a half.

It was evident from the beginning of the children's six-month stay in the Lab that Jeff, who was eight years old, was well behind the others in school skills. While in school, he talked little ("not at all," reportedly, when he entered the school at age six), although he was clearly quite talkative on the playground as he interacted with the other children. Jeff was having difficulties learning to read; his math skills were limited mostly to counting, and even here he sometimes failed to make one-to-one correspondences. At the same time, Jeff's behavior suggested that lurking behind these "learning disabilities" was an active and inventive mind at work. Indeed, there was something very impressive about Jeff—he was tall and thin, very well coordinated ("the fastest runner in his age group"), and he had another quality that I can only describe as a kind of internal dignity.

My work with Jeff differs in an important way from the previous experimental situations and their results: whereas the rhythm studies focused on differing, often conflicting hearings *across* individuals, this study focuses on the conflicts in hearings and in the processes of constructing those hearings that one child confronts in the course of his own work. The story of Jeff is, then, the story of the "cognitive work" he does and the risks involved as he learns to restructure and to coordinate his varied and often dissonant ways of making and representing simple tunes to himself.

Thus, as a result of the relatively long period during which Jeff and I worked together, I was also able to gain a better understanding of what is sometimes called cognitive change, sometimes cognitive restructuring, or sometimes even an "Aha!" experience—a sudden flash of insight. But when we carefully trace the course of Jeff's work, it becomes clear that what we might take, at the moment, as an "Aha experience" is in fact the result of a long process through which, over time, Jeff slowly comes to see (quite literally) and hear in new ways. It becomes clear, for example, that the child, like the adult scientist or artist, gains significant new insight only over a long period wherein he has time to test, to explore, even to play, and in that process to restructure, to risk cognitive disequilibrium, and to struggle with the incongruences that inevitably arise. "The sudden insight in which a problem is solved, when it is solved suddenly, may represent only a minor nodal point, like the crest of a wave, in a long and very slow process . . . the development of a (new) point of view" (Gruber 1981, p. 5). This is Howard Gruber talking about Darwin, but it could apply just as well to Jeff, the small boy in this story.

In my work with Jeff, as in my work with the fourth-grade children that resulted in the first rhythm drawings of the Class Piece, research and teaching are reciprocal—the one informing and enriching the other. For example, instead of excluding interventions, as one might in a more traditional experimental situation, in my work with Jeff I use them as an important part of the work to be done. And as in the dialogues with Met and Mot, I perturb the situation sometimes in a planned way, but often as an improvisation in response to an on-the-spot hunch. The interventions, then, are a way of maintaining a conversation back and forth with the material. In particular, they are a way of testing a running hypothesis concerning how Jeff might be representing the problem, the materials, and the situation to himself. As in the rhythm experiments, the work with Jeff led to important clues which I later tested through the design of experimental situations in which larger groups of subjects participated. Perhaps most important, the questions, puzzles, and confusions that evolved in the course of these six months went far beyond the questions I had initially put to myself—indeed, with Jeff's help, I too quite literally came to see in new ways.

In this and the next two chapters I trace Jeff's work with the tune "Hot Cross Buns." The work involves two different settings: in the first Jeff builds the tune using a computer along with a synthesizer as sounding medium; in the second he builds the tune using a set of Montessori bells. The two media make a striking contrast. In the computer situation, Jeff must begin with names for things that are already predetermined by the design of the computer program; it is these names, when used as commands to the computer and synthesizer, that produce sounding results. With the bells, Jeff begins with unnamed, hands-on objects that he can move about; and it is the objects and his actions on them, without any symbolic intermediary, that directly produce sounding results. However, in both situations I ask Jeff to make his own paper-and-pencil descriptions, which help to illuminate his inner strategies for making sense of the tune.

In the remainder of this chapter I go thrice-over Jeff's computer session: first I give a move-by-move description of the session; this is followed by a dialogue with Met and Mot in which we discuss the surprises and puzzles that arise in Jeff's work with the computer; then I conclude with comments on this dialogue. Chapter 7 begins with a detailed description of Jeff's first session with the Montessori bells, during which he builds Hot Cross Buns, and ends with a conversation about it with Met and Mot. In Chapter 8 this conversation continues as I tell Met and Mot about the instructions Jeff invents for playing Hot Cross Buns on the bells. As I do so, we discuss the various problems he encounters and also the discoveries he makes along the way. Once again, our conversation is followed by my remarks on it. These conversations set up many of the puzzles and questions that are confronted in Part III, which is entirely devoted to Jeff's development as he works with the bells building, rebuilding, and making instructions for the tune "Twinkle Twinkle Little Star."

THE COMPUTER AND THE PROJECT "TUNEBLOCKS"

Having discovered early on that Jeff's math skills were quite limited, I chose to work first with him on a music task that involved the computer,

but no computation and little use of the computer keyboard (since reading and spelling were also difficult for him). The game we played is called
"Tuneblocks." I had invented the game in response to what I had learned
from the rhythm studies: when people listen to a rhythm or a melody,
especially individuals with no formal music training, their "units of perception" tend to be figures rather than notes. It is also clear that figures
are different kinds of entities from notes, which are the units of description in standard music notation (SMN). To make the point clear, try a
little experiment: sing the *first phrase* of "The Star-Spangled Banner" to
yourself. You probably had no trouble hearing and stopping at the end
of what you hear as the first phrase, but can you say, quickly, without
going back over your singing, how many *notes* you sang? I suspect not.
If I am right, the experiment strongly suggests that our conventional
units of description, the notes that you would see in a printed score of
"The Star-Spangled Banner", are at a much more fine-grained level of
structural detail than our units of perception, and they are quite different
kinds of entities as well.

With this in mind, and with the possibilities presented by the computer, it was easy to set up a tune-building game in which *musical figures*
rather than notes could be the units of description. These figures would,
then, be the building blocks with which a tune-builder could work. In
this way, novice tune-builders could benefit from the closer congruence
between their intuitive units of perception and the units of description as
given in the game.

Put yourself in Jeff's place as he began his work with Tuneblocks.
Seated at a computer, you are asked to reconstruct the tune "Hot Cross
Buns." To begin, you simply type the word HOT, and instantly you hear
the whole tune "played" by a synthesizer we called the Music Box.* You
can, of course, listen to HOT as many times as you like. The task is to
rebuild HOT using just two figures or Tuneblocks, each of which is a
small meaningful *segment* of the tune.† The blocks have been named,
respectively, HA and HO. When you type HA, you hear the whole segment of the tune that goes with the words, "One-a-penny, two-a-penny."
Typing HO, you hear the whole segment of the tune that goes with the

---

*The original Music Box was a digital synthesizer invented by Marvin Minsky. Terry
Winograd, then a graduate student in the Artificial Intelligence Lab, in turn had built the
music primitives so that commands in Logo could "talk" to the Music Box.
†I have omitted certain commands (such as striking the ENTER key and typing PM
for Play Music) in order not to encumber the reader's grasp of the basic features of the
game.

Figure 6–1

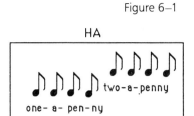

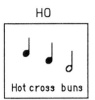

words, "Hot cross buns." I can, of course, transcribe the two blocks so that you can see their "contents" at the note level (Figure 6–1). But keep in mind that for the player who is playing the game, this level is not present at all; that is, the player's functional units of description, the names HA and HO, are at the more aggregated level of figures, and these descriptions immediately result in the "performance" through time of these whole, meaningful structural segments of the tune.

The goal of the game is to arrange the blocks—that is, to type in their names one after the other, including repetitions if necessary—so that when they are played back in the lined-up succession that you have requested and that you can see on the computer screen, you will hear the whole tune. Before going on to see what Jeff did, imagine for a moment how you would build the tune HOT using just the two blocks.*

JEFF BUILDS HOT CROSS BUNS WITH TUNEBLOCKS

Jeff and I worked together on building "Hot Cross Buns." While I helped Jeff by demonstrating instead of just describing, he could also experiment by himself. After telling Jeff that we were going to play a game called Tuneblocks, I explained that the game was to build up a whole tune, like Hot Cross Buns, out of blocks which the computer could play. It was, I suggested, a little like putting together a jigsaw puzzle—if you arranged the cut-up pieces of the puzzle in the right order, you would put the whole original picture back together again. The blocks for Hot Cross Buns, I told Jeff, were called HA and HO. Each of them was a cut-up "piece" of that tune, and when the blocks were arranged in the right order, they would play the whole tune.

I will describe this first session just as it happened. The session took about 20 minutes, and I have divided Jeff's work during that time into five parts. The boundaries of these parts are structural boundaries—that

---

* The correct answer is, of course, HO HO HA HO.

is, each marks what I see as a change of some kind: for example, a change in Jeff's focus of attention, a new intervention, or a new puzzlement. As you read, think of yourself as the observer of this session. How would you account for Jeff's comments, his various moves including singing and drawing, and also the reasons for and influence of my interventions? Jeff's comments and the descriptions of his singing are shown in bold type.

Throughout the session I helped Jeff type commands to the computer. His typing was, of course, slow and studied—search and find, one letter at a time. I began by helping Jeff to type HOT, explaining that this was how to tell the computer to play the whole tune, Hot Cross Buns.

I

With my help, Jeff types HOT and listens to the whole tune.

Jeanne: Good. Now try HA and listen to what that sounds like.

Jeff slowly types H-A, and the Music Box plays the block named HA—that is, the melody that goes with the words, "one-a-penny, two-a-penny."

Listening to what the Music Box played, Jeff says:
"It skipped one."

Jeanne: Interesting. Now let's see what HO sounds like.

Jeff types H-O, and the Music Box plays the tuneblock HO—that is, the melody that goes with the words, "Hot cross buns."

Listening to what the Music Box played, Jeff says:
"That's the first one."

II

Jeanne: OK Now how about if you be the computer and sing HO?

In responding to my request, instead of singing the *single* block, HO, that the Music Box had played, Jeff sings two—that is, he
sings HO-HO.

Jeanne: Hmm. Try the computer's HO again, and listen to the music very carefully.

Jeff types HO again, and listens.

Jeanne: Now ask the computer to do HO HO.

Jeff types HO HO, listens, but looks confused.

Jeanne: Now can you be the computer, and sing *just* HO?

In response to my request, Jeff
sings HO (pause) HO.

III

Jeanne: Do you think you could draw a picture of HO?

Jeff makes the following drawing:

$$| \quad | \quad |$$

Jeanne: And now how about a picture of HO HO?

Jeff makes another drawing:

$$| \ | \ | \quad | \ | \ |$$

IV

Jeanne: That's terrific! Now can you be the computer and sing HA?

Jeff sings just that part of HA that goes with the words, "one-a-penny." That is, Jeff
sings the first part of HA.

Jeanne: How about asking the computer to do HA, once more?

Jeff types HA again and listens to what the Music Box plays.

Jeanne: Now can you draw a picture of HA?

Jeff draws the following picture:

$$| \ | \ | \ | \ | \ | \qquad \text{(one note missing)}$$

Then, after tracing over his first drawing with his finger, Jeff draws HA again, slowly:

$$| \ | \ | \ | \ | \ | \ | \qquad \text{(correct number)}$$

V

Jeanne: Great! So how does the tune go so far? See if you can get the computer to play the tune as far as you've got it.

Jeff types HO HO HA, and listens. He hears the melody that goes with the words, "Hot cross buns, hot cross buns; one-a-penny, two-a-penny."

Jeanne: Good, and now what comes next?

Jeff looks at me, looks away, but says nothing. I wait; there is a long pause.

Jeanne: How about getting the computer to play the tune so far, and then you *sing* what comes next.

Jeff types HO HO HA again, listens, and then sings correctly the melody for the final words; that is, he sings:

Jeanne: And what is that that you just sang?

Jeff is again silent and there is another long pause.

Jeanne: Let's see what happens if you try adding a HO at the end—after your HO HO HA.

Jeff types HO HO HA once more and (begrudgingly) adds HO. He listens to the Music Box playing back the results, recognizes HOT, but, shrugging his shoulders, seems to take it as magic.

How are we to understand Jeff's comments, his productions, and his puzzlements? In fact, as we shall see, many of the issues that arise in Jeff's session with HOT are similar to those we have encountered before in trying to understand the children's drawings of rhythms. Therefore, I will ask the reader to follow Met, Mot, and myself once again as we try to "give Jeff reason." It will be useful to refer to the account of Jeff's session as we continue our conversation.

MET AND MOT PUZZLE OVER JEFF'S WORK ON HOT

JEANNE: Now that you've worked through Jeff's first session, listening to the Music Box play each of his requests and carefully reading his responses, what do you think?

MET: You said the whole session only took about twenty minutes, but a lot happens and some of it is pretty strange. Let's go over the whole thing again slowly.

JEANNE: Good.

MOT: First of all, the sound of the Music Box is so dehumanized. As the Red Queen said somewhere else, "That's a poor thin way of doing things."

MET: Well, you get used to it after a while. What intrigued me was how little Jeff actually says—a couple of things right at the beginning and that's it. It makes it hard to tell what he's thinking. For instance, remember what Jeff says right at the beginning when he hears the block HA?

MOT: Sure. He says, "It skipped one." And I suppose the "it" that did the skipping was the computer—a kind of willful machine that didn't have the good sense to start at the beginning.

MET: Probably so. But then when he hears the block HO, he says, "That's the first one." It seemed to me that there was a kind of contradiction there.

MOT: What do you mean?

MET: Well, Jeff says that the computer skipped "one" when it played HA, and then when he hears HO he says "that's the first *one*." What bothers me is that he uses the word "one" in those descriptions of what he heard to refer to different objects—different segments of the tune. The "one" that the computer skipped when it played HA is the whole first part, but the HO block is only part of that part.

MOT: So it's our old problem of what is an entity, a "thing." That's interesting, but it didn't bother me so much. What I found really strange, though, was when Jeanne asked Jeff to be the computer and sing the block named HO, he sang HO-HO—two blocks instead of the *one* that the Music Box played. Why do you think he did that, Jeanne?

JEANNE: At the time I couldn't understand it at all, but now I think have a better idea of what was going on.

MOT: Are you going to tell us?

JEANNE: Yes, and it's related to Met's concern about Jeff's use of "one." After thinking about it for a while, I realized that in programming the blocks I had probably broken the tune up differently from the way Jeff was hearing it. I suspect that I made two blocks, HO HO, out of what Jeff heard as just one unbreakable object. For Jeff, everything that came before HA was just one entity, not two.

MET: I suppose that one unbreakable object was the "one" that Jeff was talking about when he heard HA and said, "It skipped *one.*"

JEANNE: Exactly.

MET: But when he typed HO and heard the computer play only part of that whole, he should have gotten it straight. After all, the name you give to an object is what you define it to mean—just what you program the computer to do.

JEANNE: That may be obvious to you, Met, but for people a name isn't as firmly attached to its meaning or to the object it refers to as it is for a computer. And in this case, Jeff's integrity, his own way of hearing the structure of the tune, took precedence over the meaning I had given to the name HO.

MET: What do you mean, Jeff's "integrity"? It seems to me he just didn't get it.

JEANNE: Think about it this way, Met: When you invent a name, it's a way of *giving meaning* to an object; you bound a bit of the universe that you're attending to so as to differentiate it from its surround; in a sense, you bring that circumscribed bit of phenomena into existence. But the meaning *you* intend isn't necessarily obvious to someone else. In fact, learning something new often involves finding the meaning that another intends for some word or name; it's another instance of getting into another person's head.

MET: But doesn't it usually work the other way around? In school, we're usually *given* the definition of a word; we aren't expected to invent it.

JEANNE: That's the way it's supposed to work, but it often doesn't. For instance, in this case I defined the meaning of HO by the way I programmed the computer. Nevertheless, if I'm right, Jeff took the name and gave it a different meaning, attached the name to a different object. And what's important is that he attached the name to an object that matched his own internal hearing of the tune.

MOT: And what you're calling his internal hearing was reflected in the first words he said when he heard HA. I mean, he stuck to the idea that the "one" the computer skipped when it played HA was really one thing.

JEANNE: Yes. And so when I asked him to sing HO, he sang what he heard as that *one thing.* That part of HOT that was defined by my computer program as HO HO was just one thing for Jeff, whereas I had programmed it that way because from my point of view it was not one thing but two.

MOT: What you're saying is that for Jeff, the name HO was the name for all the HO stuff that comes before HA. So when you asked him to sing HO, that's what he sang. That way he used *your* naming but kept *his* hearing.

MET: And I suppose that's what you mean, Jeanne, by Jeff's integrity.

JEANNE: You got it.

MOT: But Jeanne, I'm curious, why did you break up the tune into just those blocks?

JEANNE: Good question, Mot. I think my strategy was to listen for the smallest figure that comes back again as a whole in the course of the tune—what I would call the smallest meaningful structural entity that repeats. That was the block HO. And whatever wasn't a HO block, I just made into one other block—that was HA.

MOT: I guess that makes sense. But it's certainly not the only way to chunk the tune.

JEANNE: True enough. And the funny thing is, in making up the game my whole idea was to give entities to novice players that would be comfortable for them—"things" to work with that would match their intuitive hearing of a tune. At the time, the blocks I made just seemed obvious to me. It took Jeff's confusions—just the ones we've been talking about—to show me that it wasn't so obvious after all.

MET: So what you're telling us is that your strategy for chunking the tune was at odds with Jeff's. For one thing, you were at a finer level of structural detail than Jeff was. And the result of that was to create boundary conflicts between his hearing and yours.

MOT: Yes, you really put Jeff in a kind of bind—caught between his hearing and yours. I'll bet these kinds of problems come up a lot in schools—for instance, the teacher and the student using the same words but meaning different things. In fact, I'll bet it happened a lot to Jeff in school.

JEANNE: The trouble is, as you're discovering yourselves, it's not so easy to find out that *that* is the problem.

MET: Anyhow, if the theory about Jeanne making boundary conflicts for Jeff is right, then Jeff is pretty quick at resolving them, getting into Jeanne's head if you want, when she asks him to draw.

MOT: Yes, but wait a minute; you're leaving out a whole part of the session. After Jeff first sings HO HO and before Jeanne asks him to draw, she asks him to listen to the music for HO again, and then to listen to HO HO. And when she asks Jeff to "be the computer and sing HO" once more, he goes right ahead and sings two HO's all over again.

MET: And I suppose that's Jeff's sticking to the integrity of his own hearing again.

JEANNE: I would say so, yes.

MOT: But I was wondering, Jeanne, why did you ask him to *listen* to HO HO? I think that just got him more confused.

JEANNE: It was just an on-the-spot hunch. I guess I was groping for some way to help Jeff deal with what we were just talking about—words and what they stand for: I figured if he typed HO again and listened to it, and then right away typed HO HO, spelling it out slowly and all, it would help him make the connection between the names and what I meant them to refer to—the music they made.

MOT: I see. And besides, hearing the Music Box *imitate* his own singing of the repeated HO's—coming back to him from the outside in, so to speak—that could have helped, too.

MET: But it didn't.

MOT: I think that's too flip, Met. Because now I remember that the second time Jeanne asks him to sing HO, he hesitates in between the two HO's. I think he realizes there is some kind of problem, some kind of mismatch going on, and he's working on it.

JEANNE: I agree with you, Mot. Jeff is certainly in flux, here, but . . .

MET: We know—the chaos of confusion is a cooking medium for great ideas.

JEANNE: I don't think I ever put it that way, but I can't say I won't in the future. Thanks, Met. Anyhow, Jeff is still being true to *his* hearing of the tune, but the firmness of his conviction is certainly a bit shaken. Do you remember what happens next?

MET: Then you ask Jeff to draw pictures of both HO and HO HO. Sorry to mention it, but those names sound awfully silly when we keep saying them. Where did you get them, anyhow? It sounds like something Alice's friends would dream up.

JEANNE: Well, I thought of HO as part of the word HOT—the first part, as Jeff said. And once I thought of HO, HA just came naturally. I never expected to be having a conversation about all this.

MET: Anyhow, drawing really worked. I wonder why?

MOT: Was that another of your "on-the-spot hunches"?

JEANNE: It was just that. But why do you think drawing helped Jeff to finally get it?

MOT: Finally? You make it sound as if he'd been struggling for a long time. Considering he had to really turn his head around, I think it was amazingly fast.

MET: I just got an idea.

MOT: Let's hear it.

MET: It's like the kids' drawings of rhythms; or, for that matter, like me when I'm trying to think: picking up a pencil helps me to focus my attention; it slows me down and makes me pay attention. And when I put something down on paper, then everything that was sort of floating around in my head holds still; I can look at it, talk to it, have a conversation with it.

MOT: I know what you mean, and I like the way you put it, Met. In fact, Jeff's drawings look like the kid's drawings of rhythms—the ones that used space for time. It's as if he had *clapped* the rhythm of the tune: you can see three lines equally spaced for HO; and for HO HO definitely two repetitions of the same three lines with a bigger space between them—a bigger space-of-time. He really got the difference between HO and HO HO there. It's great!

JEANNE: Anything else?

MET: You sound like my shrink. But actually, yes. I think drawing helps Jeff get down into the details—way down into the "contents" of your blocks.

MOT: And speaking of shrinks and hang-ups, remember how hard it was for me to pull a piece of a rhythm out of its context and look at it as a separate entity? By asking Jeff to draw, I think you're helping him to do just that. It's almost a new task, a different kind of problem. Asking him to draw has the effect of making him stop going along the tune-path so as to focus on your little part of it—a single HO. And once he's found the first one, he can put it together with the next one.

MET: I think that's right, Mot, and if we put your idea of stopping together with my idea about level of detail, I think it explains what Jeff does right afterwards, too. Remember what happens when Jeanne asks him to sing HA?

MOT: No, what?

MET: He sings just the *first part*. Remember? (Met sings):

MOT: Yes, just the first part of the music for HA. But what's that got to do with drawing?

MET: Well, as we just said, drawing helped Jeff get down into the details of HO. So, once down there, he tries the same procedure for HA, too.

MOT: I still don't get it.

MET: Sure you do. Consider what Jeff has learned so far.

MOT: I suppose he's learned to chop the one *big* part that he initially heard into two *little* parts.

MET: Right. And since that's apparently where Jeanne's head is at, he tries it again: he chops one big part—this time the music for HA—into two little parts.

MOT: And there's something else, too. Did you notice that the music for HA not only divides into two inner parts, but they sound like they are symmetrical, too? And in that sense they are like the two inner groupings of the first big part—I mean the two HO's. After all, Jeanne could just as well have made two blocks out of HA just like she did for the first big part.

MET: Yes, but there's a difference between the inner groupings of HA and the inner groupings of the first big part—the two HO's are exactly the same. Still, it's sort of true what you're saying, especially if you think about the rhythm of the words. The rhythm of the two inner parts, "one-a-penny; two-a-penny," is identical. And in the melody, the pitch stays put *within* each part, but it moves up as it goes from "one-a-penny" to "two-a-penny." Like this (Met draws):

MOT: By the way, is each of the little inner groups of HA the same length as each HO block?

JEANNE: Now let's see what *you've* learned, Mot. How could you tell?

MOT: Well, it seems like they are. Each of the inner groups of HA has about the same number of notes as one HO block, I think.

MET: Here we go again! It's not the number of *notes*, Mot, it's the number of *beats*. If you want to measure time, you have to count beats, not claps or notes. Here, let me show you. You clap the rhythm of the two HO's and I'll clap the beat. (Mot and Met clap.) OK, now let's make a space-for-time drawing of your claps and my beat:

Mot's claps and Met's beats for HO HO

MET: So how many beats, time-units, were there in all?
MOT: You clapped 8 beats and I clapped 6 notes.
MET: So how many beats in just one HO?
MOT: I guess 4, since there are 8 beats in all and one HO would be half as long as two.
MET: OK. Now let's do the same thing with HA. (Mot and Met clap HA and then make a space-for-time drawing of the rhythm and the beat):

Mot's claps and Met's beats for HA

MOT: I can hardly believe it. All those notes and only 4 beats! That means the music for *all* of HA, both parts together, is the same length of time as the music for just *one* HO.
JEANNE: Met, that was beautiful. You really ought to think about going into teaching.
MET: Actually, it's kind of fun.
JEANNE: And watching that little lesson made me realize something else, too.
MET: What's that?
JEANNE: It made me realize that there was probably another reason why I chopped the tune into just the two blocks—HO and HA.
MOT: I'll bet it's because both of them, both HO and HA, are the same length.
JEANNE: Right! I guess it's my natural bent for symmetry, or what we call "balance" in the trade. If the phrases in a tune are all the same length, we say it has "balanced phrase structure," and, in fact, almost all pop songs, folk songs, and nursery-rhyme songs are like that.
MET: That's weird language—as if time had weight. We've talked

enough about time and *space,* but "balance" has to do with relative *weight.* Do you musicians handle time so much that you think of it as weighing something—a longer time weighs more than a shorter time?

MOT: Wait a minute; I just realized something, too. If you're paying attention to symmetry, then you would probably group the whole tune into two "balanced phrases"—to use your language, Jeanne. HO-HO would be the first big part, and HA-HO would be the second big part. Like this (Mot draws):

JEANNE: You're right again, Mot. And that is just the way I think of the structure when I'm listening to the *larger grouping*—what I would call the higher-level structure of the tune. I would probably call your parts, I and II, "phrases," while I would think of my blocks, HO and HA, as the *inner grouping* of those two large phrases.

MET: So, getting back to Jeff, I suppose we would have to say that when he sings just the first part of HA, he's down to the inner grouping of your inner grouping. How can this simple tune get so complicated? I'm beginning to feel sorry for Jeff.

MOT: Me too. After all, a person could quite reasonably hear boundaries at any one of these so-called "levels," and each boundary marker carves out "things" of different sizes and shapes.

MET: I think it all depends on where you're focusing your attention—how far into the details of the tune you want to, or even *can,* go. You know, if you go far enough down, you would pay attention to *every note;* every note would be a "thing."

JEANNE: Yes, Met, and sometimes that creates a real problem. For instance, if you start from a printed score where notes, one after the other, are all you've got, then you have no choice but to start from the bottom of the structural organization—the level of greatest detail. The problem then becomes how to construct the higher-level groupings; how to hear and to project the higher-level phrases, for instance.

MET: Yes, we talked about that before. Actually, I guess Jeff is getting a pretty big dose of *possibles.* Right here in this first session you've really got him scrambling up and down the structural ladder.

MOT: It seems that our collective theories about the value of drawing must be right. Because when Jeanne asks Jeff to draw HA, he extri-

Figure 6–2

"playing-drawing" the Class Piece

cates himself from all these too many possibilities. Actually, there's something interesting here: drawing HO helped Jeff to climb *down*— to *break up* the first big part and make it into two—but drawing HA helps him to climb *up*—to *put together* into one thing what he sang as two.

JEANNE: Yes, that's very true, and I hadn't thought about that before at all. Of course, the way Jeff drew the music for HA is probably relevant here.

MET: Why? What did he do?

JEANNE: It was like the younger kids' drawing of rhythms; I described their way of putting the rhythm on paper then as "playing-drawing." Remember, their drawings of the Class Piece looked like this (see Figure 6–2). Watching Jeff was like watching those children: I could see him tapping out the rhythm of HA with his pencil (separate lines instead of continuous ones like the littler kids made), and since he was playing the rhythm with a pencil, his tapping left a trace. The trace left behind is what you see as his drawing of HA. He did it very quickly.

MET: Quickly? That could explain why he left out one "note" the first time he tried.

MOT: True. And it might also explain why he drew the *whole thing*, not just the first part that he sang. It's like my path again—making it and following it at the same time. If you're singing the pitches you can hear two little chunks because the pitches do change. But if you're just tapping out the rhythm, then the two parts of HA, if there are two parts, run right into each other, and that makes you just keep on going. I mean, it's different from HO HO because even if you're just tapping out the rhythm, the pause at the end of each HO makes a clear boundary between them. Just look at Jeff's picture of HO HO, or I'll draw it myself:

$$| \ | \ | \quad | \ | \ |$$

And now look at his picture of HA:

||||||\

By the way, did you notice that the lines in Jeff's drawing of HA are closer together than they were in his drawing of HO?

MET: Yes, and that's good evidence for your notion, Mot, that Jeff's got the idea of a space-for-time drawing: faster notes have less space between them.

MOT: And the idea of "leaving a trace" also helps to explain how he managed to get it right the second time he tried. It's like what Met said before: once he's got it there on paper, it "holds still" so he can look at it, talk to it, and it "talks back" to him too.

JEANNE: Yes, that's exactly what happened. After he had made his first drawing of HA, Jeff went back over it, slowly this time, and you could see him sort of singing the music to himself as he traced the trace. That way he discovered that he had drawn one too few lines/notes. Then the second time he made all 8 notes. But I think we should move along. What did you make of the last part of the session?

MOT: There were two things I couldn't understand. First of all, after all this drawing, you came back to help Jeff finish building the tune. You asked him, "How does the tune go so far?" He really had a good handle on it. Remember, he typed out HO HO HA. But when you asked him, "What comes next?" he apparently just sat there. What was the problem? And second, we'll never know because you just gave it away. Why, after all this, did you just give him the answer; just tell him to type HO?

MET: But now *you* left out something important, Mot. Before Jeanne "gave him the answer," as you put it, she asked Jeff to listen to the tune so far and *sing* what comes next. And he sang it perfectly. What puzzled me was how he was able to do that, but when you asked him right afterwards . . . what did you say?

JEANNE: I said, "And what was that you just sang?"

MET: Right. And here was a chance for Jeff to say something, but according to what you've told us, he didn't say a word!

JEANNE: Your puzzlements and also Mot's second question about why I gave away the answer are very astute. I have to say that when I looked back over this last part of the session, I felt not only stupid, but also sad. If you think back to the few words Jeff said about the music for HO right at the beginning, and put them together with my last question, "And what was that you just sang?" I suspect that the two of you, being so insightful, will find the reasons for Jeff's silence, too. But I certainly didn't get it at the time.

MET: Do you mean when he first heard the music for HO and said, "That's the first one"?

JEANNE: Exactly.

MOT: Well, it does seem pretty obvious now: if HO is "the first one," it can't very well be "the last one," too.

MET: I have trouble with that idea. The HO at the beginning and the HO at the end are exactly the same! But the way you put that, Mot, does make me think about something else. Did you notice that in the few words Jeff does say, he always seems to be talking about actions: for instance, "it"—the computer or whatever—"skipped." In fact, he talks about the tune itself as if it were a linked series of actions, and each action has its place along the way—as if HO is the "first one" in the series. I could imagine myself saying quite different kinds of things if I had been playing the game; more like describing the *properties* of the melody. For instance, I might have said about HO, "It goes down and it's got a long note at the end," or about HA, "It's faster and repeats the same notes a lot."

MOT: Yes, Met, I'm sure that's just what you would have said—*properties*, again, like all the longs and shorts, or all the Tuesdays, and now all the HO's. And being into properties, of course you wouldn't have any trouble recognizing those "invariant properties" to which you give the name HO, whenever or wherever they happen. But being a felt-path person myself (or at least still identifying with those who are), it's not so easy for me to hear the end of this tune as the same as the beginning. In fact, it's like the Class Piece: a long as an "ender" may be the same as a long that's a "beginner" if you're talking "properties," but they sure aren't the same if you're listening to *function!* If you would just follow the path, taking things as they come, instead of jumping off and comparing pure properties out of order! For instance, you would hear that the music for the last HO (I don't even like calling it by the same name) not only makes an ending, but it makes the ending of one long phrase—the music for HA runs right into it. And when you hear the ending of that long phrase, it certainly doesn't sound "exactly the same" as the beginning of the whole tune.

MET: Don't get so excited, Mot. I suppose you do have a better feel for the way Jeff might have been hearing it. But you don't have to get mad at me just because I have a different view—or a different way of hearing. After all, isn't that what this conversation is supposed to be all about?

MOT: Sorry. Anyhow, Jeanne, am I right that you felt stupid because of your last question? I mean, after Jeff sang the end of the tune, you said, "And what *is* that?" Given *Jeff's* view of the tune, *his* way of hearing, what could he have said?

JEANNE: Are you asking me to take sides here, Mot? The simple answer is, yes, that is why I felt stupid. But I think what Met was saying is very important. Do you know why?

MOT: Oh, I suppose because it *is* another view.

JEANNE: Yes, and he put it very well. His examples made some very common assumptions quite clear—assumptions about properties and classification and naming—that are often deeply buried and thus hard to articulate. It's important to get them out in the open because they are, I think, the kinds of assumptions that lead people, even with the best of intentions, to think that a child like Jeff (and I suspect there are many like him) is a "slow learner," or has a "bad ear," or is "unmusical." And it's doubly important because these assumptions and the values attached to them—while left unsaid, even unrecognized—are just those that we too easily take for granted as the stuff of "knowledge."

MET: That's a pretty strong statement.

MOT: Is that why you gave Jeff the answer? So he wouldn't feel bad?

JEANNE: I suppose that was partly it. I also had the feeling that Jeff might be tired—I had probed and poked enough for one day. As Met said a while ago, I had really given poor Jeff a big dose of *possibles*.

MOT: But then why did you feel sad?

JEANNE: Because instead of waiting, giving Jeff a chance to find his own way, to listen to himself think, I gave away an answer which at the time he couldn't use. The answer I gave him did get the computer to play the whole tune, but instead of having a feeling of success after all that work, I think Jeff felt disappointed, left out. It was some kind of magic. The tune had been completed by me in cahoots with the computer, not by him.

MET: Was he willing to come back for more?

JEANNE: Oh, yes; there's lots more. We can go on to the next session tomorrow.

COMMENTS ON OUR CONVERSATION

There is, indeed, much more to come; what we have seen so far is only a beginning—the opening scene in a continuing saga. Thus, I will limit my comments to the questions that the reader might have despite our best effort to "give Jeff reason" and to issues that will come up again in various guises as we follow Jeff's work into the next session. There are three general issues: (1) the "structural ladder"; (2) paths, properties, and multiple hearings; (3) imitation and drawing.

The structural ladder. Met and Mot, quite insightfully, I think, confront the issue of the structural ladder head-on right from the beginning of our conversation. Mot asks, for instance, what Jeff means in his double use of the word *one* when he describes the tuneblock HA as "It skipped one," and then the tuneblock HO as "That's the first one." And later, the issue turns on the respective meanings we assume in giving names to things. This leads Mot to question my choice in segmenting the tune as I did. As she puts it: "Why did you break up the tune into just those blocks?" After all, she argues, "it's certainly not the only way." Met summarizes the issues clearly when he comments that Jeff is "getting a pretty big dose of *possibles*," and then goes on to say, "Right here in this first session you've got him scrambling up and down the structural ladder."

Through all of this we are, in fact, circling around within the *hierarchical structure* of HOT. For just as the structure of rhythms is hierarchical, so is that of melodies. And just as hearings of rhythms can differ depending on the structural level to which individuals attend, so can the hearings of melodies. As Met says, "It all depends on where you're focusing your attention—how far into the details of the tune you want to, or even *can,* go." Mot argues that Jeff and I are marking off different structural boundaries, and that I, in making the blocks, "put Jeff in a bind." The reader who may not be entirely convinced will be helped if I lay out the structural hierarchy of HOT now in more formal fashion.

Recall for a moment the hierarchical structure of the Class Piece (see Figure 6–3). Notice that if you focus your attention at Level 1, you hear a rhythm with a single boundary marking off only *two* larger figures—

Figure 6–3

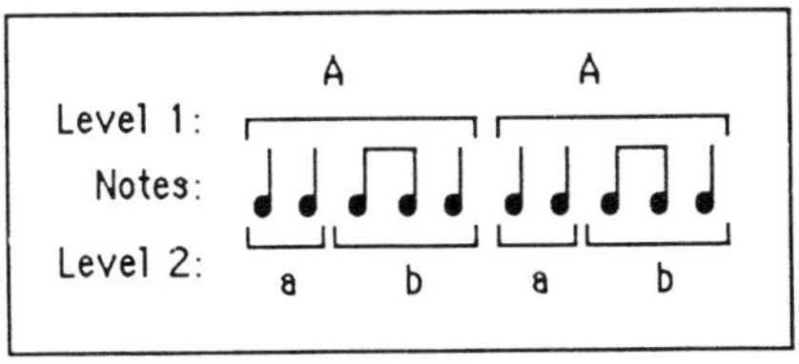

the hierarchical structure of the Class Piece

Figure 6–4

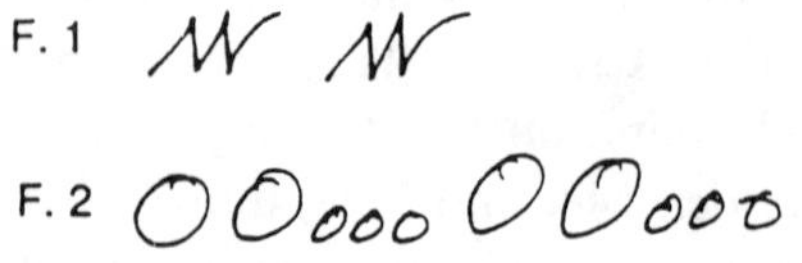

F. 1   /\/\/   /\/\/

F. 2   ○ ○ ₒₒₒ   ○ ○ ₒₒ ∿

figural drawings of the Class Piece

two structural entities, with the second the same as the first, thus A A. But if you focus your attention at Level 2, then you hear a rhythm with *four* structural entities. That is, each large figure is further articulated into two smaller ones, and within each of these pairs the second is always different from the first, thus *a b a b.*

Now consider the two figural drawings of the Class Piece made by the children (see Figure 6–4). As I pointed out in the discussion of the typology, F.1 drawings are less differentiated than F.2 drawings. That is, in making the drawings labeled F.1 (which I described as "playing-drawing"), the younger children clearly demonstrate their attention to the grouping of their claps into two large gestures. In contrast, the older children, who made F.2 drawings, show not only the two large gestures but also their "inner grouping"—that is, each large gesture is further divided into two smaller ones. Using the drawings as clues to hearings, we can see that the younger children focus their attention at Level 1 of the structural hierarchy, while the older children focus their attention at Level 2 of the hierarchy.

Now consider the hierarchical structure of HOT, as shown in Figure 6–5. The diagram shows three levels of the structural ladder for HOT, all of which come into the arguments between Met and Mot, though as

Figure 6–5

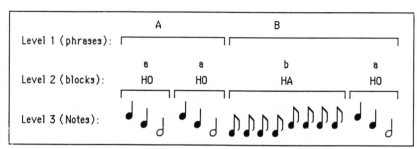

the hierarchical structure of HOT

we shall see, these levels are not exactly the ones that Jeff "scrambles up and down." Notice that going from the top (Level 1) down, structural entities become more finely articulated, more differentiated. Level 1, then, is the *least differentiated*. These are the entities that Mot and I called "phrases"; I have labeled them A and B, respectively. Level 2 is *more differentiated;* it shows the inner grouping of phrases A and B. These mid-level entities are the "givens" of the game, blocks HO and HA. I have labeled them (in conformance with convention) *a* for HO and *b* for HA. At this mid-level, the structure of the tune would be described as *a a b a*. Levels 1 and 2 taken together correspond exactly to Mot's drawing of "balanced phrases":

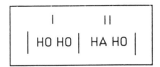

The lowest, *most differentiated* level of structure (Level 3) is made up of notes; these are the "contents" of the blocks. At this level, as Met says, "every note is a 'thing.'"

Paths, properties, and multiple hearings. As with hearings of the Class Piece, hearings of the tune will be quite different depending on which hierarchical level you attend to. And these "possibles" are, of course, exactly the crux of Jeff's puzzlements—the "chaos of confusion" that I unintentionally thrust him into. For example, if your attention is at Level 1, then you will hear the whole tune as only *two* large gestures, two "balanced phrases," each different from the other. And if you "enter" the tune in the middle, as Jeff did in listening to the Music Box play HA, then indeed "one" has been skipped, and that "one" is the single phrase A. But if your attention is at Level 2, you will hear the whole tune as *four* smaller gestures, the blocks: the first pair (the inner groupings of A) each the *same* and thus *a a;* the second pair (the inner groupings of B) *differ-ent* from each other and thus *b a*. This contrast between same and different within the structures of A and B is an instance of our continuing concern with function and context: the last iteration of the HO block makes an ending, while the first iterations are beginnings. And this differ-ence contributes to Jeff's confusions at the very end of the session. Mot puts it this way: "The music for HA runs right into the ending. It's just one long phrase. And when you hear the ending of that long phrase, it certainly doesn't sound 'exactly the same' as the beginning of the whole tune."

In considering a focus at Level 3, the note level, a new and interesting distinction emerges. It seems that a hearing at this level is not only more fine-grained, but it also may be rather different in kind. If, for example, you are attending solely to "notes" as individual sound events and not at all to how they group together to form gestures or figures, then this would be not just a hearing at a particular *level* of attention, but a different *kind* of attention as well. It appears at first that this is the level of attention and also the kind of attention that Met prefers. For example, he prefers to describe blocks in terms of what he calls "properties"—HO "goes down and it's got a long note at the end." But notice that in this favored description, Met is describing *relative* pitch and duration—he does not, for instance, say how far down in pitch or how long in duration. Moreover, notice that while his description does refer to notes, it also refers to and is bounded by a structural entity at Level 2, the block HO. Thus, despite Met's claim (and Mot's barb about "invariant properties" in her heated reaction to Met), his description is neither wholly at Level 3 nor limited to "pure properties." Still, his description is certainly quite different from those of Jeff and others who "follow the path, taking things as they come."

What emerges, then, are different aspects or dimensions of structure, and it is important to distinguish among them. For instance, hearings may differ with respect to *level* of attention within the structural hierarchy, on one hand; and, on the other, a hearing may be *figural/functional* in its focus in contrast to a focus on *formal properties*. In addition, as with the children's drawings of rhythms, hearings may certainly focus on a mix of aspects and dimensions; in fact, they are probably most often just that—"hybrids." For example, a hearing may include more than one *level* at a time, and a person may also shift her attention from one *aspect* to another. Thus, to make these distinctions is once again to expand the universe of "possible hearings" and in doing so to broaden the terrain in which to pursue the presumed goal of musical development, namely the capacity to make multiple hearings. Indeed, it is exactly in this way that even such simple melodies as HOT grow complex.

However, this growing potential for complexity in trying to "give Jeff reason" should not be confused with the reasons that Jeff himself gives through his own actions and words. For example, it seems clear that while Jeff's hearings do move between Levels 1 and 2, and even down to the "inner grouping of the inner grouping" of Level 2 in singing HA, he does not, nor does he have any reason to, "climb down" to Level 3, the note level of structure. In Jeff's next session he will, in fact, build HOT using individual pitch-making materials, working necessarily then at the note level. Watching Jeff in this new context, it will be interesting to return to the issue of multiple hearings and to the distinctions between levels and kinds of focus.

Imitation, drawing, and paths. Looking back now to what and how Jeff learned in the course of this first session, recall Mot's interesting point about imitation and why it might have helped Jeff: "hearing the Music Box imitate his own singing of the two HO's—*coming back to him from the outside in*—could have helped, too." Hermine Sinclair, in an article entitled "Interactive Re-creation of Knowledge," makes a similar point. She says of very young children, "Even very simple reciprocal imitation . . . offers both partners an occasion to see their own actions from the outside as well as from the inside and this may facilitate reflexion on the action *as an object of thought*." Obviously, neither Jeff's actions in singing nor the actions of the Music Box in playing can be *seen* by the two "partners," but perhaps this makes Mot's point stronger. For, as Sinclair suggests, an imitation of one's own performance can "facilitate reflexion on the action" and, in the case of singing, help the singer to look at his otherwise invisible production so as to make it an "object of thought" (Sinclair 1990, p. 54).

It is interesting in this context to associate imitation with drawing. For making a drawing of a rhythm or a melody is a kind of imitation, too—albeit importantly transformed by the new medium. I have previously emphasized the possible traps inherent in such transformations—the conventions of line-ups in static paper-space, for instance, which we see again in Jeff's drawings. But thinking about drawing as a kind of imitation suggests another view: it can also provide the maker with an "object of thought." For example, as Jeff plays/draws the rhythm of HA, he is imitating and also *externalizing* his invisible memory of that music. And as Met says of himself, "When I put something down on paper . . . I can look at it, talk to it, have a conversation with it." As we move on to Jeff's next session, we will see, in particular, how Jeff's drawn imitations of his felt paths become clues (sometimes very puzzling clues) to his internal thought, and how they also serve as an important vehicle in his continuing musical development.

COMPUTERS AND PROGRAMS AS SYMBOLIC INTERMEDIARIES

In using a computer to build tunes, names and naming, along with the assorted symbols used to express them, necessarily become important issues. To make the computer and the Music Box "perform," instructions must be given in some symbolic form. However, the choice of words or numbers and the meaning given to them—what they refer to—is entirely a matter of the programmer's will (sometimes his caprice). And even though programmers may try hard to segment the universe to which their programs apply into useful bits, and to give names to these entities/actions that will be congenial to prospective users, mismatches between user and programmer are bound to occur. Certainly this was the case between me, the programmer/teacher, and Jeff, the user/student.

Mismatches, even when the domain is not music, are like symbolic versions of different hearings, and as such they often lead to confusion and frustration on the part of the user. Moreover, the misfit is commonly not recognized as such, but rather seen by the user as simply his own mistake or even his own "stupidity with computers." But if this same user takes a more exploratory, even playful stance, *mismatches can serve a productive purpose:* they can provide an opportunity to probe differing assumptions—the user's own way as well as the programmer's way, for example, of representing a particular tune. And in the largest sense, mismatches can sometimes illuminate the assumptions of a whole domain, since programs often embody those conventional, supposedly "given" units of description that are commonly associated with a given field.

Indeed, the term "mismatch," with both its more and less positive results, describes much of what happened in Jeff's first session. The computer and the programmer's program functioned as a *symbolic intermediary,* giving back to Jeff a kind of distorted reflection of his own hearing (like a mirror with a peculiar flaw). Looking and listening, he was able to sense *my* hearing of the tune, and, given enough time, he might have discovered (as we eventually did) his own as well. But it was clear from what I knew about Jeff, and from what I had seen in the first session, that names, symbols, and their referents were especially thorny issues for him. Thus, it seemed likely that continuing to use the computer might be more confounding than illuminating; rather than contributing to his learning, it might be an unnecessary obstacle. In the next session, therefore, I shifted our activities to hands-on tune-building materials—materials, that is, in which there was no symbolic intermediary between Jeff's actions and their sounding results. The materials I chose were a set of bells originally invented by Maria Montessori with the help of her music specialist, Anna Maccheroni. As it turned out, our work with the Montessori bells continued through many sessions, which I will describe in the chapters that follow.

CHAPTER 7

Building "Hot Cross Buns" with the Montessori Bells

THE MONTESSORI bells were designed by Montessori and Maccheroni to be used in their classrooms as one of many sets of objects known as the "sensorial materials." The bells are a rather extraordinary technological invention in themselves. Each individual mushroom-shaped metal bell is attached to a wooden stem, with bell and stem, in turn, standing on a small wooden base. A complete collection of Montessori bells includes one set with the bases painted white, and another set that includes matching pitches but with the bases painted brown. As part of the sensorial materials, the two sets are typically used by children to listen for and pair brown and white bells that match in pitch. The bells, which are free to be moved about on a table, are played by striking them with a small mallet, or "dinger" as we called it (see Figure 7–1).

The bells are carefully tuned so as to play different pitches (a complete set of white bells includes the 8 pitches of the C major scale from middle C to the C above; a complete set of brown bells includes the 13 pitches of the chromatic collection from middle C up to and including the C above). However, unlike other pitch-playing materials, all the mushroom-shaped metal bells *look the same*. Differences in pitch, then, are distinguishable only by actually playing on the bells. Montessori, in her wisdom, was thus able to focus children's attention on "pitch-sense" alone. With most pitch-making materials, cues such as size, shape, or

Figure 7–1

a child building a tune with the Montessori bells

position in an array can help the user to tell relative differences in pitch without listening—for instance, a xylophone bar that is relatively *longer* is also *lower* in pitch; a piano key to the *right* of another is also relatively *higher* in pitch. But since the bells all look alike, and are free to be moved about, differences in pitch can be determined only by listening—that is, without the help of cues from visual or tactile "senses."

As with all the tasks that I have described thus far, the particular way in which I came to use the bells evolved from observations in classroom settings where I saw children solving problems in surprising and puzzling ways. And as with the rhythm drawings, I subsequently designed more constrained experimental tasks in order to test hunches about the meaning of these puzzles. And again as in the rhythm experiments, to account for the results of these bell experiments it was necessary to question deeply held assumptions—for example, assumptions concerning the nature of melodic structure and, in particular, the implications built in to our "units of description" as these refer to pitch and pitch relations.

The experimental situation always includes two parts. First, I ask participants to build a tune. I will say, for instance, "Can you build Hot

Cross Buns (or Twinkle Twinkle Little Star) with the bells?" Second, I ask participants to "make instructions so someone else could play [the tune] on the bells as you have set them up." As might be expected, the construction strategy and the resulting finished product, together with the subsequent invention of "instructions" for playing the tune, provide important clues to builders' inner strategies for making sense of the tune, the situation, and the task. And the two differing media give a broader scope to these clues: in the construction task, clues to the player's inner strategies, her means of organizing the material, are *embodied* in her actions in building the tune and in the resulting bell arrangement; while in the notation task, clues are gleaned from the player's paper and pencil *descriptions* as these take graphic or symbolic form.

Some seventy individuals have informally participated in these bell tasks over the years, with ages ranging from six-year-olds all the way up to adults. The results of the bell experiments are particularly interesting because they generally confirm the robustness of figural in contrast to formal strategies, a distinction that was so central in differentiating among subjects in the rhythm experiments. Not surprisingly, however, just as there are important differences between a clapped rhythm and a sung or played melody, there are also important differences in the ways in which these strategies are expressed.

In particular, a melody includes not only temporal relations but pitch relations as well, and pitch relations differ from temporal relations in critical ways. For instance, the temporal relations of a rhythm or melody can aptly be described and measured with reference only to their *internally* generated relationships. That is, since the surface durations themselves generate a beat that serves as the unit of measure, no absolute measure outside the melody is necessary. But pitch relations are different. While we can speak of internal and relative pitch relations, such as the melody "goes up" or "gets higher" (just as a rhythm "gets faster or slower"), in order to say *how much* higher, we must make use of a reference structure that has an absolute existence outside of the tune itself. It is in terms of this outside fixed reference that we measure "pitch distance," and it is also with reference to this structure that pitch-names (such as D or G) gain meaning. Pitch-names, then, refer to property classes—classes of objects like the pitch-class D or G. And these pitch-names are inventions which (along with other notational conventions like the musical staff) we use to define and also to refer to *places* along this fixed reference structure.

But property classes (like the class of all Tuesdays) do not come full-blown with names already attached to them; in fact, grasping their meanings always depends on the previous mental construction of the appropriate conceptual framework. Indeed, the long history of the evolution of modern pitch notation is the story of a communal construction of just such a conceptual framework (see Treitler 1989). Similarly, the mental construction of this framework on the part of an individual plays a critical role in the course of that individual's musical development. And, as we shall see, it also plays a critical role in the transformations implicit in moving between figural and formal tune-building strategies, and between figural and formal hearings of melodies as well.

For instance, figural constructions and descriptions of melodies, like figural drawings of rhythms, are characteristically responsive to structural function and context—in particular, the function of a pitch-event within the figure of which it is a member. In turn, those who make formal descriptions characteristically ignore function and context; two pitch-events that share a common pitch property (two C's or two G's) will be labeled as the same in an invented formal "notation." But in invented figural "notations," members of the same pitch-class may be given different labels if they occur in differing situations and with differing structural functions. And as with rhythms, individuals with more fully developed strategies for making sense of melodies are able to make multiple hearings of the same melody—that is, they may hear a pitch-event as either the same or different depending on the listener's or the performer's focus of attention.

But all of this creates a dilemma in describing the experimental bell tasks: in order to make the moves, decisions, and strategies of a tune-builder clear to the reader, I must tell the reader the *names* of the bell-pitches, naming them with their conventional letter names (D, G, and so on). However, these names, like most conventions associated with a community of professional users, have a whole set of implicit assumptions built in to them. For example, the letter names assume that a pitch is an invariant *property,* and that the name D or G names the *class* to which all D's or all G's belong. In turn, these names implicitly assume the "fixed reference structure" in terms of which these names gain meaning. Thus, by giving away the names of the bell-pitches, I am in serious danger of distorting the meanings that novice players give to their own actions and decisions—for example, attributing to the materials, as if they were givens, formal features that for the participants still remain to be constructed. Moreover, when readers are already privy to the names of the bells—information that is significantly different in kind from the directly sensory experience of novice players—readers may easily fail to recognize and appreciate the creativity and the cognitive work that are involved as novice players *invent* strategies, *make* decisions, and *devise* original notation systems. By giving away the names of the bells, I also put readers at risk of failing to recognize and appreciate the learning that occurs over the course of a participant's work.

I can see no way out of the naming dilemma except to invent some new names to describe a cluster of new entities that the bell tasks spawn. It will be helpful for readers to become familiar with them:

1. *Bell-pitch:* An object (bell) that has the *property* pitch-P (for example, G-bell or C-bell).
2. *Bell-path:* The spatial *arrangement* of bells on the table, including all the forms this takes in the course of constructing the tune.
3. *Action-path:* The sequence of *actions* made on the bell-path in playing the tune.
4. *Tune-path:* The sequence of *pitch-events* as they occur in the tune's unfolding.
5. *Notation-path:* The sequence of pitches in the tune as represented in *standard music notation* or in the participant's *invented notation*.
6. *Table-space:*
   a. Work-space: the area of the table occupied by the cumulating bell-path; the space where the work of construction takes place.
   b. Search-space: the area of the table occupied by the bells in the mixed array which have not yet been included in the cumulating bell-path.

JEFF BUILDS HOT CROSS BUNS WITH THE BELLS

With all these hazards in mind, let us return to Jeff. Jeff's first session with the bells, as I suggested earlier, was the first of many. He enjoyed working with them, and since his work was so interesting and productive, we turned to bell tasks whenever he was not busy with other activities. This first session, in which Jeff builds Hot Cross Buns, sets the stage for all the others, so I will describe it in some detail.

Jeff and I worked with the bells in a space partially separated from the other children and from the computers. We sat together at a table on which I had casually arranged eight Montessori bells—five with white

Figure 7–2

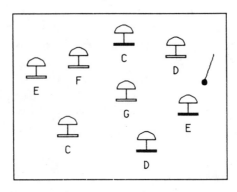

five with white bases, three with brown

bases, three with brown (Figure 7–2). The white bells play the pitches C-D-E-F-G, and the brown bells play the matching pitches C-D-E.

After showing Jeff how to use the "dinger" to play the bells, I suggest he begin by playing the "matching game." The game, I explain to him, is to "find all the bells that sound the same." I show Jeff what "sounding the same" means by playing two bells that share the same pitch—for instance, the two E-bells. I also explain that *bells that have bases of the same color never match*—that is, white and white, brown and brown never match, only a brown and a white bell can make a match. Jeff spends only a few minutes at this game—long enough for him to find the three brown and three white bells that match (the C, D, and E-bells) and for me to see that Jeff understands and can hear "same pitch." We then go on to the task for the day: to "build HOT with the bells," and to "make instructions so someone else can play HOT on the bells."

Jeff is a remarkably adept tune-builder even in this first session. He works in a consistent way—focused, persistent, and with what seems a clear sense of goal. I start him out by showing him "a good starting bell"—that is, the E-bell. Once started, Jeff quickly develops a strategy for building the tune. His strategy is procedural and recursive. The steps are as follows:

1. Remove the target bell from the search-space and place it in front of the others on the table—that is, in the work-space (Figure 7–3).

2. Play the found bell that is already in the work-space, and then test in the search-space for the next bell in the tune. For each test

Figure 7–3

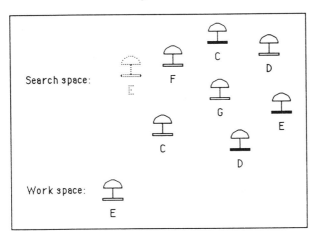

place the target bell in the work-space

of a new bell, always begin by playing the bell(s) already in the work-space. Repeat this procedure for each try on a new test bell. For instance, with the E-bell already in the work-space, Jeff plays:

Work-space	Search-space
E-bell →	F-bell (no)
E-bell →	G-bell (no)
E-bell →	D-bell (target!)

3. When a test bell is found that matches the next pitch-event in the tune, remove it from the search-space and place it in the work-space to the *right* of the bell(s) already in the work-space (Figure 7–4).

4. Continue with the same strategy, always *starting from the beginning* of the cumulating bell-path in testing each new bell for next-in-tune.

Using his construction procedure, Jeff adds bells to his bell-path *in their order of occurrence in the tune.* In searching for next-in-tune, he has no trouble recognizing the target bell, and thus quite quickly builds up the pitches for the first tuneblock—that is, HO (Figure 7–5). But notice that Jeff limits his tests and thus his cumulating bell-path *only to*

Figure 7–4

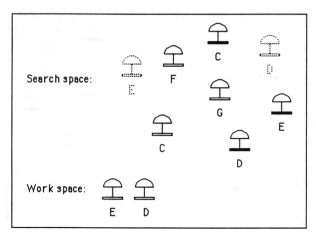

place it in the work-space to the right *of the bell already in the work-space*

Figure 7–5

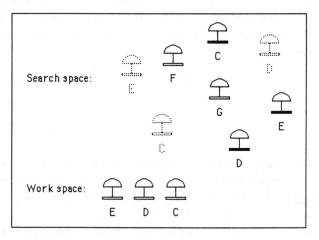

quickly builds up the pitches for the first tuneblock—that is, HO

white-based bells. Why he does so is puzzling, but his preference for white bells, as we shall see, has important implications later on.

At this point in his work I intervene, curious, now, to see what Jeff makes of his construction:

Jeanne: Can you play the tune so far?

Jeff responds by playing through the bell-path left to right once, just going "straight ahead," and then, turning back to the beginning of the bell-path, he traces his initial action-path through the bells once more. The result is, obviously, the music for the *repeated* blocks, HO HO (Figure 7–6).

Jeanne: Good. Now how about building the rest of the tune?

Jeff responds to my request by going in search of a bell that will match the pitch for next-in-tune—that is, a C-bell for the first event in HA. Following his usual procedure, Jeff starts from the beginning of the bell-path, plays all of the tune-so-far (that is, HO HO), goes into the search-space, and tests a white bell (F). But this time, instead of playing one stroke on the test bell as he had done before, he plays *four faster hits on it*. Rejecting the F-bell, Jeff tests the only remaining white bell (G), which he also plays with four faster hits and also rejects. This small change in Jeff's testing strategy, playing four repeated hits on a test bell, is intriguing. It suggests that in testing a bell as potentially next-in-tune, Jeff treats the test bell as if it were already in the tune. That is, for each test, Jeff starts from the beginning of the tune already in his work-space, and going into the search-space he tests a new bell *as if it were already a continuation of the tune*. Thus, in playing each test bell with four faster strokes, Jeff treats each test bell as if it might already play the repeated pitches for "one-a-pen-ny"—the beginning notes of HA.

But now Jeff is faced with a problem. Since he has limited his search to only white bells, and since there are no white bells left in the search-space except those he has rejected, what shall he do? There are only two possibilities: he can give up his limiting search strategy and try brown bells, in which case he will, of course, find the target C-bell for the beginning of HA; or he can stay with only the whites. If he chooses the latter course there is only one possibility, and this also involves a change in his search procedure—he must reuse the white bells already in his bell-path, the only white ones he has not yet tried in searching for the beginning of

Figure 7–6

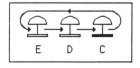

E   D   C

the music for the repeated *blocks,* HO HO

HA. Jeff chooses the latter option. Playing through the tune-so-far (that is, HO HO), he *turns back to the beginning of his bell-path* and tests the white E-bell (the first bell-pitch already in his cumulating bell-path). As with his previous tests, Jeff plays *four fast hits* on the E-bell (clearly testing for "one-a-penny"), and again rejects it as a "fit" for next-in-tune. Starting again, he plays the tune-so-far, turns back on his bell-path to test the white D-bell, and rejects it as well. Now, *without trying the final C-bell*, Jeff puts down his dinger and stops. For the first time in this session he looks quite discouraged.

And now I am faced with a problem: How can I help Jeff to go on without giving away a solution to his problem, as I had done before when he was building HOT using the computer? I make a suggestion:

> Jeanne: Do you think you could find a *brown bell* that matches the last bell in your bell-path?

In response to my question, Jeff plays the white C-bell (the last bell in his bell-path), then goes into the search-space and tests a brown bell (E). And interestingly, in searching for a match, Jeff plays the test bell with just *one stroke*. He shakes his head—no. Going back again to play the white C-bell in his work-space, Jeff goes into the search-space, tests another brown bell, and this time finds a match—the brown C-bell. Removing the brown C-bell from the search-space, he places it *above the white C-bell* already in his bell-path to make a matched pair (Figure 7–7).

> Jeanne: Good. Now can you find a brown bell that matches the white bell in the *middle* of your bell-path?

Jeff plays the white D-bell in the middle of his bell-path, goes into the search-space, and this time finds the brown match right away. As before, he removes the brown D-bell from the search-space and places it above

Figure 7–7

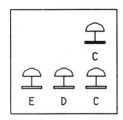

to make a matched pair

Figure 7–8

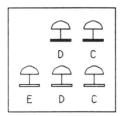

another matched pair

the white D-bell in his bell-path to make another matched pair (Figure 7–8).

With the paired C and D-bells before him on the table, I turn Jeff's attention back to tune-building.

> Jeanne: Do you think you could use the two new brown bells to go on with the tune?

Jeff responds to my suggestion by returning to his previous search procedure. That is, he plays the tune from the beginning, playing through his bell-path twice to make HO HO, and then, moving just above the last white bell-pitch (C), he tests the matching brown C-bell. But this time, instead of playing it just once as he did when matching, he *plays the brown C-bell with four fast strokes*. And recognizing it as a "fit" for next-in-tune (that is, the bell-pitch for "one-a-pen-ny"), he removes the brown C-bell from its pairing with the white C-bell and adds it to his cumulating bell-path. That is, he places it to the right of the white C-bell. But this time Jeff *leaves a gap between* the previously added bell—the last bell in HO—and the new bell (Figure 7–9).

Going on, Jeff repeats his search procedure, but he now includes the beginning of HA—that is, he moves through his bell-path to play HO HO, goes on to play four hits on the new brown C-bell for "one-a-pen-ny," and then moves up to test the matching brown D-bell, which he also plays four times. Removing the brown D-bell from its pairing with the white D-bell, he adds the brown D-bell to his cumulating bell path (Figure 7–10).

I intervene once more:

> Jeanne: Now can you play the whole tune on the bells?

Jeff responds: he plays HO HO (turning back his action-path to play the second HO), continues straight on to play HA (striking each bell four

Figure 7–9

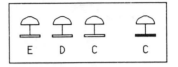

but leaves a gap between

Figure 7–10

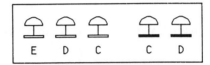

he adds the brown D-bell to the cumulating bell-path

times for "one-a-pen-ny, two-a-pen-ny"), and then, *turning back again to the beginning, he plays HO once more*. Jeff's performance of HOT is complete and perfect. Clearly, in working with the bells, he has solved the problem that was left unsolved in his computer session: the HO that functions as a beginning, "the first one," works now as the last one, too. In constructing HOT with the bells, adding each pitch-event as it occurs in the tune, next-next-next, the same built-shape (HO) can function as both the beginning and the ending of the tune. What has contributed to Jeff's success? I try an on-the-spot experiment:

> Jeanne: That's great; you built the whole tune and played it perfectly. Now I'd like you to try something else. Do you remember that the brown bells and some of the white bells matched?

Jeff nods his head (yes).

> Jeanne: Do you think you could find the matches again?

In response to my request, Jeff begins by striking the brown C-bell just *once* as in his previous search strategy for matches, passes over the immediately adjacent white C-bell, and goes all the way *back to the beginning of his bell-path to test the first white bell* (E). Striking it once, he rejects it as a match. Then, returning to the brown C-bell at the beginning of HA, he again plays it once and tests the *second* white bell (D). No. And now, *pointing* to the brown C-bell and the adjacent white C-bell, he says:

Figure 7–11

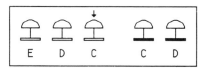

that one is lower

"They won't match 'cause that one (pointing to the white C-bell at the end of HO) is *lower*." (Figure 7–11).

But having said so, Jeff tries the adjacent brown and white bells anyhow. Immediately recognizing a match, he *looks very surprised!*

Jeanne: That was a surprise, huh?

Jeff nods his head (yes). And now I make another on-the-spot experiment:

Jeanne: Well, since those brown and white bells you just played sound the same, you don't really need them both to play the tune, right? I'll bet you could play HOT without the brown bell since you have a white one like it already.

Jeff pauses and looks at me quizzically. Then, to my complete surprise, he takes the white C-bell in his left hand and the brown C-bell in his right hand and *switches their positions* (Figure 7–12). And having done so, Jeff confidently plays HOT once more all the way through using the newly switched bells as regular members of his bell-path. That is, he plays the *brown* C-bell for the end of HO and the *white* C-bell for the beginning of HA.

Jeff's last move is perhaps the most puzzling event in this session, but there are a number of others as well. To help in unraveling these puzzles, I will ask Met and Mot to join me in another of our continuing conversations.

Figure 7–12

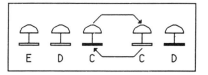

switches their positions

MET AND MOT PUZZLE OVER JEFF'S
CONSTRUCTION OF HOT

JEANNE: Well, what do you think of Jeff now? Surprising, isn't it?

MOT: Not so much surprising as baffling. I thought I had a fairly good handle on how Jeff's mind works (using myself as a model, I suppose), but some of the things he does in this session I haven't got a clue about.

MET: Yes, I found some things pretty confusing, too. But still, I'm impressed. For instance, Jeff seems to catch on right away when Jeanne asks him to match bells—which means, of course, matching *pitches*. And then he is quick to switch over to a different kind of task when Jeanne asks him to build HO. By the way, does *Jeff* ever talk about HO and HA?

JEANNE: No, he doesn't. In fact, you may have noticed that he only *talks* once in the whole session.

MET: Yes, I did notice that. But I've been wondering, why do you think he only used the white bells in the beginning?

MOT: I wondered about that, too.

MET: I have a hunch, but it's pretty far out.

MOT: I think we're going to be trying out a lot of hunches here. Out with it, Met.

MET: Well, if it were me, I might have remembered the thing about whites only matching browns and never matching themselves. And since I could hear that the three notes in HO were all *different*—it goes down, you know—it would make sense to stay away from the browns.

MOT: What? Would you mind running through that again, please?

MET: OK. See, it's a matter of probabilities. Browns are matches for whites, and I'm not looking for matches because HO has three *different* pitches. So, if you think about the probabilities, I *might* get a match with a brown, but I'm sure *not* to get a match note if I stick with the whites.

MOT: Probabilities, huh? Sounds like something you might think of, Met, but for Jeff it seems to me very unlikely.

MET: You asked. Got any better ideas?

MOT: Nope. Have you got the answer to this one, Jeanne?

JEANNE: I'm afraid not. But I admire Met's hunch partly because it's so typically Met. But also because, who knows, Jeff might have some kind of intuitive feel for probabilities, too. He certainly is efficient.

MET: There I'd have to disagree with you. For instance, why does he always play the whole tune, starting over again from the beginning every time that he goes in search of a new bell—what you call "next-in-tune"? It takes so long, and he repeats everything so many times; especially later on as the tune grows. It seems pretty inefficient to me.

MOT: Now I've got a hunch about that.

MET: Yes?

MOT: Actually, it's about paths. Take a poem or a song that you've known all your life; they become like paths—you have to go with them from beginning to end. You can't just start in the middle; you have to start from the beginning and keep going. Wait, let's try it. Met, try to sing "The Star-Spangled Banner" starting in the middle somewhere.

MET: OK. (long pause; then Met sings: "What so proudly we hail . . ."). See, I did it. But I have to admit that I had to sing the beginning of the song to myself first. Hmm, I never thought of that before. You mean Jeff has to play through the tune from the beginning each time to sort of catch up with where he left off?

MOT: Yes, I suppose you could put it that way.

MET: But that still doesn't explain why Jeff has to play every test bell four times when he's looking for the beginning of HA. Isn't *once* enough to hear if he's got it right or not?

MOT: But you see, it's all part of the same thing. To tell if it *is* the right bell, Jeff first has to create the context, the environment, that leads up to it—just as you had to sing the first part of the Star-Spangled Banner to yourself before you could get the next part. He has to put himself *on* the tune-path, go as far as the bell-path goes, and test a *possible* continuation. And in order to really tell if it is the continuation, he has to act as if he's actually going on with the tune when he plays that test bell. And that means playing the bell four times *as if it really were "one-a-pen-ny."* But if the test fails, as it did for the first white bell Jeff tries, then the context is broken and he has to start again—create the context all over again. So maybe it's not efficient as in *fast,* but it is efficient as in *sure.*

MET: OK, I guess you convinced me about that one. And since we're speaking of efficient use of the bells, there's a question I've been wanting to ask: Why did you include the brown bells in the first place, Jeanne? After all, you can build all of HOT with just the white bells—or for that matter with just the brown bells. All you need is C, D, and E, and one bell of each will do.

MOT: *You* know that there are only those three pitches in HOT, Met, but surely you can't assume that Jeff does.

MET: I suppose not. But he might have found that out if he had only those three bells.

JEANNE: True. If I had given Jeff only the C, D, and E bells, he might have found out what *we* already know; but I was interested in finding out what *Jeff* already knows. For instance, why do you think Jeff has so much trouble with the beginning of HA?

MET: That's another thing that really baffled me. Why can't Jeff hear that HA begins with the same pitch that HO ends with? Is there something interesting about *that*? He can obviously hear bells that match in pitch; that's clear already in the first matching game. Are you trying to say that getting stuck when he tries to go on to the beginning of HA tells us something about what Jeff already knows? What's your wisdom on that one, Mot?

MOT: None, yet. But in the spirit of our conversations, let's assume that it might, and go in search. What if we back up a little. Do you remember what happens right after Jeff has finished building HO? I think Jeanne asks Jeff to play through the tune-so-far.

MET: Right.

MOT: And he plays through the three bells in his bell-path once, and then *turns back* and plays through them again. That, by the way, tells us something that Jeff knows. He knows that in some circumstances he *can* use the same bells over again. Bells can be reused when a whole little motive is repeated right away; it's just more of the same. And that's pretty good evidence that he also already knows that those three bells together form a single higher-level entity—they are HO. Furthermore, in this tune it's efficient because by going back over them, he makes the whole first part with just those three bells. It's funny because by going *backwards* on the bell-path, he goes *forward* in the tune. You can't do that with the computer. I mean, you can't reuse the same word; you have to go on, type it again.

MET: I have a feeling we're getting into all that time-space stuff again. You seem to be saying that in order for Jeff to go forward in time, he has to go backwards in space.

MOT: Well, yes, I suppose I am. But let's not get into big philosophical discussions now; I want to go on (or go back) to Jeff's problems at the beginning of HA. Having played HO HO, instead of reusing the C-bell, he starts looking for a *new* bell.

MET: Yes. First, he tries the two white bells that are still left in his search-space—I think they were an F-bell and a G-bell. And when they fail, he switches to the only other white bells he has, namely the ones that are already in his work-space. That kind of surprised me.

MOT: Oh, why?

MET: Well, because Jeff is thinking of the same bells in a completely different way now. In reusing the HO bells in his search for the beginning of HA, Jeff transforms the meaning of the bell-path. Or maybe you could say the bell-path takes on a double function and also multiple meanings.

MOT: Go on; I don't get it.

MET: Think about Jeff's search strategy, which you just explained to me so eloquently. For each test, whether he's going into the search-space or not, he first uses his bell-path to make a performance of HO HO— in that way generating the context for his search. So, after he's used up the white bells in the search-space, he again plays through the tune but this time instead of going into the search-space, he goes back to the beginning of his bell-path and plays the first bell-pitch (the E-bell) four times.

MOT: Of course, because he's looking for the beginning of HA; that's been his procedure all along.

MET: Aha! So at that moment the E-bell and the work-space, too, for that matter, change their meaning, or you could say, they change their *identity*. You see, just a moment before, the work-space was holding the cumulating bell-path—the three bells that Jeff used to play HO HO. But when Jeff *reuses* them now, he turns that work-space into a search-space and the bells into "unidentified objects." And we have sure evidence for that when Jeff plays the E-bell four times. The same E-bell that a moment before was identified as the beginning of *HO* is now turned into an unknown object that Jeff is testing as a potential candidate for the beginning of *HA*.

MOT: So are you saying that Jeff gives his work-space and the bells in it two different uses—what you call a "double identity"?

MET: Exactly.

MOT: But what do you make of the fact that Jeff tests the first two bells in the HO-path (the E-bell and the D-bell), but then he stops without trying the last bell—the C-bell, the very one that would have worked for the beginning of HA?

MET: I couldn't understand that at all. Maybe he just got discouraged after two tries and gave up. Why didn't you ask him to try that C-bell, Jeanne?

JEANNE: I guess I learned something from the computer session, too. I didn't want to give away an answer that Jeff couldn't use.

MET: You mean he couldn't have used that white C-bell?

JEANNE: Well, yes, in a way that is what I mean. You see, I had a hunch based on what I had seen other tune-builders do and from what I had seen of Jeff's work in the computer session. I suspected that Jeff would probably build up a bell-path by adding pitches in order of their occurrence in the tune—next-next-next.

MOT: And that's exactly what he does.

JEANNE: Yes. And once a single bell becomes a member of the bell-path and is incorporated as a functioning element in the tune, it will always maintain its particular "identity," as you put it, Met. In other words, while *we* might know that two tune-events share the same pitch-property, like the end of HO and the beginning of HA, my hunch was that, for Jeff, that same pitch-property would need to be *embodied* in two different bells—one as the end of HO and the other as the beginning of HA. In that way each separate bell could stand for and thus embody two different structural functions.

MOT: Almost literally "stand for"—two bells standing up there in the bell-path, each representing tune events with different functions.

JEANNE: Yes, and that, in fact, is why I included the "doubles"—the pitch-matched pairs—in the first place. I suspected Jeff would need them both. So, with all that in mind (of course it was an on-the-spot hunch, again), I figured that even if I encouraged Jeff to test the C-bell that he already had in his bell-path, it wouldn't help him—it would just create a kind of "identity crisis." But by getting the brown bells into the action, I figured I was giving Jeff a route out of his fix without giving away a useless answer. And this route, namely the possibility of using a matching brown bell for the beginning of HA, seemed more consistent with the way he was representing the tune and the situation to himself at that moment. In any case, it was a way of testing my hunch about what Jeff knew already.

MET: So your hunch was that if you introduced another bell with the same pitch, you would save Jeff from having to confront an identity conflict. Without another bell, that one white C-bell would have had to embody, as you put it, two different structural functions. Instead, you proposed the matching task. That way you sidestepped the crisis that you would have perpetrated if Jeff had had to give that poor C-bell a new identity. When you switched Jeff's attention to the matching task, the result was that the white C-bell was no longer a functioning member of the tune at all; it was just a solitary, functionless, unattached bell-pitch looking for a match.

MOT: Putting it that way, Met, makes me realize something I had never thought of before.

MET: What's that?

MOT: It made me realize that *setting* a problem or a task creates a context, too. And if you change the task-context you also give the same objects new meanings, new functions, and new relations to each other.

MET: What you just said, Mot, reminds me of what happens when I get really stuck in working on a complicated computer program.

MOT: Really? How is that?

MET: Well, sometimes when I get really stuck, I'll just walk away from it, go for a swim or something. And then it will hit me—I suddenly see that I'm trying to solve the wrong problem. And once I see what the problem really is, all of the same elements take on different meanings, functions, and relations. It's just like what you said about the bells when Jeanne changes the task-context. And when that happens to me, I mean when I've got the right frame for the problem, then all the pieces fall into place and the solution seems easy.

MOT: How come these music examples end up being about everything else in the world?

JEANNE: That depends on how you look at them—what you find in them. And you two are becoming awfully shrewd at pulling out profound meaning from very little musical material.

MET: I suspect you have something to do with that, too, Jeanne. However, I just thought of something else: did you notice that Jeff uses position in space as place-markers for identity? In fact, you can literally see the bells changing identity as Jeff moves them around. For instance, when the brown C and D-bells are matches, they sit together with their white twins, like this (see Figure 7–13). But after he's found the matches and you ask Jeff to use the same bells to continue the tune, he changes their position—moves them over to the right. Now they are no longer matches; they are new members of the tune—absorbed into his cumulating bell-path—first the C-bell and then the D-bell. And the change in position "holds" the change in identity (see Figure 7–14).

MOT: It's almost like an invented notation—Jeff uses the position on the table to refer to or define the meaning of the bell. It reminds me of what you just said about "all the pieces falling into place" for you.

Figure 7–13

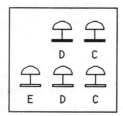

sit together with their white twins

Figure 7–14

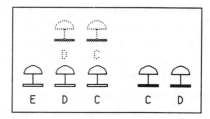

change in position "holds" the change in identity

Maybe that's why we use language like "falling into place." For Jeff it's literally so, but I don't suppose that in fixing your computer programs you were actually moving pieces around into different places as they changed their identity.

MET: Actually, I was in some cases.

MOT: In fact, speaking of using space to mark identity, Jeff even uses *empty space* to mean something. Did you see how he leaves an empty space between his HO-path and his HA-path?

JEANNE: What do you think that space represents, Mot?

MOT: I assume it's a boundary-marker between the two figures.

MET: Yes. And by marking that boundary, Jeff makes the bell-path become a kind of embodied description of the tune—or at least its two structural building blocks. Three white bells for HO and two brown bells for HA. It's great!

MOT: True. But for the same reason, the bell-path could have created the "first one/last one" problem again.

MET: What do you mean?

MOT: Just this: remember in the computer session when Jeff has typed HO HO HA?

MET: Sure. Big troubles followed.

MOT: Well, Jeff is in essentially the same place in the construction of the tune in this session. So when Jeanne asks him to play the whole tune, the question is, what will he do when he gets to the end of HA this time? If he doesn't realize that the HO at the beginning is the same as the HO at the ending, he would probably go into his search-strategy to look for another E-bell to begin a new HO-path. But he doesn't. He plays through HA, and coming to the end of his bell-path, he goes right back to the beginning and plays through the already existing HO-path once more—no problem. And to do that he really has to go *backwards* on the bells in order to go *forward* in the tune—not just back over three bells for a quick repeat of a figure, but back to a figure that he had used as the *beginning* of the tune. So now, within the context of the tune itself, Jeff gives a new identity to the same group of bells. He uses them to play two different roles—beginning and end. How come this doesn't create an identity crisis? And why is it all so simple for Jeff now, when it seemed so impossible when he was building HOT with the computer?

MET: Let me speculate. For instance, maybe giving him the answer in the computer session—telling him to type HO at the end—wasn't so useless after all. But probably more important, constructing the tune with the bells—building it up at the note level, next-next-next, as you say, actually handling the bell-pitches as physical objects that he can hit and that talk right back to him with a sound—all of that is very different from typing some silly words to the computer and mysteriously getting back some weird invisible sound. I think working with the bells gives Jeff a much better *grasp* of the tune—if you'll pardon the pun.

MOT: I'm really surprised to hear you, the computer hacker, talking about computers that way.

MET: But you see, I'm also a tinkerer, and I appreciate the difference between pushing symbols around and pushing around things that you can actually handle. After all, a word doesn't mean anything by itself—you can't "grasp" its meaning the way you can grasp a bell or a block of wood and then see what you can do with it. The meaning of a word is a convention—a kind of agreement between you and the person who made it up, or at least between you and its community of users. But as we've both been saying, Jeff has invented ways of using the bells themselves as a kind of notation. Well, not exactly all by themselves; as I said before, their position in table-space "holds" their identity—tells you what they mean. And that's very different from some arbitrary word—either as a sound or as a squiggle on paper. The bottom line is that Jeff just seems to do much better with things that literally stand *up* in space rather than standing *for* something on paper. What's your view on Jeff's success story, Jeanne?

JEANNE: I think the two of you have just about covered the collection of plausible explanations. I also think that in your last speech, Met, you made not one but a whole collection of profound philosophical insights. And as we go on watching Jeff, those issues of things and symbols, of reference and meaning, are going to come back again and again. But let's talk about the end of the session. Any ideas about that?

MET: You mean the big switcheroo at the very end? That was truly amazing!

JEANNE: Yes, for instance.

MOT: But wait. I really need to know what happens right after Jeff succeeds in playing the whole tune through. Remember, you ask him to find matches again. Why did you do that, Jeanne?

JEANNE: I'm not quite sure. Were you surprised at what happened?

MOT: More than surprised; I was quite astonished. I just can't understand why he has to start all over again to find a match when he had the paired C-bells sitting right there on the table only a few moments before. Can't he remember?

MET: You know, Mot, I think you and I are beginning to switch identities. That's the kind of question I usually ask.

MOT: So can you provide my usual kind of answer?

MET: As a matter of fact, I think I can. The simple answer is, no, he can't remember. But as *you* may remember, Freud and others tell us that forgetting is not simply a deficiency; often there is a reason behind it. And I think in this case it's not hard to "give Jeff reason." It's your point, Mot, about setting a new problem. It seems that when he is inside of one task-context, he holds onto the meanings that the bells acquire in that context, and any previous identities just go away.

MOT: OK, let me go on for myself now. At the moment when Jeanne asks Jeff to find the matches again, he has just been using the bells as tune-events—first to build HA and then to play the whole tune. While he's doing that job, the bells are clearly identified as members of the tune—as place-markers and functions. And on your theory, while that's going on, the previous matches go away, but more than that, the very *identity* of the bells *as matches* is gone, forgotten.

MET: Right. It's a little like only being able to run one computer program at a time.

MOT: That might even account for why Jeff starts out by trying to match the C-bell at the beginning of HA with the E-bell at the beginning of HO.

MET: You'll have to say more about that.

MOT: Maybe he is having a real "identity crisis"—caught between the bells as tune-functions and the bells as simply pitch-matches. You see, while he's building the bell-path and also in the course of playing HOT, the brown C-bell has the function "beginner"—the beginning event in HA. And similarly, the white E-bell has the function "beginner" in the figure HO. So, even though these two bell-pitches are certainly not pitch-matches, Jeff might be thinking of them as *functional "matches"*—they're both "beginners."

MET: I think that one is pretty far-fetched—your association, not Jeff's. Starting his testing with those two bells could have been completely arbitrary. Do you have any evidence?

MOT: Not really. Except maybe this: Jeff tries to match the brown C-bell with the white E-bell first, and then with the white D-bell. But then he stops without testing the white C-bell. That white C-bell is certainly provocative—remember that Jeff also stopped without testing that bell when he was looking for the beginning of HA. But this time we have some clues because he finally talks.

MET: That's right; he doesn't try that bell because he *predicts* they won't match. He says that the brown and white C-bells won't match because the white bell is "lower." What could he mean? It's true that the C-bell is the lowest pitch in HO, but I can't believe that Jeff was talking about that. And besides, what has this got to do with your idea about "functional matches"?

MOT: Well, this may sound strange, but HO *feels* really ended—I mean when you get to the C-bell, it feels as if you've arrived, settled down.

MET: Down?

MOT: Sorry, I didn't even mean to make a pun—it's such a familiar expression, settling down, for feeling at rest. Anyhow, that white C-bell just feels like a "downer." And the beginning of HA couldn't be more different. I *know* that the two bells play the same pitch, but that same pitch in the context of HA sounds completely different—like it's taking off, not arriving. So, I agree with you that Jeff probably doesn't mean lower in *pitch* when he says that the white bell is "lower." I think he's using the word to refer to a feeling or function. And if I'm right, this could be evidence that Jeff is still in the world of tune-functions, maybe even "*function*-matches," and hasn't really switched to *pitch*-matching at all. Anyhow, those two C-bells are a perfect example of bells that embody the same pitch-property but different structural functions.

JEANNE: That's right, Mot. In fact those two tune events are different in every respect *except* for their shared pitch-property. First of all, in duration—the ending white C is much longer than the beginning brown C. Then there is pitch-direction: the white C is approached from above, and that means the pitch-direction is downward—we shouldn't throw that out altogether. Unlike the white C, which is the bottom of a downward motion, the brown C comes from and leads into a repetition of itself—the repeated pitches for "one-a-pen-ny." So the feeling of the brown C as moving *forward,* taking off as you said, is generated not only because of its shorter duration—faster, if you want—but also because its repetition creates a sense of moving faster but standing still at the same time—all of which generates a feeling of *tension* in contrast to the *stability* of the white C. And finally, remember that HA begins after the *second* HO—what Mot called "more of the same." This repetition of a whole figure reaffirms the stability of the white C and, in doing so, marks a big structural boundary, what we call a structural *down*-beat. In contrast, not only does the brown C "take off," thus marking a beginning, but it also marks the beginning of a figure, HA, which, as a whole, functions as a structural *up*-beat—it leads into, swoops *up* to, the return of HO.

MET: And another thing: because of those repeated notes, Jeff has to play four faster hits on the same bell—we've been witness to that during every one of his searches. I suppose playing four faster hits on the same bell *feels* very different from playing one hit on a bell and letting it ring for its full duration.

JEANNE: Good point, Met. And all these factors or features conspire together to give that shared pitch what Mot calls a different *feel.* In particular, it's the contrast between at rest or *stability,* on one hand, and, on the other, *tension,* which is always moving toward, seeking out, stability. In fact these particular differences in "feel" between tension and stability, and the continuous swing between them, are critical to nearly all of the emotions that music creates. And interestingly, this same movement between tension and stability is also very closely related to what we mean when we talk about differing structural functions.

MOT: So when Jeff predicts that the white C-bell is "lower" than the brown C-bell, the one thing he is *not* talking about is pitch. I guess he packages together in that one word, "lower," all the particular musical features and relations that combine to generate that feeling.

JEANNE: Exactly. Indeed, that's probably what we all do when we're deeply involved in listening to much more complex pieces. I doubt very much that we attend to "same pitch," for instance, except maybe when we "go analytic." Although that can be important, too.

MET: It's our favorite theme again: an event can be heard as both same and different depending on what you're paying attention to. And that helps me understand what seemed so baffling to me a while back. Even though those two bells are the same in pitch and next to each other in space and time, they aren't next to each other in a *hearing* of the tune because there's a *structural gap* between them. As you *listen* to HOT, you don't go across that boundary, and you certainly don't compare pitches.

MOT: Our favorite theme, indeed; in fact this sounds like our first conversation about the Class Piece. Back then I said something about not paying attention to what goes on between two figures. I was inside of one, then inside the other, and the "in between" didn't exist. There we were talking about rhythm figures, but I suppose it works the same way with melodic figures. The important thing is that in going along those paths, we don't *hear* across boundaries. As we said at the time, to *compare* two claps or two bell-pitches, you have to jump off the tune-path.

MET: And bingo! Now I just realized something else. When Jeff switches on his pitch-matching program the first time—right after he has built HO—that's exactly what he does: he *jumps off the tune-path*. Once off, he compares bell-pitches irrespective of their place-value or function. And that way he has no problem hearing matches. But when Jeanne asks him to find matches the second time—right after he has built HA and played the whole tune—he still has his tune-building program on; he's on the path and his pitch-matching program is turned off. So in order to find matches, he needs to turn his pitch-matching program on, and that means starting all over again.

MOT: Or putting it the way you did before: Jeff has access to multiple representations, but it's either one or the other. It's as if the two ways of representing the bells exist in separate spaces. In fact, as we've seen, they literally do.

JEANNE: Wonderful. You've just summarized the major work that Jeff is about to launch into. It took me about a month of working with him to begin to grasp what you both just said about multiple but iso-

Figure 7–15

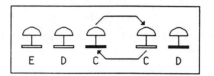

picks up the two bells and switches them

lated representations. The big problem that Jeff is going to face now is how to coordinate them, and in that process to build some new ones, too. But we have to finish up now. What about the very end of the session—the "big switcheroo," as you called it, Met?

MET: You mean after Jeff finally does try the two C-bells and, comparing across the boundary, discovers the surprising match?

JEANNE: Yes, exactly. And then I try to tease him or tempt him into getting rid of the brown C-bell. I said something like: since you've already got another bell that sounds the same, you don't really need them both to play the tune, right?

MET: But Jeff was not about to be tempted; another example of his integrity, I suppose. Instead, he just picks up the two C-bells and switches them, like this (see Figure 7–15).

MOT: What do you make of that, Met?

MET: I think there's something really important there. In fact, it may be the beginning of the big work Jeanne was just talking about—a kind of transition on-the-way-to coordinating multiple representations.

JEANNE: Can you say a little more?

MET: By switching the two bells, Jeff is implicitly saying that two bells inside the tune can match, and because they can, either one can be a *stand-in* for the other. But at the same time, he's saying that he can't do without the place-markers along his path. So it's an important leap because he's in both representational spaces at the same time—the match-space and the tune-space. He recognizes bells as matching, but he's not about to give away their identity as functions. And since functions are "held" by their spatial positions in the bell-path, even though the bells play the same pitch, he needs them both.

JEANNE: Bingo, indeed! See you next time.

CHAPTER 8

Making Instructions for Playing *"Hot Cross Buns"*

AFTER JEFF had successfully built HOT, and with his final arrangement of the bells still on the table, I gave him paper and pencil and asked him to make instructions so that someone else could play HOT on the bells just as he had them set up. In the course of carrying out this task, Jeff's instructions evolved and changed in quite unexpected ways. To give readers an appreciation of these events as they occurred, I will describe Jeff's work as a running account in the continuing conversation with Met and Mot, using their questions and their search for answers as a means of pointing out the puzzles that occur along the way. As I recount these events, I also encourage Met and Mot to question the bases for my interventions. Through my responses, I intend to exemplify to the students (and to readers) the value of a research methodology that includes on-the-spot experiments as a vehicle for testing hunches about the meaning of momentary events in a child's work. The conversation is also meant to give readers a sense of the long and often circuitous process involved in "giving a child reason." Once completed, this process is frequently forgotten, leaving behind only the final results of the quest as if arrived at in a single moment of insight.

MET AND MOT USE THEIR NEW INSIGHTS TO GRAPPLE WITH
JEFF'S INSTRUCTIONS

JEANNE: I'm glad we could get together so soon because we still have to look at the second part of Jeff's session—his "instructions" for playing HOT on the bells. A lot of knotty problems came up in this part of the session, so I think it would be best if we just go through it together.

MOT: Let's get to it.

JEANNE: Actually, there was an issue that we kept returning to last time that is very much to the point as we look at the evolution of Jeff's instructions. It was what Met initially called "identity," and along with that, the intriguing inventions Jeff made for *marking* a bell's identity when that changed. As you put it, Met, their position in table-space "held" the meaning of the bells.

MET: Yes. Since the bells all look the same and they have no labels on them, a person needs to find some way of knowing *where* they are and *what* they've got. So for Jeff, a change in the *spatial disposition* of a bell depicted for him (and also for us) a change in its meaning—for instance, at one moment a matching pitch property and at another a functioning member of a figure.

JEANNE: And since the issue of identity is very close to the meaning Jeff gives to the bells, it will become important again in this part of the session as he searches for paper-and-pencil ways of indicating the meaning he intends for the bells.

MOT: In fact, we even talked about Jeff's use of table-space and the arrangement of the bells in it as the invention of a special kind of *notation scheme*. Even the tune structure—the two basic building blocks or motives—was *described* by the way he grouped the white and brown bells together and by his use of empty space, too. But Met also talked a lot about the differences between using hands-on objects arranged in space as a way of defining meaning, and using symbols (words or numbers) as a way of representing what you mean.

JEANNE: And that's just the place to start thinking about Jeff's invented "instructions." These instructions are, after all, another kind of invented notation—this time using paper-space rather than table-space, and marks *on* paper instead of real objects *in* real space. You remember, the bells were set up like this at the end (see Figure 8–1). And with the bells sitting there on the table, I said to Jeff, "Can you make some instructions so that someone else could play HOT on the bells

Figure 8–1

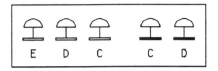

set up like this at the end

just as you have them set up there on the table?" I gave Jeff crayons and paper, and he started his instructions this way:

MOT: That looks exactly like what he drew in the computer session when you asked him to draw a picture of HO.

MET: That's not so surprising—same tune and same boy.

MOT: Except it's not so simple, Met. There he didn't have any bells—just the sound coming out of the synthesizer. So one thing is for sure: whatever the lines stood for in the computer session, they didn't stand for bells.

MET: That's true. I think we finally decided that in Jeff's first drawing of HO, the lines were more like rhythm—as if Jeff were clapping the rhythm of the tune. That was because they looked so much like the children's drawings of the rhythm pieces. Do you think these lines could stand for the rhythm?

MOT: There's really no way to tell yet. I suppose they could stand for hits on the bells—the rhythm of playing on them; that would be the same as clapping the rhythm. But I think it's more likely that they stand for the bells themselves—like stick-figure pictures of the first three bells on the table. It's fascinating that a representation of two such different things—rhythm and the bells—could look the same.

MET: Isn't it, though. How can we find out which Jeff intends them to be?

JEANNE: Good question, Met, and at the time I was just as puzzled as you are. So, I used my old ploy. I asked Jeff to "add some numbers that would help people know what to do." This is what he did:

MOT: That doesn't help much. He could have put those numbers in if the lines stood for bells on the table, but the same numbers would work if the lines stood for claps or hits, or even for pure, invisible melody notes. In any one of those, the numbers 1 2 3 would mean the same—simply the first, the second, and the third "thing" in the tune. And a "thing" could be a clap, or a hit on a bell, or the bell itself.

MET: But if the lines are pictures of the bells on the table, then Jeff might be using the numerals to give a *name* to each bell.

JEANNE: How could we test that? Or specifically, how could we distinguish between the numbers as names for the bells and numbers that show, simply, that there are three "things" in HO?

MET: Maybe we can get some clues from what Jeff does next. For instance, if they are names, then the names will have to "travel" with each bell—stay attached to each one—just as our names stay attached to us.

MOT: Hmm, that's a problem. Because if the lines *are* pictures of the three bells, then the only way Jeff could go on to show instructions for the next HO would be like this:

MET: And that would disconfirm my theory about the numbers as names.

MOT: Why is that?

MET: Those numbers can't be names because you defeat the purpose if you give more than one name to a thing—for instance, Bell 1 can't also be Bell 4. Those instructions are like a picture-map, the kind people make for treasure hunts. The lines stand for the bells, like pictures of places and things on one of those maps, and the numbers tell you what direction to go—the sequence of moves from one place to the next.

MOT: I see what you mean. But what else *could* he do to show that you are supposed to go back and repeat those same three bells again?

MET: How about this:

/ | | / | |
1 2 3   4 5 6

MOT: That's certainly a whole different thing. Now the lines can't be pictures of the bells anymore.

MET: Why not?

MOT: It's obvious. Jeff has only three bells on the table, not six—he played HO HO on just those three bells. Remember, that was something Jeff knew—to reuse the same bells for the second HO. And that meant going *back* in space in order to go *forward* in the tune and also in time. That's what I tried to show with my numbers.

MET: But, Mot, you know as well as I do that that's the way we do it. I mean, it's another convention. Everyone knows that if you want to represent going "forward" in time, you go from left to right in paper-space. So drawing the three lines again means something that happens *later*, or to do something *after*, not that there are three new bells.

MOT: I suppose so, *if* you know the convention.

MET: And Jeff obviously does. Remember, he used that convention in the computer session for his drawing of HO HO. That was exactly the same as what I just drew:

Jeff's drawing of HO HO in the computer session

MOT: True. But in the computer session Jeff didn't have any physical, graspable objects that were occupying real space. I mean, there was only something to listen to but no things to draw pictures of.

MET: What you're saying makes me realize something. I guess you would have to say that the second three bells in my drawing are in some kind of imaginary or *symbolic* space. See, in your drawing, there's a direct *correspondence* between objects in table-space and "objects" in paper-space—if you consider the lines as "objects." It's as close as you can come to just picking up the bells and sticking them onto the paper. So I suppose my drawing is more symbolic than yours since I use an *imaginary space* to stand for later or after. But it is a convention that Jeff seems to be familiar with.

MOT: Keeping all that in mind, now I'm confused by your numbers— 4 5 6. Did you mean them to be names?

MET: You're right, they can't be. I intended the second group of three lines to stand for the same three bells, but the numbers obviously aren't names; they show you the sequence of *actions on* the bells— just like yours do. It makes you realize how complicated this business of naming, actions, space, and time really is. You have to make up your mind what is going to move and what is going to stand still. But I want to know what Jeff actually does.

JEANNE: OK. But before I show you, you need to know that I asked Jeff to start over again from the beginning of his instructions each time as he went along. I didn't want him to erase anything. That way I kept a record of any changes so I could look back over the evolution of his final product. Doing as I asked, Jeff left the first three lines as they were and underneath he started over again and added:

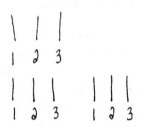

MET: But that confirms my theory! Now it's clear that the lines stand for the bells and the numbers are, in fact, names. Jeff is more consistent than I was.

MOT: How do you know that?

MET: It's really very clever. Repeating the lines uses the convention of time going from left to right—*after* is to the right. And repeating the same numbers for the second group of three lines tells you that the second group of lines means the same three bells again. Both you and I used numbers to show the sequence of actions, but Jeff holds the numbers steady—they don't mean actions at all; they consistently name the bells, travel with them as I said.

MOT: But you know, going from left to right now means two different things. The action-path on the first three bells goes literally left to right, and that's exactly mirrored on the paper—what you called a "direct correspondence." But with the repetition—the second group of bell-pictures—the literalness breaks down: in paper-space, going right now means onward in time or after, next. So the instructions go to the *right* in paper-space, but when you're actually playing the bells in table-space, you have to move to the *left* to get back to the beginning of the bell-path. I see what you mean about a treasure hunt map: Jeff's instructions are *not* like a map—he hasn't drawn a picture that you can move on as you do in actual table-space.

MET: Very true, Mot. Jeff is using our conventional symbolic space as I did in my drawing. And I suppose using numbers as names is pretty symbolic, too. How do we ever learn all this stuff?

JEANNE: Actually, some kids have real troubles—Jeff for one. As you can see, he has internalized some of the critical conventions, but he's inventing his own, too.

MOT: So asking Jeff to make instructions is really a neat way to find out what he knows already.

JEANNE: That's the idea, Mot. And from what *you* know so far, how do you think Jeff will go on with HA?

MOT: From what we've seen, I suppose something like this:

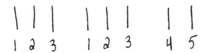

MET: Yes, that's consistent with the numbers as names for the bells. The two new bells for HA are the two new lines, and the numbers are the next two number-names. Is that what he does?

JEANNE: Well, not exactly. Jeff started from the beginning as I asked him to, but then he added:

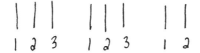

MET: Uh oh! There goes my theory about the numbers being names. That's really puzzling.

JEANNE: Isn't it, though. I was totally confused by that one.

MOT: So, what was your on-the-spot hunch this time?

JEANNE: I was making the same assumptions you were: the lines stood for the bells on the table and the numbers were names for the bells. But with this addition, the two new *lines* made sense—they were pictures of the two new bells, the HA bells—but what did the *numbers* mean? Clearly they did not refer to the same bells that Jeff had labeled 1 2 before.

MET: So what did you do?

JEANNE: To check out my assumption about the two new lines, I asked Jeff to play the tune on his drawing.

MET: Good idea. What happened?

JEANNE: That checked out as I thought it would. Jeff "played" his drawing. Following along, pointing to the lines, he tapped out the rhythm of the tune on the first set of three lines and then the next to make HO HO. Going on to the two new lines, he tapped four faster "hits" on each of them.

MOT: So the two new lines were clearly pictures of the bells for HA. Those four faster hits certainly tell us where Jeff is in the tune. But what did you do about the numbers?

JEANNE: Nothing very useful, I'm afraid. I pointed to the first of the two new lines (the first one in HA that Jeff had marked "1") and said, "Is this 1-bell the same as this 1-bell?" and pointed to his very first line in HO. As you can imagine, Jeff just looked puzzled and didn't say anything.

MET: That question must have made no sense to Jeff. Just using the expression "1-bell" was probably totally incomprehensible. It only makes sense if you are assuming that the numbers *are* names. And even then, it's kind of funny language.

MOT: It also takes for granted that the lines are bells. And if so, it must have been completely obvious to Jeff that the bells pictured by the new lines weren't "the same" as the bells pictured by the old lines. What did you do then?

JEANNE: I gave up on direct questioning and switched gears. You see, even without really understanding what those numbers meant, there was still another problem. . .

MOT: Wait a minute, I have an idea. First of all, just think about the troubles Jeff had at the beginning of HA when he was *building* the tune.

MET: OK, I'm thinking.

MOT: Now remember all the ideas we had about that—especially about the difference in function between the white C-bell and the brown C-bell—the ending C of HO and the beginning C of HA. And add to that the stuff about the "structural gap" that you don't cross over when you're actually listening. Putting all that together with these new numbers, it seems to me that the 1   2 here might mean something like a *new beginning*.

MET: I must say that makes a lot of sense. In fact, come to think of it, Jeff is doing exactly what some of the kids did with numbers in the rhythm drawings—numbering up *inside of* each figure separately. I remember one of them:

in the rhythm drawings, numbering up inside of each figure separately

Jeff's numbering is exactly the same!

MOT: So does that mean that Jeff's numbers never were names for the bells?

MET: They can't be names like a permanent label on a bell—a name that names some unchangeable *property* of it, like its pitch. Jeff really keeps the figures of the tune separate from one another. "1" seems to be the name for the *first bell inside of a figure,* but it isn't the same as a pure label on a particular bell. It seems like numbers don't name bells; they name the *place* of a bell in a figure.

MOT: It's pretty consistent, though, as long as you are paying attention to figural boundaries. It's the boundaries that define the *context* for naming.

MET: So what was the context for naming when you put the numbers 4 5 under the two new lines?

MOT: It had nothing to do with figures or functions. I suppose it was just a count-up—the number of bells on the table.

MET: You mean like the kids who did count-up numbering in the rhythm drawings?

MOT: Sort of, but those were claps, and bells are not at all the same as claps.

MET: But there's something that makes me uneasy here. Jeff's instructions will only work for *these* exact bells in *this* exact order. In fact, the arrangement of the bells on the table is like a *one-purpose instrument.* It only plays this one tune, and his instructions only work for this instrument.

JEANNE: That's a very shrewd insight, Met. It makes you begin to think about what would be involved in making a general-purpose notation—one that could work for any melody and any instrument.

MET: Standard music notation seems to do that, but it's not so easy to think about how that works and exactly how Jeff's instructions are different from standard notation.

JEANNE: You're right, it's not so easy. In fact, that is a critical question, especially if you think about how Jeff might get from his instructions to the assumptions implicit in standard notation. I do want to say, though, that I think you are absolutely right about Jeff's numbering of the two new lines. And understanding that—what Jeff knows already—is going to be very useful later on in helping him to develop an understanding of the conventions that underlie standard notation. I'm particularly impressed with how you came up with evidence for how Jeff was using numbers—thinking back to the kids' drawing of rhythms, and all. Anyhow, I was going to tell you about how I gave up on Jeff's numbering and switched gears to try to deal with another problem.

MET: And what was that?

JEANNE: It's the problem of the four faster hits on the two new bells— or the two new lines. He hasn't shown that at all in his instructions.

MET: That's right. And it wasn't a problem in HO because there was always one-bell, one-hit. So what did you do about that?

JEANNE: As I said, I switched gears. I asked Jeff to *clap* HA—that is, to clap the rhythm of "one-a-pen-ny, two-a-pen-ny"—and then to draw a picture of his claps.

MOT: How do you come up with these things?

JEANNE: It always seems perfectly obvious at the time. There is something that I want to find out about, and I guess I've just gotten into the habit of making little off-the-cuff experiments to do that.

MET: Well, it doesn't seem all that obvious to me. Anyhow, what happened?

JEANNE: Jeff clapped the rhythm—no problem. And then he tapped it out on the paper, leaving a trace like this:

Jeff tapped the rhythm out on the paper

MOT: Dots this time instead of the lines he used in the computer session.

JEANNE: Yes, and as you'll see, that difference between dots and lines proves very useful. But then came a surprise. When Jeff finished making his drawing, he said, to my astonishment, "four claps and four claps." Seeing an opportunity, I grabbed it and said, "Could you show that in your instructions?" What do you think he did?

MOT: He could put the four dots under each line like this:

MET: Or he could make four lines and repeat the 1 under each line. That would make use of the symbolic space convention where going left to right means onward in time, and the numbers would still name the bells as the first and second ones in the new figure:

$$| | | | | | | |$$
$$1 \; 1 \; 11 \; 2 \, 2 \, 2 \, 2$$

JEANNE: Actually, he did something quite different. This time, he took what he already had on the paper and changed it like this:

MET: So he just crossed out one set of numbers and substituted another set. And do you know what?

MOT: What, Met?

MET: In substituting the 4's for the 1 2, he's totally switched what the numbers stand for. In fact, he's switched them from one dimension of the tune to another.

MOT: I don't get it.

MET: Well, his first numbers refer to a bell according to its *position in a figure*, but the second numbers, the 4's, refer to *how many times you are supposed to play each bell*. So the lines still stand for the bells on the table, but now the numbers stand for actions on them.

MOT: So what you're saying is that Jeff has transformed the picture of his *claps*—where there's a dot for each clap, and paper-space is used to show time between claps—into symbols under the bells, where paper-space has no purpose except to "hold" the number. But in a way, he had already taken that step—I mean when he finished making the dot drawing and said in words, "four claps and four claps."

MET: That's true. But what's really important is that Jeff is again keeping dimensions isolated from each other—switching from one to another. You see, numerals can stand for *either* the place of a bell-pitch in a figure—like his first numbering of the HA bells, 1 2; *or* they can stand for how many times to play a bell—like the 4's he adds now. He slips from one to the other, but he has no way to get them together— to coordinate them.

JEANNE: Exactly right, Met. And at the time, I wanted to push that slippage a little. I wondered if Jeff was really making a clear distinction between those two dimensions, and if he could hold that distinction steady. So I asked him, first, to just clap the whole tune—that is, to focus on just the rhythm—and to make a picture of his claps. As in the computer session, he clapped the rhythm and then tapped it out on the paper, this time leaving a trace like this:

● ● ●   ● ● ●   ●●●●▾●●● ● ●

a trace of the rhythm of the whole tune

MOT: The first part looks exactly like his pictures of the bells—only dots, again, instead of lines. But the dots now stand for claps while the lines stood for the bells. And the bigger space between the two groups of three *dots*, I suppose, stands for a bigger space-of-time—a longer duration. I remember that when we first looked at the lines Jeff made for HO in the computer session, we assumed that the space between the two groups stood for a figural boundary; but I suppose it could have stood for the longer duration there, too. After all, it's the longer duration that helps to make the figural boundary. It's very confusing.

JEANNE: Indeed it is. And I wondered if it was equally confusing for Jeff. Specifically, I wondered if he was clear about what the dots represented as compared with the lines. To find out, I asked what seemed like a reasonable question, but as before, his answer taught me otherwise. Pointing to the lines he had first made in his instructions for playing HOT on the bells, I said, "What are these?" To which Jeff answered, simply, "Lines."

MET: Straight answer, all right—what you see is what you get.

JEANNE: That was, however, certainly not what I expected. I followed up with, "And what do they stand for?" Jeff told me, but not in words; he *showed* me instead. He picked up the dinger and made the motions he used for striking the bells.

MOT: Well, that's clear enough. Those lines that Jeff put on paper when you first asked him to make instructions really *are* instructions—the lines mean *playing* on the bells, not just the bells themselves. I mean, the lines aren't just pictures of bells standing there on the table; they tell you to *do* something. They show you how to play the tune.

JEANNE: You're absolutely right, Mot, and as you'll see, it's just as true for the dots. When I asked Jeff, pointing to the dot-drawing of his claps, "And what are these?" he said with his wonderful consistency, "Dots." So, once more I asked, "And what do they stand for?" To which he replied by making the motions with his hand that he used when he was drawing-playing the rhythm on the paper with his pencil.

MET: And that's pretty clear evidence that Jeff knows exactly what he's doing: the dots are for clapping, the lines are for playing on the bells.

MOT: But it is remarkable how he can move from one kind of thing to the other as you shift his focus.

MET: It's also remarkable what Jeff's separate and distinct descriptions are doing for me.

MOT: What *are* they doing for you, Met?

MET: Well, just this: in shifting from one dimension to another, Jeff is making me become aware of the *existence* of these dimensions. In my usual experience of playing and singing melodies, these dimensions are so interlocked with one another that to separate them is an exercise in abstraction.

JEANNE: Can you say what you mean by "abstraction" there?

MET: I mean that in ordinary experience—singing a melody, playing a melody on an instrument, or just listening—all those dimensions are buried in what we experience as simply "the melody." The pitch and the rhythm, for instance, don't exist as separate features. And I think it's the same sort of thing once you have learned how to read words, or numbers, or even music notation: you don't even notice the graffiti, so to speak—dots, lines, or any other squiggles. It's as if you see right through them to their meaning. So what I meant by "abstracting" is to pull out separate features from "the melody," or to stare at the marks on paper and ask yourself what each one individually means.

MOT: But aren't you really talking about "multiple hearings?"

MET: Maybe so; go on.

MOT: What you just said makes me realize that Jeff has wonderful capacities for shifting his focus so as to hear this tune in multiple ways—much more so than you or I. He can already *do* the very thing that Jeanne is telling us is the mark of the sophisticated, "musical" musician.

JEANNE: Just so, Mot. But the trick is going to be to encourage Jeff's inventiveness and his close contact with the many faces his world shows him, and still to enrich these with an ability to control and coordinate this many-splendored world.

MOT: Can you show us what Jeff's final instructions looked like? What did he do with the final HO?

JEANNE: As you might expect, it was no problem. Here are his completed instructions for playing HOT on his bells:

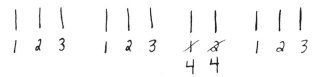

completed instructions for playing HOT

MET: Wonderful.

JEANNE: You've both been great in helping me make sense of this whole session. Now I need to go off and think about the more general implications that may lie hidden in what we've learned.

COMMENTS ON OUR CONVERSATIONS

The issues that emerge in Jeff's work during this first bell session, especially the puzzles and ambiguities that Met and Mot point up as they interrogate his work, are just those that we will see Jeff confronting again and again as he goes on with his work in the next months. Interestingly, many of these puzzles and ambiguities rest on the tensions between figural and formal strategies for making sense of and organizing musical relations. As Jeff goes on, we will see him confronting these tensions head-on. At the same time, *through* the very confusions that Jeff will face, along with the disequilibrium that accompanies them, the terms "figural" and "formal" will gain greater clarity and more functional meaning. But it is important to emphasize that Jeff's course is not a simple, unidirectional one *from* figural *to* formal knowledge, where the latter takes over from the former. Rather, after slow and often confusing periods of transition, Jeff is finally able to move freely in and out of his multiple ways of representing tunes to himself, mapping one onto another, choosing one or another, and thus richly apprehending the multiple intersecting dimensions of simple tunes.

We see a small hint of Jeff in transition even in this first session. It is the moment that Met calls the "big switcheroo," when I intervene after Jeff has successfully built HOT (Figure 8–2). In trying to account for it, Met says, "It may be the beginning of the big work Jeanne was just talking about—a kind of transition on-the-way-to coordinating multiple representations." And indeed it is; but if it is a transition, what are the "multiple representations" of the tune that Jeff is moving between, and what is the evidence? Met proposes a partial answer to this question

Figure 8–2

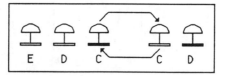

the big switcheroo

when he says: "Jeff is implicitly saying that two bells inside the tune can match, and because they can, either one can be a *stand-in* for the other. But at the same time he's saying that he can't do without the place-markers along his path. So it's an important leap because he's in both representational spaces at the same time—the match-space and the tune-space."

As they go on to discuss Jeff's session in making instructions for play-ing HOT on his bells, Met and Mot together make a number of other insightful comments about Jeff's capacity to make "multiple representa-tions," as evidenced, for example, in his shifts from one dimension of the tune to another. And they also are quick to notice that Jeff is "always keeping dimensions isolated from one another." At the end of our con-versation, I suggest that the trick is going to be to help Jeff "control and coordinate this many-splendored world." In order to think about these issues more clearly, since they have implications that extend over such a wide terrain, I will propose a more general framework within which to look at these and other characteristics of Jeff's moves in this first session.

Let me call this terrain "making meaning" in an effort to bound it, but not too tightly. By construing the terrain in this way, I want to emphasize a view that is, by this time, familiar, but I would like to put it now more strongly: in entering into the tasks I put to him, Jeff must first *determine* what the elements of the task may be. And in doing so, he is also con-structing or invoking a *coherent mental universe* within which elements and relations that become relevant to him can be assigned meaning—a universe that can include them. Within this constructed universe, Jeff can then give meaning to *particular* actions, events, objects, elements, and their relations as participating members within that universe. On this view, the details of Jeff's work—his construction strategies, the resulting bell-paths, his action-paths on them, together with his "instructions" (or notation-paths)—become evidence for (or at least clues to) the structure of the coherent mental universe that he is creating along with the vari-ous meanings that Jeff gives to particular elements and relations that in-habit it.

I mean to suggest by the term "coherent mental universe" something like what F. C. Bartlett in his book *Remembering* calls an "organized setting" or a "momentary setting." He says, for example: "There is not the slightest reason . . . to suppose that each set of incoming impulses, each new group of experiences persists as an isolated member of some passive patchwork. They have to be regarded as constituents of living, *momentary settings* belonging to the organism, or to whatever parts of the organism are concerned in making a response of a given kind, and not as a number of individual events somehow strung together and stored within the organism" (Bartlett 1932, p. 201). Jeff's actions, his moves, his constructions become, then, the means by which, as Bartlett goes on to say, "not exactly to analyze the settings, because the individual details that have built them up have disappeared, but somehow to construct or to infer from what is present the probable constituents and their order which went to build them up" (p. 202).

As we have seen, and as Met and Mot observed, Jeff constructs (mostly as a result of my interventions) more than one such organized setting. But as the students also observed, each of these settings, though coherent and consistent within itself, remains self-contained during most of Jeff's work in this session. For example, as Jeff starts his work, the bells within the mixed array are, so to speak, "neutral" in their meaning. But as he begins building HOT, Jeff invokes a construction strategy in which the array itself is given meaning—it is what I have called a search-space. In turn, upon going into the search-space, Jeff invokes a mental setting in which he can assign meaning to a bell as a tune-event. And when, in searching, Jeff recognizes a bell as the object of his search, he can assign it *particular* meaning as next-in-tune. Finally, in placing the found bell in his cumulating bell-path, Jeff gives the bell *unique* meaning: it marks a necessary and particular *place* in the unfolding tune, and it "holds" or embodies a unique structural function within the figure of which it is a member.

But there is another mental setting within which Jeff assigns quite different kinds of meaning to bells. He does so when I intervene in trying to help him out of the problem he faces at the moment when he momentarily gives up in his search for the bell-pitch with which to begin the new figure, HA. Recognizing that Jeff will need to "get the brown bells into the action . . . [to] use a matching brown bell for the beginning of HA," I set a new task, namely, the matching task. And in doing so, I trigger a new mental setting, a new self-contained universe for Jeff. Within this setting (Met calls it Jeff's "pitch-making program"), the object and meaning of Jeff's search changes; going into the search-space, Jeff now gives meaning to bells as either "match" or "mismatch" with respect to pitch-property alone.

That each of these is a separate and distinct mental setting for Jeff was demonstrated throughout his continuing confusions around the white and brown C-bells. For instance, Jeff first finds and incorporates the white C-bell as the last event in HO (Figure 8–3). In doing so, he invokes an organized setting in which a bell is given meaning as a *unique tune-*

Figure 8–3

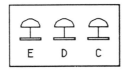

as the last event in HO

event, a place-marker with a particular structural function. And within this setting he gives the white C-bell a particular meaning. At this moment the white C-bell might be described as "third one in the tune-so-far" or "ender."

But when I shift Jeff's attention to the matching task, he invokes an organized setting in which bells can be assigned meaning only as *match or mismatch.* Within this setting, the white and brown C-bells are given meaning appropriate to this setting—they are *pitch-matches.* To "hold" this meaning, Jeff places the matched bells together (Figure 8–4). Now recall that when Jeff has successfully matched the two pairs of brown and white bells, I ask him to return to tune-building, and at my suggestion he uses the brown C-bell to construct the beginning of HA. It is at this point that we have the strongest evidence that, indeed, Jeff is invoking separate and distinct organized mental settings, and that within each, the identical bells are given quite different *kinds* of meaning. The evidence is in Jeff's rearrangement of the position of the bells in table-space—their positions "holding" (as Met says) their respective "identities." When the white and brown C-bells are serving as pitch-matches, they are in the configuration shown in A in Figure 8–5. But when Jeff uses the brown C-bell as the first event in the new figure, HA, he moves it to form the configuration shown in part B of the figure.

Figure 8–4

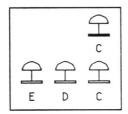

places the matched bells together

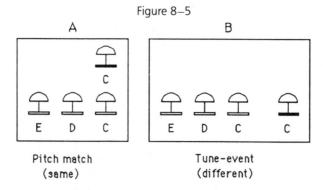

Figure 8–5

Pitch match
(same)

Tune-event
(different)

As Jeff changes the bell-configuration, table-space becomes like a "tablet" where each spatial configuration "holds" the particular meaning he has given the bell within each organized setting. In configuration A, Jeff can give the meaning "same pitch" to the paired bells—a meaning that *does not exist* in the tune universe. When he is in configuration B, Jeff can give the two identical bells with identical pitches two different meanings, "ending" and "beginning"—meanings that *do not exist* in the pitch-matching universe. Thus the set of possible constituents within one organized setting is not shared by the other; the constraints of the two bounded settings are mutually exclusive. It is this sense of mutually exclusive constraints that Met is groping for when, invoking Freud, he says that "forgetting is not simply a deficiency . . . when [Jeff] is inside of one task-context, he holds onto the meanings that the bells acquire in that context, and any previous identities just go away." Thus, each arrangement of the bells "holds still" the meanings Jeff intends. In this sense, a spatial configuration becomes a *reference* for these meanings. And since each of these arrangements includes objects that occupy three-dimensional space, and actions within this space that are events in real time, the spatial configuration is also a *concrete entity.* I shall, therefore, call each of these arrangements in table-space a *reference entity*—an embodied and enacted description of an organized mental setting and the constituents that inhabit it.

Looking back at these reference entities, we see a "log" of Jeff's work in making meaning. In turn, looking back at the changing series of instructions, we see a log of the changing meanings he gives to paper-space, to numerals, and to other graphic marks—for instance, dots in contrast to lines. As in the construction task, each of these changes in meaning suggests a shift in Jeff's organized mental setting, and most often these were in response to the shifts in task context that I generated for him. As Mot says, "Setting a problem or a task creates a context, too. And if you change the task-context you also give the same objects new meanings, new functions, and new relations to each other." In subsequent sessions we will see Jeff shifting his focus and his mental organized setting as *he* wishes rather than in response to my suggestions.

In the light of this more general framework, along with the notion of organized mental settings and reference entities, I return now to questions I posed earlier concerning the significance of Jeff's switched bell-path, as I shall now call it (Figure 8–6). What are the meanings the switched bell-path holds? How is the organized setting that it implies different from that implied by Jeff's own final construction of HOT, and in what sense is this move evidence that Jeff is in transition? Met gives an insightful but only partial answer: "[Jeff] is in both representational spaces at the same time. He recognizes bells as embodying pitch-properties, but, at the same time, he's not about to throw away their identity as functions. And functions are 'held' by their positions in the bell-path. So, even though the bells play the same pitch, he needs them both."

As Met already suggested, there is a critical cognitive leap implicit in this move. While Jeff has rearranged his reference entity several times before, each time he did so he invoked mental settings that were distinct from one another and *self-contained*. But in making the switched bell-path, Jeff makes a transformation of a different order: in this reference entity his two organized settings *intersect*—both are present simultaneously. On one hand, what we see is an elaboration of the mental setting that Jeff invoked initially in the matching game. That is, Jeff "says" through his actions that one bell can *substitute* for the other, but only with respect to their *shared pitch-property*. This is not a trivial point, for in making this move, Jeff demonstrates his awareness of a possibility that we saw no evidence for earlier. It is this: if Jeff is willing to let two *differ-*

Figure 8–6

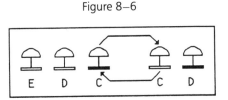

Jeff's switched bell-path

ent bell-objects substitute for each other, he can only do so if he can differentiate the object, bell, and its spatial position from the *internal and invisible pitch-property* that it embodies. Moreover, in making the switch, he demonstrates that he can hold this hidden property steady across objects and across their differing positions in space. In short, the switch is a move in the direction of *noncontextual classification,* where a property maintains its identity, remains invariant, despite a change in context—that is, a change in the position and the function of the object in the tune. As Piaget succinctly puts it, the internal property maintains its constancy "despite the route traveled." These capacities to classify events with respect to their shared properties and to hold these properties invariant despite change in context are clearly reminiscent of those I previously associated with formal rhythm drawings—for example, the drawing I labeled M.2 in the typology. Indeed, it is just these aspects of Jeff's move in making his switched bell-path that express in nascent form the characteristics that I will later associate with a formal representation of a tune.

But at the same time, by insisting on keeping both the white and brown C-bells present in his bell-path, Jeff also gives meaning to the two bells as constituents of the competing organized setting—that is, the *functional* tune universe. Here each of the bells is unique, since it marks a unique *place* and a unique *structural function* within the separate figures of which it is a member—one an "ender," the other a "beginner." And these characteristics of Jeff's move are, in turn, reminiscent of those I associated with figural rhythm drawings—for instance, F.2 in the typology.

We see, then, in Jeff's actions and the resulting switched bell-path the beginning transformations toward a single and more complex mental setting—one that can encompass features and relations that before could only be given meaning as constituents in separate and competing organized settings. Moreover, the switched bell-path is particularly significant because it appears to include features and relations that I previously associated respectively with figural and formal mental representations of rhythms—representations that, like Jeff's organized settings, remained largely separate and distinct in the children's drawings. Met had a glimmering of the significance of Jeff's move when he observed that the switched bell-path "may be a kind of transition on-the-way-to coordinating multiple representations."

That the switched bell path does, indeed, suggest the possibility for multiple representations becomes quite clear if we consider what would

Figure 8–7

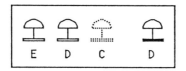

removed the brown C-bell altogether

have happened if Jeff had simply followed my suggestion and removed the brown C-bell altogether (Figure 8–7). How does this bell-path differ from Jeff's final construction—what is gained and what is lost? First of all, as a reference entity it would no longer embody or implicitly refer to the *figural* structure of the tune since the two basic building blocks, HO and HA, have lost their realization, their concrete embodiment in table-space. Moreover, the unique function of bell-pitches within figures is obscured—the single white C-bell "absorbs" into itself the differences in structural function previously "held" by the presence of both the white and brown C-bells in Jeff's final bell-path construction. And the action-path in playing the tune on this bell-path confounds rather than reveals the structure of the tune.

To make this point more vivid, imagine playing the tune on this contrived bell-path just up to the beginning of HA: arriving at the white C-bell and the end of the first figure, instead of *going on* to the beginning of the next figure, HA, you would have to *stand still in one place*. Further, the critical boundary between figures would have no spatial dimension. You would move "forward" in time and in the tune but never change your place in space; even though you would be "in" the next figure, you would never cross over a spatial boundary—everything would be just as it was. It reminds me again of Alice, this time as she runs through the woods with the Red Queen:

> The most curious part of the thing was, that the trees and the other things around them never changed their places at all: however fast they went, they never seemed to pass anything. "I wonder if all the things move along with us" thought poor puzzled Alice. And the Queen seemed to guess her thoughts, for she cried "Faster! Don't try to talk."
>
> . . . just as Alice was getting quite exhausted, they stopped, and she found herself sitting on the ground, breathless and giddy.
>
> The Queen propped her up against a tree, and said kindly, "You may rest a little now."

Alice looked around her in great surprise. "Why, I do believe we've been under this tree the whole time! Everything's just as it was!" (Carroll 1960, pp. 209–210)

In short, this bell-path reflects only a single organized setting. In it, pitch-identity, instantiated by the singular white C-bell, subsumes the marking of figural boundaries and unique figural functions. This contrived bell-path derives from a mental universe that cannot include or give meaning to figural, situational features of a tune. And yet, as Met points out, such a reference entity in its consolidation of bell-pitches is more "efficient." Moreover, if we take the capacities that are involved in holding properties invariant over change in situation or context—capacities usually associated with formal mental representations—as a mark of "progress," then this proposed bell-path and the organized mental setting that produces it could be seen as being at a higher level rather than a more impoverished one.

But as I have argued all along, while figural and formal representations of rhythms or melodies may occur at differing times in the course of development, they both capture legitimate and important aspects of musical structure. And as I have also argued, the mark of the sophisticated musician is the capacity to shift focus, to select for attention multiple kinds of features and relations and to coordinate them in various ways depending on "when and what for." As we go on to the next phase of Jeff's work with the bells, we will see instances of just that process being acted out—but not without the disequilibrium that so often accompanies significant learning.

PART III

The Story of Jeff's Development

CHAPTER 9

Jeff's Figural Construction and Notation for "Twinkle"

IN ALL the subsequent sessions that I will discuss, Jeff is concerned with only one tune, "Twinkle Twinkle Little Star." In the course of his work—constructing and reconstructing the tune with the bells and inventing instructions for playing the tune on his changing bell-paths—we will see Jeff passing through three stages which I will call, not surprisingly, figural, transitional, and formal. However, in the course of the discussion, I will need to offer some caveats concerning the notion of "passing through" and also reconsider my terms "figural" and "formal."

To help readers grasp the multiple dimensions of the tune itself, and to appreciate the kind of learning that is involved in Jeff's development, I will analyze the structure of Twinkle in some detail. In doing so, I will also step back from time to time to provide some basic background for readers with no formal music training. These "didactic digressions" will make explicit the shared musical intuitions that are at work as Jeff (along with the rest of us) makes sense of the familiar music of our culture. Readers can participate in the analysis by singing along as I describe the fine-grained relations within the tune.*

---

* For readers with some knowledge of common musical terminology, particularly an understanding of what is called "tonality" and its generative relations, the analysis will provide an opportunity to rethink the meanings of these common terms—especially what they have learned, even what they have come to take for granted, in using them.

177

A DIDACTIC DIGRESSION

Figure 9–1 shows a diagrammatic sketch of the first part or A section of Twinkle, which readers may refer to as they follow the analysis. I will discuss only the A section because this is as far as Jeff gets in the tune. The diagram shows the direction of pitch-motion (up and down) and also movement around two fundamental pitches—C and G. Blacks in the diagram indicate shorter durations, whites indicate longer durations. A white note with a ⅄ indicates a boundary that is incomplete, while a white with a ⊥ indicates a boundary that is complete, closed-out.

The diagram makes it clear that the A section of Twinkle includes two distinctly different figures, a.1 ("Twinkle twinkle little star") and a.2 ("How I wonder what you are"). These two figures are not only different but also strongly *complementary* to each other. The complementarity is expressed first by the differences in *pitch-motion* within each figure: singing the first figure (a.1), notice that you go *up* in a leap, while in singing the second figure (a.2), you go *down* and you do so *stepwise,* the stepwise motion filling in the pitch gap left by the leap in a.1. Second, and most important, complementarity is created by differences in "boundary conditions," specifically differences in *structural functions* at the boundaries. Singing a.1 again, you will hear and feel its boundary (on the word "star") as *incomplete,* needing resolution; the second boundary (on the word "are") you will hear as *complete,* thus resolving the incompleteness and the tension set up at the first boundary.

These hearings are universally shared by those who have grown up listening to the common music of our culture. It is, therefore, important to ask: What are the pitch relations that generate the differences in *struc-*

Figure 9–1

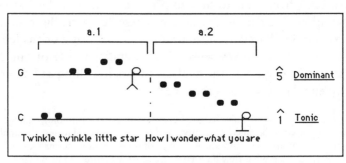

the first part (A) of Twinkle

tural function that we hear at these boundaries? Answers to this question also give us important insight into the internalized "rules" that guide us as we *make* the sense that we seem simply to find in singing or listening.

Notice that in the diagram the two lines labeled C and G, respectively, delimit the functional "pitch-space" of the tune. Using these lines as place markers within the pitch-space of the tune, you can see that the tune begins on C and that the next *new* pitch is G. Twinkle could begin on any pitch, but given the particular pitch collection provided by the bells, the first bell-pitch in the tune will be a C-bell and the next bell-pitch will be a G-bell. Thus, a.1 leaps up from C to G. It is the *reciprocal interaction* between the two pitches, C and G, that gives meaning to both. That is, we apprehend and attribute functional meaning to both pitches only insofar as *each one determines the function of the other*. And it is the particular reciprocal relations between these two pitches that create the "setting" for the rest of the tune. Indeed, it is because Jeff, like all of us, has learned and internalized the "rules" that generate these reciprocities that we can perceptually assign particular and different functional meanings to the pitch-events that follow. For example, with this setting established, we hear a.1 move away from stability or rest toward tension at its boundary. In turn, we hear a.2 as moving back down stepwise, filling in the gap left by the leap in a.1 to arrive at stability and the release of tension generated at the end of a.1.

The following analogy may help in understanding the notion of "reciprocal interaction" as necessary to generating meaning. Consider a dot all by itself on the page:

●

With respect to defining "a space," a setting in which to make meaning, the dot by itself is insufficient. And in this sense the dot, alone, has no meaning. Now I will add another dot:

●

●

We now have a *relationship!* And as a result of the reciprocal relationship between them, we can meaningfully see and talk about, for instance, above and below, inside or outside "their" space, or we can measure the distance between. And given the two dots, we can make a line:

Now we can speak of connectedness in contrast to disconnectedness, or measure the slope of the line and perhaps think about its stability or instability. But none of these relations exists with only one dot; each of them depends on the reciprocity between the two dots—each one determines the meaning and the function of the other within the space that they themselves define.

Similarly, the C-bell (or any bell) played all by itself has only a *potential* for meaning, but, like a dot, no inherent meaning. But when we add another pitch, as in arriving at the G-bell in playing Twinkle, then we have a relationship. We can hear and speak of above and below, inside or outside the "pitch-space" they enclose, and we can *measure* the pitch-distance between them. Moreover, in singing the tune, we can hear the move from one pitch to the other as a "leap," and we can (as in a.2) fill in the pitch-space left by that leap. And most important, in listening to the C-bell followed by the G-bell, our internalized "coherence-making rules" strongly suggest that, in their reciprocity, the G-bell sounds less "stable"—that is, if we follow it with another C, that pitch will now sound "stable," at rest.

(The reader can demonstrate the generality of this reciprocity by making a little experiment: sing any pitch, then sing the pitch that goes with the second "twinkle" (that is, an interval of a fifth) and stop. You most likely have a feeling of "cliff-hanging." Now sing the first pitch again, and notice that the instability has resolved. This demonstrates that it is not the specific pitches C and G that create this effect, but any two pitches with the same relationship, the same pitch-distance between them.)

Notice that the C and G lines in the diagram are also labeled as scale-degrees 1 and 5. (The ˆ above a number indicates that it is a scale-degree.) These labels reflect the relative position of the two pitches when the whole set of bells is ordered from low to high.* Thus, the ordered series and their labels serve as a kind of grid with which we can measure the

---

*This labeling is implicitly "formal," and this will become important in the observations of Jeff's work. It is derived as follows: by convention we label the pitch that is heard as most stable "1," or what is called the "tonic." Given the collection of pitches provided by the bells, C is heard as the most stable, so we label it as "1." If we now order this collection (C D E F G . . .) from low to high, starting with C as "1," we construct the C major scale. And counting up along this scale, giving consecutive number-names to each pitch, G comes out as scale-degree "5":

C D E F G A B C
1 2 3 4 5 6 7 8

Figure 9–2

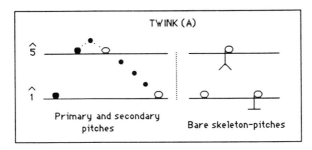

pitch-distance or "interval" between any two pitches. The interval between C and G, or scale-degrees 1 and 5, is a "fifth." Looking at Figure 9–1, we can see that scale-degrees 1 and 5 function as "points of orientation" around and between which the other secondary pitches move. As such, C and G on scale-degrees 1 and 5 form the underlying *pitch-skeleton* of Twinkle. The left-hand side of Figure 9–2 shows the pitch-skeleton of Twinkle, with the secondary pitches drawn smaller; the right-hand side shows just the bare-bone skeleton pitches and also indicates the differences in structural function generated by this reciprocity—instability (5) and stability (1).

Singing Twinkle once more, you will hear that the secondary pitches either *embellish* or *fill in* the moves between the fundamental skeleton pitches. For example, within a.1 the initial move to 5 is embellished or *prolonged* by the stepwise move up away from it and back down again (on the words "lit-tle star"). In Figure 9–2 I have shown this prolongation by dots; the effect is much like that of a rubber band held still, stretched, and snapped back again. Within a.2, the secondary pitches are heard as filling in the gap between the dangling 5 (G) at the end of a.1 and the return to the 1 (C) at the end of a.2 (that is, as you sing the words "How I won-der what you," with "are" arriving again at 1).

Finally, notice that the two figures within A are "balanced" in two senses. First, they are equal in their total duration—each has the same number of beats; second, they are complementary in that the first (a.1) generates an essential tension while the second (a.2) resolves this tension. This latter complementary relationship between two figures is conventionally called an "antecedent-consequent relationship."

All of these features and relations of Twinkle conspire together to generate a fully defined and complete mini-structure. Indeed, this same structure is found again and again in common folk tunes and also, in

Figure 9–3

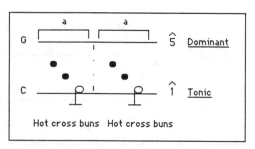

repetition of a single motive precludes complementarity

elaborated form, in much more complex compositions. These features and relations successfully generate a fully defined and complete mini-structure precisely because they include among them a critical set of what I have called "structural simples." Some of the pitch-relations that characterize these structural simples can be clearly recognized by comparing the structures within the A section of Twinkle, where they are *strongly present*, with the structures within the A section of HOT, where these critical relations are noticeably *impoverished*. Looking at the diagram of HOT in Figure 9–3, you will notice, in particular, that repetition of the single motive *a* in HOT precludes the complementarity that is such a critical feature in the relations between the two inner figures of Twinkle. The repetition also precludes the essential tension between boundaries. That is, because of the repetition, pitch-motion in HOT *moves only between scale-degrees 1 and 3,* thus failing to generate the important reciprocal relation between scale degrees 1 and 5. And it is precisely because of the absence of this latter relation—the very one that is most critical in generating the "organized setting" with which we assign functional meaning to pitch-events in the unfolding of a tune—that HOT also fails to define fully the "complete mini-structure" that we hear in Twinkle.

This rather detailed analysis of Twinkle should help the reader to understand some of the differences between Jeff's work with HOT and his subsequent work with Twinkle. In particular, it will help in an understanding of the series of transformations that Jeff's construction strategies undergo, along with the series of transformations in his instructions for playing Twinkle on the resulting bell-constructions. The analysis should also help readers to appreciate Jeff's transitions and confusions as he learns to participate in what I will now call "figural/formal transactions."

JEFF'S FIRST CONSTRUCTION OF TWINKLE

When Jeff built his switched bell-path at the very end of his session with HOT and the bells, we saw in it a fragile moment of transition. In retrospect we will see that moment as foreshadowing more extended and also more poignant periods of transition that occur only much later in Jeff's work. In this first session with Twinkle we see Jeff working in his most purely figural way.

Jeff's first session with Twinkle occurred several days after he had built HOT with the bells. In preparation I arranged a mixed array of bells on the table (Figure 9–4). Notice that for this task I have included 11 bells in all: the white bells include all the pitches of the C major scale, and the brown bells include matching C, E, and G-bells.

After Jeff had played through the bells casually for a few moments, I proposed that he try building Twinkle with the bells. Looking quite sure of himself, Jeff immediately went to work. His strategy was much the same as it had been in building HOT:

1. Add a new bell to the cumulating bell-path in *order of occurrence* in the tune—next-next-next.
2. Add a found bell for next-in-tune to the *right* of the just previous bell in the cumulating bell-path.
3. Create a *context for search* by playing the tune-so-far, then test in the search-space for a bell-pitch that matches the next tune-event.

Figure 9–4

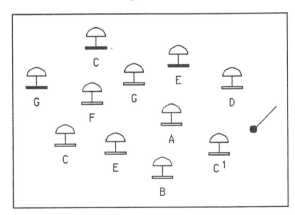

a mixed array of bells on the table

4. There must be a *new bell* for each pitch-event in the tune even if a bell with the same pitch-property is already present in the bell-path.

In short, using what I have called a figural strategy, Jeff invokes a mental setting in which each bell is recognized and given meaning as a particular and unique tune-event. And when he recognizes a bell as the object of his search and adds it to his cumulating bell-path, it marks a particular place as well as a unique structural function within the figure of which it is a member.

Giving his full attention to the task, Jeff quickly builds up a prototypical figural bell-path (Figure 9–5). Comparing Jeff's bell-path with the diagram of the tune, we see two groups of four bells separated by a gap that "acts out" in space the boundary between the two balanced figures of the tune (Figure 9–6).

Jeff's construction strategy appears at first to be much the same for both HOT and Twinkle—he adds bells to his cumulating bell-path in their order of occurrence in the tune, next-next-next. Both paths start out, then, as a chronological narrative account of the tune—its story. But

Figure 9–5

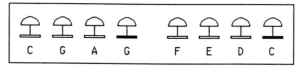

builds a prototypical figural bell-path for Twinkle

Figure 9–6

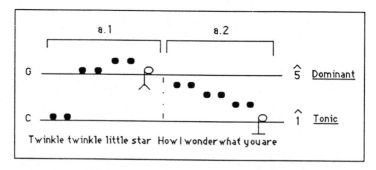

the boundary between the two balanced figures

Figure 9–7

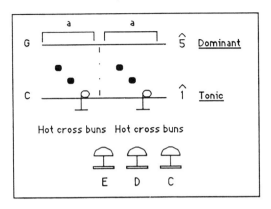

an incomplete story

the paths continue differently. Indeed, if we consider Jeff's Twinkle path to be a prototypical figural one, then his bell-path for HOT must be seen as having certain atypical features. The differences reflect differences in the *structures* of the two tunes. Recall that the A section of HOT includes only a single motive of three events, but that motive is repeated to make six tune-events in all. Comparing Jeff's bell-path for HOT with the diagram of the tune, we see that the bell-path includes only three bells, not six—just enough for one instance of the single figure "Hot cross buns." Jeff's bell-path, in all its "efficiency," tells an incomplete story (Figure 9–7). Interestingly, in representing only one instance of the single figure, Jeff recalls the confusions in his computer session with HOT—is HO one or two?

In contrast, as Jeff continues his bell-path for Twinkle, he tells a complete story. There are just as many bells as there are pitch-events exactly because all of them are *structurally* important. All the pitches and thus all the bells are necessary in generating the essential structural complementarity between the two figures.*

Differences in the bell-paths necessitate differences in action-paths for playing the tune as well. Jeff's action-path for Twinkle is in one-to-one correspondence with his bell-path—both go onward, never turning back, just as the tune itself does (Figure 9–8). But this was not the case

---

* Strictly speaking this is, of course, not entirely true, since there is only one bell for repeated pitch-events such as "twin-kle." However, there is, I believe, a significant difference between immediate repetition of a single pitch, which is a very small-scale prolongation, and repetition of a whole motive as in HOT.

Figure 9–8

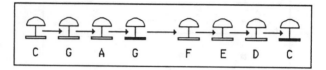

both go onward, never turning back

Figure 9–9

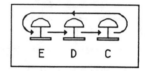

circling back to play the repeated motive again

with HOT; Jeff's action-path for HOT circled back on the bell-path in order to play the repeated motive again (Figure 9–9). And Jeff's circling-back action-path raises the same structural question as does the construction of his bell-path: is HO one or two?

But if we include Jeff's construction of HA, the bell-paths for both HOT and Twinkle share another important aspect—one that perhaps best characterizes both as figural bell-paths. As I put it in our previous conversation: "Even though *we* know that two tune-events share the same pitch-property (like the end of HO and the beginning of HA), for Jeff that same pitch-property will need to be embodied in two different bells. In that way each separate bell stands for two different structural functions." We see this aspect of figural tune-building in a particularly vivid and elegant form in Jeff's bell-path for Twinkle because he chooses to begin his construction using only the white bells, just as he did with HOT. White bells alone suffice for the first three events, each of them repeated—that is, up to "Twinkle twinkle little . . ." (Figure 9–10). But

Figure 9–10

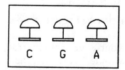

up to "Twinkle twinkle little"

Figure 9–11

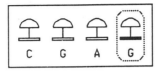

adds a new brown bell for "star"

as Jeff continues he meets a familiar problem, and his quick solution suggests that important learning has been going on. Arriving at the next tune-event (on the word "star"), Jeff searches among the white bells in the search-space but without success. This happens, of course, because it is a G-bell that he needs for the tune-event on the word "star," and he has already used the *white* G-bell for a previous event (on the second "twinkle"). But this time no intervention is necessary. Instead of giving up as he did initially in his struggles with the brown and white C-bells in building HOT, Jeff searches for and finds *a new brown bell* that matches the tune-event on "star" and adds it to his cumulating bell-path (Figure 9–11).

Continuing on, now, into the next figure in the tune (a.2), Jeff returns once more to his favored white bells. He successfully finds white bells for "how I won-der what you" (F, E, and D-bells) and adds them to his cumulating bell-path. But on arriving at the final tune-event (on the word "are"), there is no white C-bell available. Once more turning to the remaining brown bells in the search-space, Jeff finds and adds a *brown* C-bell to his cumulating bell-path and thus completes the tune (Figure 9–12).

I emphasize Jeff's use of the brown bells because it points to an essential feature of figural tune-building: just as in building HOT, Jeff needs two different bells for tune-events that share a common pitch-property but have different structural functions. By introducing the brown bells, Jeff makes it very clear again that the meaning he gives to bells in space

Figure 9–12

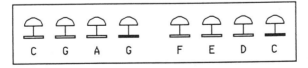

and thus completes the tune

and events in time is determined by their particular *situation* along the route of the tune. Past and future exist only in the present moment; there is no comparing backward or forward in space/time. It is the particular *sequence* of tune-events and the position and function within that sequence that give meaning both to the event and to the bell that instantiates that event. Thus it is their *situational* properties rather than their fixed pitch-properties that define tune-events.

What, then, are the situational properties of an event? They are made up of a *unique confluence* of features. For example, just as the events "represented" by the white and brown C-bells in Jeff's bell-path for HOT were significantly different in their situational properties, the events "represented" by the white and brown G-bells in Jeff's bell-path for Twinkle differ in every respect except for their shared pitch. Looking back at the diagram of Twinkle (Figure 9–1), notice the following:

- The G (brown bell) at the end of figure a.1 is longer in *duration* than the G (white bell) in the middle of figure a.1.
- The initial white G is approached by leap from below, while the subsequent brown G is approached by step from above.
- The first G marks the *arrival* of the "significant other" in its reciprocal relation with the preceding C-bell, while the brown G functions as a *prolongation* of that previous G.
- All these features join together to give the two pitches different *structural functions*—the first G a "middle," or "on-the-way," the second a "boundary-marker," an "ending," albeit an incomplete one.

Similarly, the situational properties of the white and brown *C-bells* in Jeff's Twinkle bell-path are different in every respect except for their shared pitch. Most important, of course, the white C-bell is "the first one," a beginning, while the brown C-bell is "the last one," an ending.

It is particularly interesting that because of Jeff's penchant for using up the white bells first, the two brown bells in the bell-path (G and C) clearly mark the *boundaries* of the two complementary figures. Moreover, these two bells necessarily show the only two pitches that are *repeated* in the tune. And it is just these two pitches, C and G, that form the central pitches of the tune—the points of orientation around which the other pitches move (Figure 9–13).

Finally, in leaving a gap in space between the two figures (perhaps, as with HOT, depicting a longer duration; perhaps the structural boundary) Jeff reaffirms the boundary that marks off the two figures within the

Figure 9–13

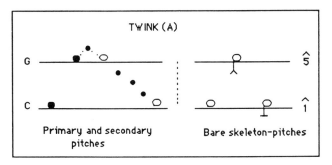

C and G, the points of orientation

A section of the tune. In all these ways, Jeff's bell-path becomes a beautiful enacted description; it tells the story of the figural/functional structure of Twinkle. As suggested in my earlier analysis, Twinkle is a kind of *Ur*-tune, a prototypical tune, realizing in bare form the relations I have called structural simples—relations that we find elaborated over and over again in complex compositions. Just so, Jeff's particularly elegant figural bell-path for Twinkle mirrors in *its* structure those fundamental relations that characterize Twinkle itself as a prototypical Simple.

JEFF'S FIRST NOTATIONS FOR TWINKLE

Jeff's instructions for playing Twinkle on his bell-path present few of the ambiguities that Met and Mot found so puzzling in his instructions for playing HOT. And once again we can attribute these differences to the differences in the structure of the tunes themselves. In particular, the two onward-moving and complementary figures of Twinkle, unlike the repeated figures in HOT, result in a bell-path and an action-path on it that are unidirectional. The bells are like stepping-stones along the unidirectional action-path; they mark the route through the tune much as claps mark the route through a rhythmic figure. I call Jeff's strategy of construction a "felt path" strategy by analogy with the felt path of a clapped rhythm. The process of constructing the tune and then playing it is also reminiscent of the familiar experience of marking the chronological occurrence of chosen landmarks as one walks, through time, along a path from here to there—next-next-next. When one traverses the path again, these temporally experienced landmarks become a description of the path—the way one remembers it. Kevin Lynch puts it this way:

[Landmarks] are frequently used clues of identity and even structure, and seem to be increasingly relied upon as a journey becomes more and more familiar ... A sequential series of landmarks, *in which one detail calls up anticipation of the next and key details trigger specific moves of the observer,* appeared to be a standard way in which these people traveled through the city. In such sequences, there were trigger cues whenever turning decisions must be made and reassuring cues that confirmed the observer in decisions gone by ... The sequence facilitates recognition and memorization. Familiar observers can store up a vast quantity of point images in familiar sequences, *although recognition may break down when the sequence is reversed or scrambled.* (Lynch 1960, p. 83; emphasis added)

Like the traveler through the city, Jeff's felt-path construction gives meaning to the bells as a "sequential series of landmarks, in which one detail calls up anticipation of the next." As each bell is added to his cumulating bell-path, it serves as a landmark marking a place on his repeated trips through the tune. But it is the particular structure of Twinkle that makes the analogy apt. Just as a walk through the city is remembered and described as a "sequential series of landmarks" guided by the direct correspondence between moves along the path and the sequential ordering of landmarks, so the structure of Twinkle leads Jeff to construct in his bell-path an *enacted* description such that there is a direct correspondence between bell-path, action-path, and the tune-path itself. In short, all of Jeff's paths are "in sync."

As we have seen, this is not the case with HOT. Instead of a direct correspondence between action-path and bell-path, the action-path moves independently from the bell-path—going forward on the bell-path, turning back, going forward again only to turn back once more. This is perhaps a "wander" through a city, but hardly a path that the traveler would want to take every day in getting from home to work (Figure 9–14).

Figure 9–14

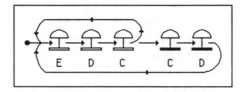

perhaps a wander through the city

Figure 9–15

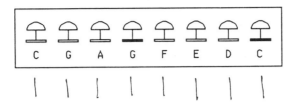

just as many lines as there are bells

Jeff's paper-and-pencil descriptions, in turn, reflect the differences in his constructions. His "notation" for Twinkle is in direct correspondence with his *enacted* description—the arrangement of bells on the table. Using the same convention as he did for HOT, Jeff makes "stick-figure" lines in paper-space that are copies of the bells in table-space. Taking the bells, so to speak, one-for-one from table-space, Jeff puts them into paper-space. Thus, unlike the notation for HOT, there are just as many lines as there are bells (Figure 9–15).* Jeff left no doubt about the meaning of the lines when I asked him to "put in some numbers so people could tell how to go on the bells." Saying, "You just go straight ahead," he did the following:

| | | | | | | | |
| 1 | 2 | 3 | 4 | 5 | 6 | 7 | 8 |

Finally, I asked Jeff if he could show "how many times you hit each bell." He responded by adding another row of numbers above the lines:

2	2	2	1	2	2	2	1
1	2	3	4	5	6	7	8

As he did for HOT, Jeff uses not only different numbers but different *kinds* of numbers to indicate these different dimensions of the instructions and the tune. Counting *on* the bells as on a number line, the lower numbers *name* the bells according to their *position* in the sequence of the tune—these are ordinal numbers. But for the upper numbers, which indicate *hits* on each bell, Jeff "counts *up*" showing the *aggregate* of hits—

---

*But notice that in making his notation, Jeff does not leave a gap between the two figures.

these are cardinal numbers. Notice, too, that Jeff can name the bells only *after* they are already embedded in the tune sequence. That is, the names (numbers) are entirely dependent on the particular sequential ordering of the bells in *this* tune. The numbers tell us nothing about the relation of one bell-pitch to another with respect, for instance, to the pitch-interval between them. The bell-path for Twinkle, like that for HOT, is a "one-purpose instrument," specially made for playing Twinkle; the number-names Jeff gives to the bells work only for the single-purpose instrument he has built.

Not surprisingly, many of the provocative issues raised by Met and Mot in our previous conversation about HOT come up again in looking at Jeff's work on Twinkle. It seems only fair, then, to give them a chance to consider these issues once more in the light of this latest session.

MET AND MOT THINK ABOUT JEFF'S FIRST
SESSION WITH TWINKLE

JEANNE: Now that you've read about Jeff's first session with Twinkle, what do you think?

MOT: The whole task seemed to be much easier for Jeff than when he was working with HOT.

MET: At least it's much easier to make sense of what Jeff is doing. Everything seems to fit neatly together.

MOT: Yes, and before I read your analysis, Jeanne, I would have thought that HOT was a simpler tune. But I guess I was thinking of "simple" in a different way—more like "fewer notes" or "not much happens." But from what you've shown us about the structure of the two tunes, it seems that "simple" depends more on the way a tune conforms to our intuitions about "well-built."

MET: I'd say that HOT is more "simpleminded" than "simple," and paradoxically, simplemindedness seems to make things harder, not easier.

JEANNE: Good point, Met. But I'm particularly interested in your reactions to Jeff's instructions. You raised a lot of provocative issues in our last conversation, many of which we never really resolved. Did Jeff's work with Twinkle help you to understand them better?

MOT: I need to get Jeff's instructions for HOT out on the table again so we can compare. Were they like this?

$$\text{\Large \textbackslash{}|\textbackslash{} \quad |\textbackslash{}| \quad |\textbackslash{} \quad |\textbackslash{}|}$$

$$\text{\large | 2 3 \quad | 2 3 \quad | 2 \quad | 2 3}$$

MET: Yes, except remember at the end Jeanne asked Jeff if he could show the four faster hits in HA.

MOT: Right. And he crossed off the numbers 1 2 and changed them to 4 4:

$$\begin{array}{cccc} | \;| \;| & | \;| \;| & | \;| & | \;| \;| \\ 1 \; 2 \; 3 & 1 \; 2 \; 3 & \cancel{1} \; \cancel{2} & 1 \; 2 \; 3 \\ & & 4 \; 4 & \end{array}$$

MET: He does something like that in his instructions for Twinkle, too. Except there he keeps both dimensions neatly separate—numbers for bells and how you go on them in one row and numbers for hits in another; two complete notations for each.

MOT: I would guess that the session with HOT helped Jeff with that. But I'm curious about something else. As you said, Jeanne, Jeff's bell-path is a really elegant description of the tune—the two brown bells marking the boundaries and also, as in HOT, a gap, a space, between the two figures. So my question is, how come when he puts in the first set of numbers for the bells, he numbers up *straight through* that structural gap instead of starting over again with 1 in the second figure as he did with HOT?

MET: I have a hunch about that: in working with HOT, the all-pervasive HO figure becomes almost like a real object for Jeff; a single, bounded chunk. That isn't so for the first figure in Twinkle.

MOT: Why is that?

MET: Think about it. Jeff uses the same three bells to play both HO's—in fact, all three HO's. Now, for one thing, Jeff's *motion* in doing that—his arm movements in going back and playing over those three bells again—gives the three bells real definition as a *group;* it puts boundaries around them.

MOT: That seems right. And besides, the pitches and durations make HO really end each time; that helps to make a "thing" of it, too.

MET: And then there was the computer session. After all, Jeanne gave Jeff *names* for the two blocks; he heard the blocks and he used them as the material, the entities, for building up the tune.

JEANNE: So in that session we could say that the figures, HO and HA, were the units of description *and* the units of perception *and* the units of construction—all three.

MOT: Well, eventually they were. But even Jeff's confusions in getting all that straight probably helped to make the two figures stick in his head.

MET: OK. So when he comes to Twinkle, all that is different. The figures have never been named; in fact Jeff worked only at the note level, building up the tune one event at a time—next-next-next, as Jeanne keeps reminding us.

MOT: But still, he did leave a space, so he was marking the two figures.

MET: Yes, but he didn't when he drew the lines. The boundary in Twinkle that Jeff marks by leaving a space in the bell-path is very different from the analogous boundary in HOT. The ending of the first figure in Twinkle really isn't an ending—it's only locally complete.

MOT: What do you mean by that?

MET: It's obvious. Taking Twinkle as a whole, the first figure *needs* the second figure to complete it.

MOT: I get it—that's the complementarity Jeanne talked so much about. We hear the first boundary as a cliff-hanger; the second figure completes what the first figure left unfinished.

MET: So, with all these differences in boundary conditions between the two tunes, it makes sense that Jeff treats them differently. Jeff goes *on* in Twinkle, numbers up right through the boundary, because the tune goes on; it doesn't start up again because it never really stops, and neither does Jeff.

MOT: It's amazing how Jeanne's analysis, which seemed so abstract to me at the time, really helps to account for the moves that Jeff makes absolutely spontaneously.

MET: Something else that interests me is that there isn't any "symbolic space" in Jeff's instructions for Twinkle; all the way through, he uses direct correspondence between bells on the table and lines on paper. But in his instructions for HOT, there are three lines that stand for three bells that aren't there—they exist in an imaginary space meaning later or after. Of course that imaginary space is clearly spawned by the repetitions and the turn-backs in the action-path.

JEANNE: Well, it's not quite true that there isn't any symbolic space in Jeff's instructions for Twinkle.

MET: What do you mean?

JEANNE: Let me tell you about something I left out of my story. To make sure I understood Jeff's instructions, I asked him to "play" Twinkle on the paper—on the lines. Surprisingly, he got quite mixed up.

MOT: In what way?

JEANNE: Well, as he moved along on the lines, he seemed to lose his place. For instance, sometimes he would go right on to the next line instead of staying put for the *two* hits on one bell that made the two repeated pitches—as on "twin-kle" or "how I." As a result, of course, he came out wrong—he got to the end of the lines and there was still more to go in the tune.

MET: What's that got to do with symbolic space?

JEANNE: You see, even though there's a one-to-one correspondence between lines and bells, *the lines are not the bells.* The bells "speak back" because, after all, they have the pertinent properties; the lines don't. The critical thing is that the lines *don't actually have the properties they represent.* And that's exactly what is meant by a "symbol." In "playing" Twinkle on the lines, Jeff has to get clearly into his mind, and keep it there, just what the line, as a symbol, is meant to stand for. So you could say that a symbol—a squiggle on paper—both reveals and conceals. The *invention* of a symbol, like Jeff's lines for the bells, is *revealing* in that it shows us at least some of what Jeff knows already. But once on paper, the symbol, in all its silent anonymity, can easily *conceal* its meaning—the *particular* aspects, relations, features of an object that the mark is meant to stand for.

MET: But there's another sense in which a symbol reveals and conceals. Learning what a symbol stands for can *reveal* an aspect of the object that you hadn't noticed before—like when Jeff's numbers made me pull apart the pitch and time of HOT. But when the meaning of a symbol becomes absorbed into your system as something you take for granted—a convention that the whole culture takes for granted—*it* is concealed, you don't see it anymore; it's transparent, you look right through it to its assumed meaning. The symbol is invisibly attached to its referent.

JEANNE: Well put, Met.

MOT: But that must take time and practice—even when the squiggle is your own invention. In fact, Jeff was having trouble hanging on to his own invented symbols. For instance, he used exactly the same lines, which certainly are anonymous, for the rhythm of HOT in the computer session and later for the bells. Remember how that confused us? Maybe he got confused, too—sort of slipped from one to the other.

MET: Good idea, Mot. That could explain why Jeff got ahead of himself in "playing" Twinkle on the lines. Think how confusing it is: the bell-pitches stand still, and you have to move *on* them. But when there are repeated pitches—like on "twin-kle" or "how I"—*you* have to "stand still" on the same bell while the hits (and the tune for that matter) keep moving forward in time. Now Jeff says, as I remember, that in playing the tune you just go "straight ahead," and Jeff's lines do just that—straight ahead, left to right. But in conventional symbolic space, that means *time* moving on. So in "playing" on the lines with no feedback from them, it's tempting just to follow along the path of lines as if each next line were the next tune-event. If you're right, Mot, that Jeff is slipping between the lines as bells and the lines as meaning hits that keep on going, then the row of lines, which is very seductive, could be pulling him along when he should be "standing still." After all, you can't tell what the lines mean by just looking at them. Try it yourself—play Twinkle on Jeff's notation.

MOT: (tries playing Twinkle on the lines) I see what you mean; with the tune in your head, it's tempting to just follow along. You have to keep reminding yourself to stay put when the same pitch repeats.

JEANNE: Yes, indeed. And a major part of Jeff's work is going to be learning to hold those two dimensions—pitch and time—steady, and also to coordinate them.

MET: And speaking of symbols, another thing that still bothers me is the business about names; a real name, as I said before, should "travel" with the thing it names. For instance, the number-names in Twinkle, as in HOT, will only work for those exact bells in that exact order. The same numbers name completely different pitches in each of Jeff's bell-paths—each bell-path is a one-purpose instrument.

MOT: Yes, and when you raised that issue before, Jeanne raised the question of how you could make a *general-purpose* notation that would work for any melody. How could you do that?

MET: I think you would have to name *properties* of the bells—the pitches—instead of the bells. But to do that you would have to invent some kind of scheme, some kind of fixed ordering of pitch-properties, that would stay put so the names of the pitches would stay put, too.

Figure 9–16

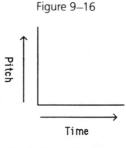

a kind of coordinate-space

MOT: Didn't Jeanne do something like that in her analysis? I mean, the pitch she labeled "1" was always the same whenever and wherever it happened in the tune. But in Jeff's numbering for Twinkle, the 1-bell and the 8-bell both play the same pitch.

MET: True. And then there's the problem of time and the *position* of pitch-events in the flow of the tune. Jeff's numbers show the position of the *bells* in the flow of the tune, not the pitches. Anyhow, the numbers are attached to bells only after they are already set up to play the tune. The question is, how can you invent a symbol-system so that you have fixed pitch-names and also show their temporal position in the tune? I think what Jeff needs is a kind of coordinate-space. Something like this (see Figure 9–16).

JEANNE: Let's stop right there and see what happens in Jeff's next session.

CHAPTER 10

Jeff in Transition:
Constructive Disequilibrium

OVER THE next several weeks as Jeff continued to work with the bells, I was interested in testing the stability of his strategies for constructing and making instructions for Twinkle, and also the reliability of my understanding of these strategies. I particularly wanted to test my hunch about Jeff's two separate and distinct organized settings—the figural one, in which he focuses on position and function within the tune, and the other setting in which he focuses on pitch-matching alone. Up to this point, these organized settings seem to have remained stable but still neatly isolated from each other. If I was correct in this hunch, then by devising ways to bring the two settings into confrontation, I could expect to see Jeff facing confusion and with it some significant disruption in the strategies that had previously led to success.

Thus, in making new interventions, I directed them toward the following questions: What kinds of situations would cause Jeff to confront the potential for conflict inherent in these two organized mental settings? What would count as evidence that such conflict was actually occurring, and what means would Jeff find for resolving conflict? Finally, and most important, what would be the nature of the learning, the cognitive restructuring, as Jeff engaged these potential conflicts?

My first probe was a repetition of something I had tried earlier during the session with HOT. One day, after Jeff had built Twinkle in his usual figural way, I asked him if he could "find bells that matched." Focusing

Figure 10–1

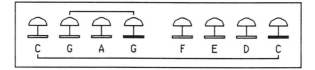

surprised to find that there were matches

Figure 10–2

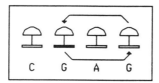

Jeff switched the white and brown G-bells

on this as a separate task, and invoking his focus on pitch-matching, Jeff had no difficulty finding and showing me the matching G-bells and the matching C-bells, although he was visibly surprised to discover that there were matches in the tune (Figure 10–1). With the matches identified, I suggested, as I had before, that since two of the bells (the two G-bells) were "the same," he could play the tune using just one of them. And as before, Jeff's earlier invention allowed him to have the best of both worlds: picking up the two bells, one in each hand, Jeff switched the matching white and brown G-bells (Figure 10–2). The two organized settings within which Jeff could give meaning to the bells were once again *simultaneously* present. But like the switched bell-path in HOT, this switched bell-path held immanent in it important implications for con-flict in Jeff's current ways of representing the tune to himself.

Some days later I tried another experiment, which turned out to be a critical one: I removed all the matching brown bells from the search-space, leaving Jeff with only *one bell for each pitch-type* (Figure 10–3). I then asked Jeff to try to build Twinkle with *just the white bells*. Jeff ob-viously had no trouble with the beginning of the tune; he found the first three bells—C, G, A—and placed them in order, left to right, in his work-space as he had always done before. But upon arriving at the boundary of the first figure, Jeff faced the critical problem: he had always found and used a matching brown G-bell for this boundary event, but with no matching brown bells available, what would he do? As usual,

Figure 10–3

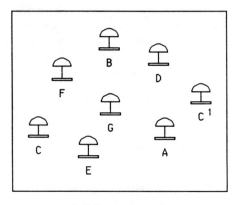

one bell for each pitch-type

Figure 10–4

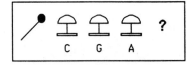

"I need another bell"

Jeff went into the search-space; he tested all the remaining bells with no success, and then stopped. Troubled, he put the dinger down, looked up, and said, "I need another bell" (Figure 10–4). As in so many similar situations, Jeff was not about to give up his stable and robust strategies. Remaining true to what he believed in, he preferred simply to stop.

A few days later I tried the same experiment again, and this time Jeff accepted the challenge—perhaps because he was more comfortable with the task and thus more willing to risk trying something new. Arriving at the critical fourth tune-event, Jeff as usual started from the beginning of his cumulating bell-path (playing as far as "Twin-kle twin-kle lit-tle") to set the context for search. But then, instead of going into the search-space, he hesitated for a moment and *turned back into his already built bell-path* to search within it for a bell that would work for next-in-tune. Testing the C-bell, he rejected it (Figure 10–5). Starting once more from the beginning, Jeff tried the G-bell. Recognizing it immediately as the next-in-tune, the target of his search, he smiled and said, "I had it already!" (Figure 10–6). Apparently realizing that it was a "lost cause" to

Figure 10–5

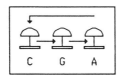

turning back, testing the C-bell, he rejected it

Figure 10–6

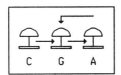

"I had it already!"

look in the search-space for the needed bell, Jeff made his work-space do double duty as a search-space as well. Jeff had tried before to turn his work-space into a search-space in constructing HOT, but there he stopped before successfully finding the object of his search. This time Jeff succeeded, and his discovery that he "had it already" held immanent in it important implications. But it would be hasty to assume that at the moment it occurred, this discovery was really a novel event for Jeff, signaling significant internal restructuring. It is more likely that the "it" he "had already" was simply an unexpectedly *found object*—the object of his search for next-in-tune.

The new implications in Jeff's discovery really only emerged as he *integrated* his "found object" into the continuing construction process and into the tune itself. Going on, Jeff tested his discovery by playing through the tune-so-far. Starting from the beginning, he played each of the three white bells twice, as usual going "straight ahead." Then, upon arriving at the critical fourth tune-event, instead of going straight ahead as he always had done before, he *switched back his action-path* to strike the second bell, the single G-bell, again just once (Figure 10–7). In doing so, he succeeded in playing the whole figure ("Twink-le twink-le lit-tle star") without using his familiar matching brown bell. Instead, he made the second bell in the bell-path do "double duty"—it functioned as both the "middle-one" in the figure (on "twin-kle") and also as the "ender" (the bell-pitch for the word "star").

Figure 10–7

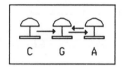

Jeff switched back his action-path

With this move, factors that had been immanent in Jeff's previous discovery ("I had it already") now became manifest. Most important, in making the switch-back in his action-path, Jeff also made the bell-path, action-path, and tune-path come apart. Jeff's bell-path (the sequence of bells in table-space) and the tune-path (the sequence of events unfolding in time) are no longer in spatial correspondence with each other; there is no longer a single, ordered series *unified by a common chronology in space and time.* It is Jeff's action-path that serves as the means for coordinating the spatial incongruence of bell-path and tune-path. That is, while the bells remain fixed in their positions, Jeff's action-path, moving independently of these fixed positions, goes both "forward" (left to right) and "back" (right to left) in space in pursuit of the sequence of tune-events. Most important, the single G-bell in a single position in *space* is now used for two events that occur in different *chronological* positions in the tune and with differing *structural functions.* In short, the G-bell becomes an unvarying element in the midst of change.

Although these moves are critical in Jeff's evolving strategies and also provide clues to potential restructuring of his inner representation of the tune, the new switch-back in his action-path can also be seen as an elaboration of two kinds of moves that he had made previously. The first is his previous switched bell-path: with that move Jeff gave recognition to a match between two bells that played two different tune-events (the two G-bells), but there he moved the bells themselves, thereby maintaining the correspondence between bell-path, tune-path, and action-path. Here the single G-bell is left standing, serving by itself the two functions for which Jeff had previously required two bells.

Second, the new discovery can be seen as a further elaboration of another situation in which Jeff has all along been spontaneously using the same bell for two different tune-events that share a common pitch. These are the moments when he used a single bell for *immediately repeated* pitches, as on "twin-kle" and "lit-tle." But the new situation differs from this earlier instance in important ways: when Jeff used a single bell for

Figure 10–8

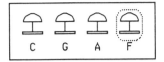

adding the F-bell

immediately repeated pitches, the two events were *adjacent* to each other in the sequence of tune-events. Moreover, the second event was basically a *structural extension* of the first—"more of the same," a kind of mini-structural prolongation. With Jeff's new discovery that a bell can be used again for two different tune-events, Jeff pushes the previous situation considerably further: the new bell-shared events are *not adjacent* to each other in the tune, and, most important, the shared events have *different structural functions* within the same figure—"middle" in contrast to "ending."* Jeff's new switch-back is, then, an elaboration of these previous moves, while at the same time leading to the critical "liberation" of features that were previously undifferentiated—the emergent recognition that the position of an object can remain fixed in space while the route traveled by the tune moves ever onward.

Indeed, evidence that significant changes are occurring in Jeff's organized settings for constructing the tune and implicitly for representing it to himself is seen in the series of confusions and conflicts that now ensue. Jeff's next move, finding the bell for the beginning of the next figure, did not yet present problems. Using his well-practiced search procedure, he started over from the beginning of the tune, hesitated only a moment at the A-bell, made the critical switch-back in his action-path to play the single G-bell again, and went into the search-space for a bell that could be next-in-tune. Finding the F-bell, he added it to his cumulating bell-path (Figure 10–8).

But now the flux of transition shows up. In preparation for his next

---

*Interestingly, on the larger structural level, as pointed out in my analysis of the tune, the second G functions as a prolongation of the first G—much as the second of the repeated pitches functions as a mini-prolongation of the first on the detailed structural level. Indeed, on simply listening to Twinkle, subjects will often say of the whole tune ("Twinkle twinkle little star, How I wonder what you are") that "It goes straight up and straight down." In doing so, they ignore entirely the detailed up-and-down motion within the first phrase, attending only to the structural-skeleton motion up to the dominant (G), with its mini-prolongation, and down again to C. But upon actually building the tune, they do not recognize at all the move to, away from, and back again to the same G.

Figure 10–9

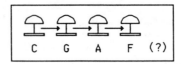

Jeff went straight ahead to the F-bell

Figure 10–10

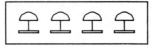

the spatial configuration of unnamed bells

search, Jeff, as usual, played the tune from the beginning. But this time, instead of turning back to play the single G-bell again, Jeff went *straight ahead to the newly added F-bell!* (Figure 10–9). The result was clearly surprising: playing through the bell-path in his usual way, making two hits on each of the bells except for the last at the boundary, he heard C C G G A A F. The "bend" in Jeff's action-path is easily subverted by the familiar spatial configuration of the unnamed bells he now sees on the table (Figure 10–10); the permanence of the G-bell within the forward trajectory of tune-events is fragile indeed.

With a bell now occupying the fourth and *last* position in the line-up, Jeff sees a configuration of bells before him that *looks* just like the old familiar one. This being the case, it is easy for Jeff to see the last bell in the line-up (actually, the F-bell) *as if* it were the bell that had always occupied that position before—the G-bell that had previously marked the boundary of the first figure. And with the new line-up seen as the old familiar configuration, it calls up Jeff's familiar action-path, and he goes straight on as if heading for the first figural boundary of the tune. So, with the new configuration *looking like* the old one, his old action-path takes precedence and the newly acquired switch-back is "wiped out," forgotten (Figure 10–11).

Looking rather bewildered, Jeff hesitated for a moment and then made a move which was not only completely unexpected, but which at the time I found quite incomprehensible. Thinking for a moment, Jeff picked up the second and fourth bells in the current line-up, G and F, and switched them (Figure 10–12). Testing the results of his switch, Jeff once

Figure 10–11

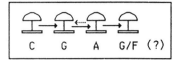

C   G   A   G/F (?)

the switch-back is wiped out

Figure 10–12

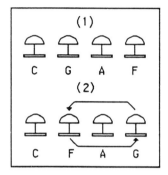

picked up the G and F bells (1) and switched them (2)

Figure 10–13

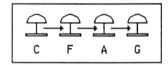

C   F   A   G

an entirely new tune

again played straight ahead, but now along this switched bell-path. As usual he repeated each of the first three bells and played the last bell only once—as if they were the familiar landmarks along his old action-path. But this time his well-trodden bell-path and action-path produced an entirely new tune: C C F F A A G (Figure 10–13). Jeff was now completely befuddled.

How can we account for this seemingly inappropriate move? Recall Jeff's earlier bell-switch when I asked him to find matches within his *figural* bell-path (Figure 10–14): upon discovering matches between the bell that occupied the *last* position in the line-up (the brown G-bell) and the bell that occupied the *second position* in the line-up (the white G-

Figure 10–14

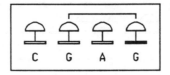

matches in his figural *bell-path*

Figure 10–15

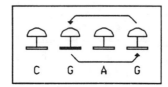

switched them instead of removing one

bell), Jeff *switched them* instead of removing one of the bells as I had proposed (Figure 10–15). Now in the current situation, where Jeff is clearly confused and looking for a fix-up, he tries the same ploy again. That is, he switches the second and last bells in the new bell-path as if the bells in the second and last positions were still matches and thus could substitute for each other. So, instead of making the new switch-back in his *action-path* (Figure 10–16), which would have done the job, Jeff switches *the bells themselves* (Figure 10–17). All these moves—going straight ahead, forgetting the switch-back, and then, in an effort to find a fix-up, trying the old bell-switch—were strong signals that Jeff's stable strategies were in flux. With all the bells looking the same and with the position of a bell in the spatial configuration no longer uniquely defining its position and function in the tune, the identity of bells in this new bell-path could easily slip in and out of focus; it was easy to lose track of which bells were where. Caught between his previously successful figural strategy, his "old way," and the new strategies that were still unstable, Jeff was disoriented; he had quite literally lost his way.

Looking hopeless, Jeff again said, "I need another bell," put down the dinger, and stopped. But this time I didn't give in. Instead, I helped Jeff to rearrange the bells as he had had them before the switch, and pointed out that a "switch-back" in the action-path made it necessary to "skip a bell" in order to go on with the tune (Figure 10–18). That was enough. Practicing the new action-path and its switch-back with each new search,

Figure 10–16

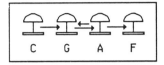

the new switch-back

Figure 10–17

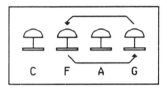

switches the bells themselves

Jeff went on to find the E and D bells, adding them to his cumulating bell-path (Figure 10–19). Now, upon arriving at the last tune-event, it also became clear that Jeff's previous confusions had resulted in some important learning. Going into his search strategy by preparing the context, Jeff started from the beginning, as usual, and played the tune-so-far. But this time, upon arriving at the last bell (the D-bell), instead of going

Figure 10–18

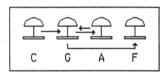

switch back and skip a bell

Figure 10–19

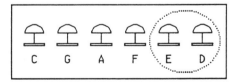

adding the E and D bells

Figure 10–20

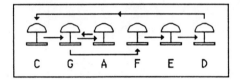

transitional bell-path and action-path

into the search-space, he immediately went back into his work-space in search of the bell for next-in-tune. Testing the first white C-bell, Jeff instantly recognized it as the object of his search. Hesitating for only a moment, he began once more from the beginning, playing the tune in his usual fashion. Then, upon arriving at the end of the current bell-path, the D-bell, he played it twice (for "what you") and immediately switched back his action-path to play the *first* C-bell once as the *last* event in the tune (on "are"). Jeff's completed "transitional bell-path" and his action-path on it are shown in Figure 10–20.

It is interesting to notice that because of the structure of the tune, the sequence of Jeff's *actions* on his transitional bell-path, rather than the bells themselves, reflect the figural grouping structure of the tune. Recall that the repetition of a pitch occurs each time at the boundaries of figures—G at the end of the first figure, C at the end of the second. And notice, too, that these two recurring pitches are also the two skeleton pitches around which the others move. Indeed, it was because of the recurring pitches at the boundaries that Jeff needed to use the brown bells at the end of each figure in his figural bell-path. But with the brown-bell matches removed, these same boundary functions are now marked *by the two new switch-backs.* That is, the two brown bells that spatially marked the end of each phrase in Jeff's figural bell-path are replaced by the two switch-backs in his new action-path. In turn, the empty space that marked the articulation between the two figures in Jeff's figural bell-path is replaced by "skip-a-bell" in his transitional action-path. Thus, in Jeff's earlier figural bell-path, the bells themselves were a static embodiment of the tune structure. With this new transitional bell-path, Jeff's actions, his *sequence of moves,* act out the structure of the tune. In this way, the configuration of bells, an *embodied description* of the tune, has been replaced by an ordered sequence of actions, a *procedural description* of the tune. A diagram of the procedural description of the grouping structure would look like the one shown in Figure 10–21. And instead

Figure 10–21

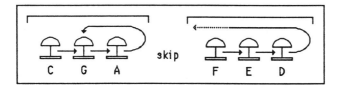

[straight ahead, turn back] skip [straight ahead, turn back]

a procedural description of Twinkle

of the spatial position of Jeff's *bells* serving as unique place-markers for guiding his way, the chronology of his practiced sequence of *actions* must now do so. Interestingly, it is just such well-practiced sequences of actions on the fixed geography of a familiar instrument that best characterize a performer's internal representation of common musical patterns and, indeed, whole compositions that he has learned well.

A great deal has happened in this session, but the implications of these events only fully emerge, as we shall see, when Jeff works on instructions for someone else to play Twinkle on his new bell-path. But it is important to recognize that it was Jeff's experience of the queasy flux of disorientation, along with his willingness to take risks that upset the very means of his earlier success, that made it possible for him to restructure his construction strategies and actions. And these new ways of building and playing Twinkle are clues that Jeff's understanding of the tune, his strategies for representing it to himself, are changing as well. Just as exploring new paths to a familiar place in the city may lead to disorientation but also to the discovery of new vistas, so Jeff's exploration of new paths has led him to discover new cognitive vistas. It remains now to see how he will view the notation task from here.

JEFF'S TRANSITIONAL INSTRUCTIONS

During the course of a single half-hour session, Jeff made four different kinds of instructions for playing Twinkle on his new bell-path. The instructions evolve through a series of rather remarkable modifications. With each modification we see Jeff shifting his focus among various dimensions of the tune and the task, while at the same time trying to resolve the potential for conflict among them. Indeed, the series of notations shows us in microcosm the disequilibrium and flux that so

Figure 10–22

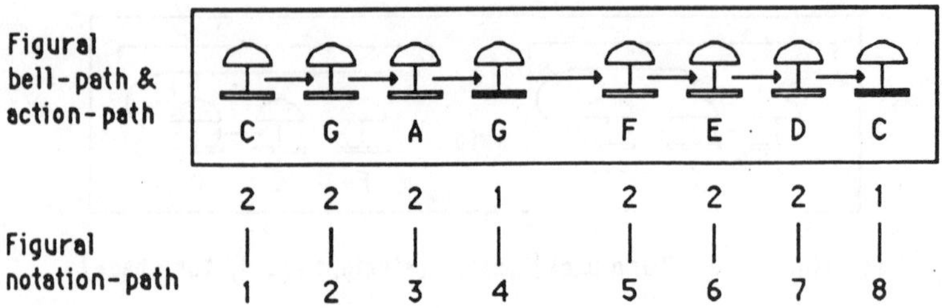

Figural bell-path & action-path								
	C	G	A	G	F	E	D	C

	2	2	2	1	2	2	2	1
Figural notation-path	|	|	|	|	|	|	|	|
	1	2	3	4	5	6	7	8

all paths were basically congruent with one another

characterize the restructuring going on during this transitional phase of Jeff's work.

Notation 1

Recall that in making his initial figural notation for Twinkle, Jeff used a direct correspondence strategy—each line in paper-space stood for a bell in table-space. And while he used numbers to stand for two different aspects of performance (ordinal numbers to show the direction of movement on the bell-path and cardinal numbers to show how many hits), still, Jeff's notation-path, his bell-path, action-path, and tune-path were all basically congruent with one another (Figure 10–22). But with Jeff's new construction, where bell-path and action-path are no longer congruent, what means will he find to make instructions?

Looking at the first of his new transitional notations, it is clear that Jeff's strategy for "making instructions" has changed:

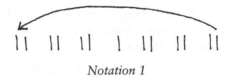

Notation 1

First of all, and quite surprisingly, instead of drawing pictures of the *bells* as he did in his figural notation—taking them one-for-one from table-space to paper-space—Jeff now uses his pencil as if it were the dinger to *imitate on paper* his actions on the bells. Imagining his actions, Jeff moves his pencil along, playing/drawing his *hits* on the bells instead of drawing the bells themselves. And interestingly, in doing so, Jeff groups his actions together in pairs; each pair of lines is separated from the next pair by a wider space, a pattern that mirrors the *repeated hits* on single bells (as on "Twin-kle twin-kle lit-tle"; Figure 10–23). Thus, by spatially

Figure 10–23

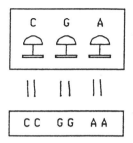

the repeated hits on "Twin-kle twin-kle lit-tle"

Figure 10–24

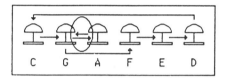

the switch-back to the G-bell at the end of the first phrase

coupling lines in his playing/drawing, Jeff shows which events and actions "go together" (stay put) in both pitch and gesture.

But notice that Jeff has invented an altogether new feature in this notation—the arrow showing the new switch-back in his action-path at the end of the tune. His instructions are becoming the kind of map that Met and Mot had proposed earlier—a map that shows in paper-space the direction of the player's actions on the bells in table-space. But there is an interesting ambiguity here: What does the arrow point to? If the trace left behind from Jeff's playing/drawing shows his *actions* on the bells, then the target of the arrow must be the *first hit*. However, the arrow is presumably intended to direct the player's actions to the first *bell;* surely the player cannot go back in time to the first hit! But as we saw in Jeff's instructions for HOT, lines standing for hits are easy to confuse with lines standing for bells. Indeed, as Jeff interrupts his imagined performance to make the new switch-back arrow, the trace of *actions on* a bell seems to become the bell itself.

And there is more: although the target of the arrow notation is ambiguous, it does clearly show the intended "switch-back" at the end of the tune. But recall that Jeff's transitional bell-path also requires another switch-back—the switch-back to the G-bell that marks the end of the first phrase (Figure 10–24). In Notation 1 we see no sign of this other

Figure 10–25

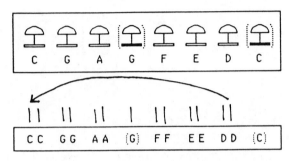

the brown G and C bells are no longer present

switch-back. The omission again provides evidence that Jeff is somewhere between his earlier and very well established figural representation of Twinkle and his not yet stabilized transitional representation of the tune. This becomes clear if we juxtapose Notation 1 with a picture of Jeff's earlier *figural* bell-path, as shown in Figure 10–25. Notice that the brown G and C bells that are no longer present in his transitional bell-path are shown in parentheses. The first three pairs of coupled lines clearly correspond to repeated hits on the C, G, and A bells; these bells are in the same positions in both the transitional and figural bell-paths. But going on in Notation 1, we see a single line for a *single hit*. This single line can only stand for a hit on the G-bell—a bell that was present in Jeff's figural bell-path but is, in fact, *no longer there* in his new transitional bell-path. So, instead of interrupting his playing/drawing actions in the middle of the tune to make an arrow showing a switch-back to the previous G-bell, *Jeff goes straight on.* In the act of drawing/playing, Jeff is again pulled along by the greater intimacy of his earlier straight-ahead action-path. In his imagined performance using pencil on paper, with no back-talk from the bells to remind him, Jeff's previous felt path—his familiar actions on the bells—once again takes precedence.

The fact that Twinkle ends where it began in both space and pitch is apparently a salient and memorable feature of the tune for Jeff—he includes an arrow signaling this in his notation, albeit ambiguous in its target. Why, then, is the switch-back at the end of the first phrase more difficult for him to hold in mind? Recall that Jeff confronted the same issue in the course of *constructing* his transitional bell-path: having discovered that he could switch back his action-path to reuse the single G-bell, Jeff went on to add the F-bell, the beginning of the second figure. But upon playing the tune from the beginning after he had added the F-

Figure 10–26

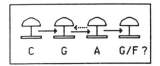

as if the G-bell were still there

bell, Jeff went straight ahead; then, as now, it was as if the bell that had occupied the fourth position in his *figural* bell-path (the brown G-bell) were still there (Figure 10–26).

There is a lot for Jeff to keep in mind. The new ways of constructing and playing the tune are still in flux, difficult to hold still. This is made clear as Jeff slips back to his more familiar, unidirectional action-path in making his notation, just as he had done in constructing his new bell-path. Indeed, it is not surprising that Jeff's figural action-path is hard for him to give up. The straight-ahead action path is particularly memorable exactly because it moved synchronously with all the other paths—going from left to right, they all moved forward together. Moreover, this familiar path had become a *felt* path for Jeff, and as an internalized gesture, it is strongly joined with his internal *mental representation* of the tune as well.

As I suggested earlier, once a *practiced sequence of actions* associated with playing a tune is internalized, becoming what I have called a *felt path*, it becomes a powerful representation of the tune itself. Ordered sequences of actions associated with common experience—the sequence of actions on the keys of a typewriter in making words, the sequence of actions in starting a car, familiar paths from here to there, as well as the practiced performance of a piece on a familiar instrument—these become our most firmly internalized ways of constructing and reconstructing phenomena. Even syntax in spoken language—our seemingly spontaneous capacity to order words correctly into meaningful sentences—may be a kind of felt path. As Karl Lashley puts it, "Syntax is a generalized pattern imposed upon the specific acts as they occur" (Lashley 1951, p. 522). Thus, to upset a felt path is to upset the very means for holding the phenomenon in mind, often upsetting the meaning and structure of the phenomenon itself. Still, the importance, even the existence, of a felt path usually remains tacit, invisible to scrutiny, as long as it functions well. We only become aware of these familiar felt paths when something goes wrong, for instance as in Jeff's case, when the geography of the phenomenon is perturbed. And if we are asked to translate these internalized, felt-path experiences into an external description of them (as I have done with Jeff, and as we do in writing/reading spoken language), the power of their functional existence, as well as their elusiveness to scrutiny, comes starkly to the surface in the difficulties we face in carrying out the task. Thus the difficulties that Jeff confronts in making his instructions are not his alone; as I shall show later, they have much more general significance.

Notation 2

Jeff tested his first set of instructions by following them along while actually playing Twinkle on his transitional bell-path. With the bells now responding, he quickly discovered that he had left out the switch-back at the end of the first phrase. This led to his second notation:

Notation 2

With Notation 2, Jeff modifies his first notation in two ways: he interrupts his playing/drawing to put in a new arrow for the switch-back at the end of the first phrase, and further, all his lines are now *equidistant* from one another rather than spatially grouped together in pairs. Perhaps this occurred because he was drawing/playing very carefully, one line at a time, in anticipation of the moment when he would make the arrow at the end of the first phrase. But in drawing this arrow, Jeff made the ambiguities regarding the referents of lines even more problematic. Once again, as in Notation 1, the arrow points to a line that Jeff initially played/drew as a hit. Moreover, instead of pointing to the second bell, the target of the switch-back in Jeff's action-path, the arrow points to the second *hit*, which, in fact, occurs on the *first* bell. While this could be dismissed as just a matter of Jeff's poor aim, there are more interesting and more persuasive reasons for his confusion here.

Consider that when Jeff draws his arrows, we can assume that he intends them to direct the player's motion to a particular *place in the bell-path*. And to do so, Jeff must shift his focus of attention from *actions* on the bells in his playing/drawing to the bells and to their *position* in his bell-path. But as he shifts his focus of attention from his actions and the trace of lines they leave, the meaning he gives to the lines, the "objects"

Figure 10–27

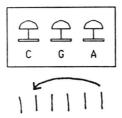

the arrow leads right to the second hit

Figure 10–28

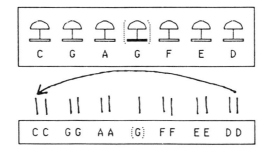

coupled lines help to coordinate actions and bells

to which they *refer,* also shifts! It seems likely, then, that with the intention of making an arrow to guide the player's actions to the second bell in the bell-path, and looking back at the undifferentiated lines in Notation 2, Jeff sees the second line, which had stood for the second *hit,* as the second *bell* instead, and the arrow leads right to it (Figure 10–27).

The equidistant, undifferentiated lines in Notation 2 further contribute to the ambiguity of referents for these lines. The coupled lines in Notation 1 performed an important disambiguating function in this regard: in drawing his hits as *coupled* lines, Jeff's instructions implicitly showed the player how to *coordinate* action-path, tune-path, and bell-path—that is, how to coordinate actions moving through time with objects (bells) that remain static in space. Recall Notation 1 for a moment, and its relation to Jeff's transitional bell-path (Figure 10–28). Leaving aside the problem of the "G-bell that isn't there," the *sequential order* of coupled lines in the notation-path maps directly onto the sequential order of bells on the table. The potential for ambiguity with respect to the referents of lines is held in check because the player can follow along seeing exactly *which* bell is supposed to be hit twice. Thus, *locally* sequential motion as shown *within* each pair of lines (the repeated hits on a single bell) can be coordinated with the more *global* sequence of actions that moves from left to right along the bell-path—each *pair* of lines does both jobs. But in Notation 2, where Jeff's lines are equidistant, he loses this implicit coordination. With the spatial coupling gone, it becomes very difficult for Jeff, as well as for a player following his instructions, to coordinate bells that stay still in real space with actions that move forward and back *on* them and that do so through time.

Jeff's confusion points up the potential for confusion that is present for all of us when we transform actions on objects in real time/space into static descriptions of them in symbolic paper-space. The confusions can be seen most clearly if we consider the multiple meanings we give to the term "place" in moving from one kind of experience and medium to the other. Consider, for example, the common convention of lining up symbols from left to right in paper-space to show *actions* "going onward" in time. We first saw Jeff using this convention in his instructions for HOT. As Met put it then, the lines in symbolic space do not represent real objects in a real place; rather, they tell the player to *do* something that happens *after* or *later than* another action (Figure 10–29). Jeff confounds actions and bells in part because he adopts this conventional use of imaginary symbolic space in these new notations as well: as he "performs" the tune on paper, lines that go left to right in paper-space stand for the imaginary "place" of actions in symbolic time/space; but in looking back at the trace left behind, Jeff sees the lines as standing for the position, the *place,* of bells in the line-up on the table, for this also goes left to right in real table-space.

Figure 10–29

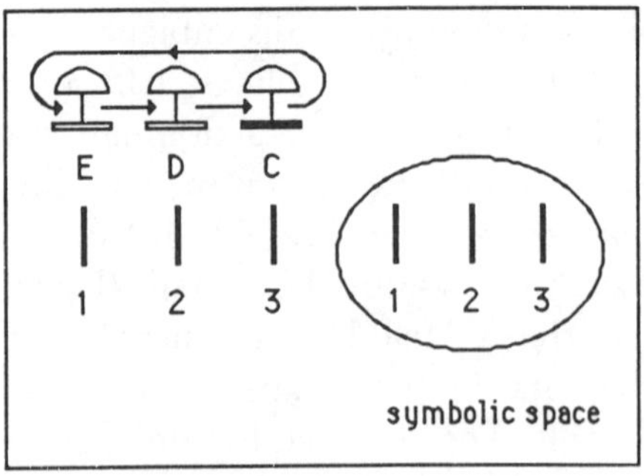

something that happens after *or* later

So a "place" can be a position in a sequence of symbols, like Jeff's lines in paper-space, but this can be easily confused with other kinds of "places" within the multiple aspects of the tune and the task. A "place" can be:

- the position of a bell in *table-space;*
- the *same* bell in table-space but two *different* "places" in the tune;
- the position of an event within the sequence of *tune-events;*
- or the "position" of an *action* along an action-path.

Given the instability within and across these multiple possible meanings, together with the ambiguities built in to Notation 2, it is not surprising that the referents for marks in Jeff's notation-path are easy victims of his transitional flux. Not yet able to hold still the various aspects of the tune and the task, Jeff is slipping among and between them all. But despite Jeff's confusions, his resourcefulness produces a third notation that helps to clarify and stabilize this sea of flux.

Notation 3

In an effort to help Jeff resolve some of his confusions, I intervened with a question. As we looked together at Notation 2, I asked him, "How will people know which bells to hit twice?" He responded with Notation 3:

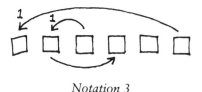

Notation 3

This notation is a rather remarkable invention, although its evolution and its meaning are probably not immediately obvious. Jeff made Notation 3 by first carefully *joining together* the pairs of equally spaced lines that he made by playing/drawing Twinkle in Notation 2. In this process, the adjacent lines that referred to repeated hits on the same bell in Notation 2 are turned into boxes in Notation 3:

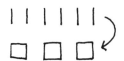

adjacent lines are turned into boxes

Figure 10–30

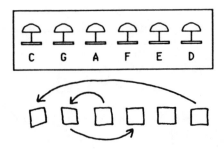

the boxes exactly correspond with the bells

Figure 10–31

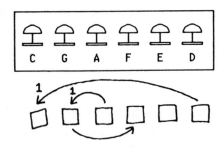

Jeff adds "1's" to the targets of arrows

And surprisingly, the new boxes in paper-space exactly correspond with the bells in the table-space (Figure 10–30). Thus Notation 3 seems almost magically to solve the problems of ambiguity inherent in Notations 1 and 2. Joining together the lines that stood for actions on the bells, Jeff transforms the lines into boxes. This, in turn, transforms the referents of the lines from *actions* on the bells to the *bells* themselves. The new sequence of boxes now unambiguously corresponds with the sequence of bells, and each box, in turn, indicates that the bell to which it refers is to be hit twice. One graphic symbol holds both meanings.

With his focus stabilized and the referents of objects secure, Jeff is now able to use his arrow notation to show clearly and exactly the targets for switch-backs and also the skip-a-bell that links the first and second phrases. And with his inimitable capacity for invention, Jeff also adds "1's" at the point of each switch-back arrow to show that the targeted bell is to be hit only once (Figure 10–31). Thus Notation 3 is a complete trail map of the terrain. While the left-to-right line-up of the boxes, following convention, shows the temporal sequence in which the bells are to be played, the arrows indicate where this convention does not hold. That is, with the action-path no longer in direct correspondence with the left-to-right sequence of bells, Jeff's arrows show when and in what direction the action-path diverges from that left-to-right sequence.

The only aspect that is not completely clear in Jeff's trail-map instructions is that the boxes by themselves are meant to show bells that are to be played twice—that is, where the player is supposed to "stay put" for two hits. Considering how the boxes came into being, this oversight is not surprising: since the boxes were made from adjacent lines, and since coupled lines initially stood for repeated *hits*, this aspect of Jeff's instructions was obvious to him. But it is not so obvious for the naive player who is expected to follow Jeff's instructions. This problem led to Jeff's final modification.

Notation 4

To help Jeff clarify this one missing aspect of his instructions, I intervened once more: I asked Jeff if he could "put in some numbers so people would know exactly how to play the tune." But my question, instead of helping, had the effect of springing things loose again.

Jeff's final modification, Notation 4, once again finds him struggling with recurring conflicts between bell-path, action-path, and notation-path, this time expressed in his shifting use of numbers. Jeff begins Notation 4 by numbering the first three bell-boxes serially—1 2 3:

begins Notation 4 by numbering the bell-boxes serially

But on his next move he crosses out the serial numbers. What accounts for Jeff's switch just at this point? The serial numbers could either be names for the bells, or they could show the temporal sequence in which bells are to be played—either meaning will work. But when Jeff gets to the critical switch-back, he is faced head-on with conflict: if he continues to use numbers as names for the bells, the bell named "2" would also have to be named "4." And if the numbers are meant to show the temporal sequence in which the bells are to be played, then the fourth action would look as if it comes *before* the third action in left-to-right time/space:

faced head-on with conflict

Jeff solves the problem, as he did before with HOT, by slipping out from under it. Crossing out the *sequential* numbers, he simply replaces them with numbers that show *how many* hits:

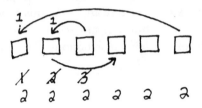

sequential numbers replaced with numbers for how many hits

So once again we see Jeff slipping between the various uses for numbers and the various meanings that each can take on: numbers can be *names* for the bells; numbers can show the temporal *sequence* in which bells are to be played; and numbers can show *how many* actions to make on a single bell. But despite this slippage, or perhaps as a result of it, notice that Jeff uses numbers consistently in this final modification—the 1's at the goals of each arrow as well as the 2's under each box tell the player *how many times to hit a bell.*

THE STORY OF THE ARROW

Jeff's solution in Notation 3 to the ambiguities and confusions of Notations 1 and 2 is particularly memorable. While it seemed at the time like a magical sleight of hand, a "quick fix," looking back we can trace the process as one of evolving modification. And following this process of evolution helps to make an important point: in making descriptions, putting marks on paper, our notations, like Jeff's, are intended as a means of communication—they are meant to tell someone else how to do what we know how to do. In just this way, Jeff's process in making his instructions was one of *externalizing* an inner "run-through" of actions made in real time/space so that someone else could do what he had done. But once the marks are out there, held still in paper-space, the trace also becomes a means for makers to examine their own inner representations. Looking *at* their own notations, they find that the process which begins as going from inside out turns around on itself to go from outside in, as well. In this way, descriptions, once made, can reveal aspects of described phenomena that were unnoticed or even inaccessible before; the traces left behind can become *things to think with*.

The evolution of Jeff's arrow can tell the story. It goes like this: Jeff's need for and use of the arrow were initially triggered by the new structure of his transitional bell-path. Within the constraints I imposed on him, Jeff, in constructing and playing Twinkle on the bell-path, learned to use and reuse a single bell for pitch-shared events that differed with respect to their position or function in the tune. As a result, the figural correspondence between bell-path and action-path was severed, and Jeff's new action-path (the switch-backs and skip-a-bell) became the means for making a new *coordination*. In making his notations, Jeff was faced with a central problem: How was he to capture this coordination in his description? As long as the sequence of tune-events, actions, and bells are all going along together—consecutively onward, next-next-next—then, in making a notation, an arrow for left-to-right motion on the page is unnecessary; it is *implicit* in our notational conventions. But when the action-path is severed from the bell-path so that it goes, at times, from right to left and skips a bell, this must be made *explicit*. Jeff adopts the arrow sign to solve this problem.

Once Jeff introduces the arrow, the conventional meanings inherent in its use help him to organize the phenomena in particular ways: problems are both set and solved as the features and relations of the tune and task are seen *through* the meanings that he and we attach to this notational sign. An arrow is a sign that directs actions; it is a signal asking us to follow its pictured movement toward its target, the *place* at its point. Because it is an action-sign, it is not surprising that Jeff thinks to use it. His notation is an action-notation: that is, it was initially both *made* by and meant to *represent* a sequence of actions. The reader is asked, so to speak, to "run the procedure" that generated it. But as Jeff embeds the arrow in this procedural description, its use and purpose change—it generates and reveals hidden problems in the notation and also becomes a means for solving them.

The single arrow in Notation 1, then, is a response to the structure of the transitional bell-path. But as a procedural description, this notation only partially succeeds (Figure 10–32). In the course of testing Notation 1—playing from it, looking at it—the new arrow helps Jeff find a signif-

Figure 10–32

the single arrow only partially succeeds

Figure 10–33

the new arrow at the end of the first phrase

icant problem as well as the possibility for its solution in Notation 2. Jeff *corrects* the line for a single hit on the "G-bell that isn't there" by *replacing* it with the new arrow at the end of the first phrase (Figure 10–33). But at the same time, when Jeff makes the arrow and then sees it held steady on the page, its conventional usage helps to reveal another problem. As a direction signal, the arrow sign is meant to direct its readers to a *place in space;* however, Jeff's lines stand for hits that "take place" in *time.* Thus Jeff's lines are mismatched with the conventions associated with the arrow. So, at the moment Jeff draws his arrow, tacitly adopting its conventional meaning, his view of his own notation changes; it is reorganized in terms of the arrow. With the arrow calling up place-in-space, Jeff no longer sees his lines as actions but rather as place markers along his bell-path—the second hit becomes the second bell, and he directs his arrow right to it.

The modification in Notation 3 is triggered by my question, which addresses the immediate problem only indirectly: "How will people know which bells to hit twice?" Jeff's first move in Notation 3 directly answers my question: he joins together pairs of lines in Notation 2 in order to show which hits "go together"—that is, the pairs of hits that belong to one bell in one place (Figure 10–34). But this move has an unexpected result. When two adjacent lines are joined together, the two become one—a single box. But the box can only be seen after the fact, *after the lines take shape on paper.* And after the new shape has been seen, after it emerges from the page, so to speak, only then does it trigger new meaning—meaning quite different from the intent of the moves that

Figure 10–34

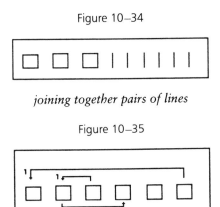

joining together pairs of lines

Figure 10–35

directing actions to places in space

created it. The coupling lines, meant to join together separate lines/actions that belong to one place and one bell, become an emblem with double meaning—the box does tell the player that the bells are to be hit twice, but it also transforms the emblem into one that stands for the object of those actions, the bells themselves. Thus an action made for one purpose takes shape on paper—becomes manifest so as to be *seen*—and in the seeing, its initial intent is quite transformed. As bells instead of hits, the boxes map out the terrain, and the arrows gain their intended meaning as directing actions to places in space rather than to hits that have gone by (Figure 10–35). And it is exactly in that invisible process—in our capacity to see one thing as another—that magic seems to happen. Think, for instance, of the architect doodling on paper; as he doodles, the marks "speak back"—they take shape, and the shapes become things to move around, to put into new relations with one another, even to reveal possibilities in the world of bricks or wood that until then were not thought of at all. But doodling as an on-the-wing process disappears, and we chalk up its often surprising results to the magic of intuition or luck when it is really history flown or thrown away.

The box emblem in Notation 3 differs from the graphics in Notation 1 and 2 in another important way. Unlike the lines in Notations 1 and 2, the box was not made by actually playing/drawing Twinkle on paper. While Notation 3 is still a procedural description—it represents a sequence of actions that the reader is meant to follow—the shapes themselves (the squares) *refer* to those actions; they are not the direct result of Jeff's actually playing the tune on paper. In this respect, Jeff's move to

Figure 10–36

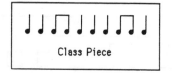

F.1

F.2

J J ♫ J J J J ♫ J

Class Piece

the moves from an F.1 to an F.2 drawing

Notation 3 is reminiscent of the children's drawings of rhythms—in particular the move from a type F.1 to a type F.2 drawing of the Class Piece (Figure 10–36). In contrasting the two types of drawings, I said at the time: "In making these shapes [F.2 drawings], the children are no longer simply transporting their actions directly onto the paper (playing/drawing); what we see instead are 'thought actions'—discrete graphic shapes that stand for, refer to, actions rather than being the direct result of the actions themselves. It would seem, then, that a critical aspect of development is the moves back and forth between reflections *of* and reflection *on* experience."

With Notation 3, then, Jeff is reflecting *on* his experience; Notation 3 is a *comment* on Notations 1 and 2. With the sequence of boxes now matching the sequence of bells, the shared sequence itself "holds" the procedure for getting from one place to the next *consecutive* one in the line-up of bells—as if they were linked by an implicit left-to-right arrow. And with the correspondence secure between the position of the boxes and the position of the bells, along with the implicit *left-to-right* motion from one to the next, Jeff can now use the arrows effectively to organize the contrary, *right-to-left* motion, the switch-backs that coordinate bells in table-space with actions on them. The arrow that marks the end of the first phrase, now firmly targeted to the second bell, "tells" Jeff how to add the next—the skip-a-bell arrow that links the first phrase to the second. And once he has closed the tune with his last arrow, the arrows help provoke one more element in Jeff's procedural description; he adds the 1's at the points of both switch-back arrows. And in doing so, Jeff completes his answer to my initial question: while the boxes show which bells are to be hit twice, the targets of the arrows are bells that must be hit only once.

Jeff's notational process began as an effort to go from his inner representation of what he knew how to do to an external description that others could see and follow. But as Jeff's initial graphics took shape, they "talked back," reshaping what he saw and also what he knew. So the initial inside-out process turned around to become, instead, a reciprocal one—outside-in and inside-out playing a game of catch-up as they inform and transform each other. And in recognizing this process, we can see the seeming sleight of hand, the quick fix of Notation 3, not as magic but rather as a history of learning. But if we fail to grab it on the wing, history disappears along with its actions; rewriting it backward from where it ends, we call its final product, like the architect's finished structure, not a matter of learning but one of pure, intuitive insight.

Still, these important innovations in Jeff's strategies of construction and notation only *prepare* for the transformations that are yet to come. The evidence can be found in those aspects of his productions that have *not* changed: his construction process is still a cumulative one; the completed bell-path, despite its important changes, is still a "one-purpose instrument" unique to Twinkle; the notation, too, despite its important innovations, is still, like his figural notation, a "dedicated" one—it instructs a person only how to play *this* tune on bells arranged in *this* way. And yet it is through the continuation of the processes and "possibles" that have emerged in this transitional phase—the increasing mobility of the once-rigid tune-as-configuration, coupled with the emergence of more general coordinating structures—that Jeff is able to achieve the cognitive restructuring that we will see finally occurring in the next phase.

CHAPTER 11

Moving toward a Formal
Representation of "Twinkle"

OVER THE next weeks Jeff continued to build tunes and to make instructions for playing them on the bells. While his new strategies suggested that important cognitive changes were going on, still his strategies for building Twinkle and the resulting constructions continued to maintain a basic consistency: he always added bells to his bell-path in their *order of occurrence* in the tune, next-next-next; his transitional as well as his figural bell-paths were built to play just one piece. Moreover, Jeff's notations were "iconic"; despite the differences that had developed, each notation was still a *graphic depiction* of a single, tune-specific path through an instrument-specific terrain.

Such iconic notations are, in fact, not peculiar to Jeff. For example, early notation for the lute, called "tablature," pictured, in bare stylized fashion, the neck of the lute and the strings, along with the "frets" that marked off the neck and the strings into equidistant intervals. Marks of some sort were added to the picture to show how the fingers should be placed to make the appropriate notes. Modern guitar and banjo notation, often seen in sheet music for pop tunes, is similar: it shows the player how to make a particular chord by showing him where on each string to put his fingers (Figure 11–1). Like Jeff's iconic notations, tablature applies to an instrument-specific terrain.

With all this in mind, I asked myself: Given what I know of Jeff's work so far, what sorts of transformations would be necessary within his cur-

Figure 11–1

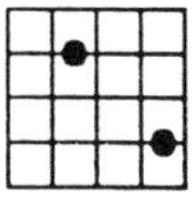

tablature

rent organized settings in order for him to develop an all-purpose instrument through which he could name bells/pitches invariantly? It became clear to me (as it already had to Met in our last conversation) that in order to arrive at such a general-purpose notation (something like our modern music notation), Jeff would need to develop a way of organizing the bells/pitches that would be *independent of any particular tune*. Such a structure could function as a "fixed reference" in relation to which names for bells/pitches would remain the same regardless of their position in the tune and regardless of their figural function. As Met put it, names should "travel" with the pitches. In his figural notation, the number-names that Jeff gave to bells had the advantage of showing the unique situation and function of an event within a tune context. This is like being able to change the name of some material (wood, glass) in response to its *function* in a building (beam/door; window/mirror), or like changing the name of a person depending on whom he is standing next to in a line. Indeed, such functional names are useful at times—as in a line-up for a game—but materials and people need to have names that "travel" with them as well.

What would the organization of such a structure for invariantly fixing names to bells/pitches look like? The most familiar version of such a reference structure is a line-up of pitch-playing objects ordered consecutively along the dimension we usually describe as going from "low to high." Given the pitch collection embodied by the bells, such an ordering would result in a major scale. In contrast to Jeff's single-purpose and changing "reference entities," the particular structure of this ordering serves well as a *fixed reference*. For example, if the internal relations among the properties of this structure were mapped onto the relations among some conventional symbolic series, it would make it possible to label invariantly the position of a bell in the series. The label given to that position could then serve as an all-purpose "index" for naming the bell/pitch associated with a tune-event wherever that event occurred in any tune. The sequence of names, A B C D E F G, that we give to the low-to-high ordered pitches in modern pitch-notation serves just such an indexical function. But it is important to notice that such a mapping is a two-way process: in order to map letters onto pitches, we must first learn and internalize the letter series as a particular linear order and also construct and internalize the low-to-high pitch series as another particular linear order. Only then can the symbol series (the letters) give meaning to the labels attached to the pitch series.

As a first step, then, I needed to ask: How could I help Jeff to construct this low-to-high pitch ordering of the bells, and then to use it as a fixed reference structure for constructing and notating his tunes? And, what was very important, could Jeff do that and still not lose his wonderful abilities for invention and his responsiveness to situation and figural function? It turned out to be a long trip, and, like Jonathan Jo's (in the A. A. Milne poem), it included a "barrel full of surprises." But we had plenty of time.

CONSTRUCTING A SCALE-TUNE

I began by testing the waters: I asked Jeff one day if he could "order the bells from low to high." This resulted in the first surprise. As I should have imagined, Jeff had his own meaning for "order." But at the same time, "order" was apparently the only part of my question that made any sense at all to Jeff: he simply arranged the bells so that they *made a nice tune*. To "order the bells" meant, as Jeff explained to me afterward, "to put them in order so they sound nice." On reflection this should not have been so surprising, since ordering the bells had always before meant putting them in order so as to play a tune that "sounded nice."

Some days later I tried another tack. Leaving aside "low" and "high," I simply sang the tune that we call a scale and asked Jeff if he could build *that tune* with the bells. I gave Jeff the complete set of white bells (all the pitches of the C major scale) as the mixed array in his search-space, started him off with the C-bell, and asked him what came next. His cumulative strategy worked perfectly here. He played the C-bell, found the D-bell in the search-space, then starting again from the beginning (C, D) found the E-bell, and in this way quickly built up this scale-tune just as he had built up other tunes—next-next-next (Figure 11–2).

The result was, of course, a row of bell-pitches ordered consecutively from low to high, the whole series forming a major scale. But it is important to distinguish between, on one hand, a *figural* way of mentally representing this series, a "tune," and, on the other, what I will call a *formal* mental representation of this series. Formally, the set would be described

Figure 11–2

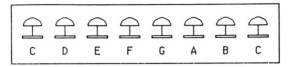

Jeff built up the scale-tune, next-next-next

Figure 11–3

a gap left in the consecutive ordering

Figure 11–4

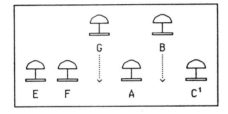

later inserted in their proper places

as an ordered series in which any one bell-pitch in the series is both higher than the previous one (to its left) and lower than the subsequent one (to its right). With a formal representation, for example, a person would no longer need always to start from the "beginning" of the series—that is, the lowest pitch; rather, the series could be built starting from any pitch. Moreover, bells would not need to be added in strict consecutive order—for instance, a gap could be left in the consecutive ordering (Figure 11–3), and the appropriate bell-pitch(es) could later be inserted in their proper places (Figure 11–4). This was clearly not yet the case for Jeff. He had built a *figural tune,* much like other tunes: he always began at the "beginning," adding bells strictly in order of occurrence; and, as in the construction of other tunes, Jeff also had to play from the beginning of his cumulating bell-path each time in searching for next-in-tune.

Vygotsky's distinction between what he calls a "pseudo-concept" in contrast to a "concept proper" is helpful here: *

> On the basis of its external appearance and external characteristics, that is, *phenotypically*, the pseudo-concept corresponds completely to the concept proper. However, *genotypically*, that is, in accordance with its emergence, its development, and the causal-dynamic connections that underlie it, the pseudo-concept is very different from the concept proper . . . Experimental analysis shows . . . that in reality the child [in making a pseudo-concept] has formed only an associative complex limited to a certain kind of *perceptual bond*. Although the results are identical, the process by which they are reached is not at all the same as in conceptual thinking . . . the child thinks the same thing in a different way, by means of different mental operations. (Vygotsky 1962, pp. 66–69)

Although Vygotsky is not referring to music here, his distinction applies to Jeff's musical learning as well. Using Vygotsky's terms, Jeff's scale-tune is a "pseudo-concept," not a "concept proper." That is, his construction is "limited to a kind of perceptual bond" where the cumulative addition of bell-pitches, next-next-next, results in a perceptually "bonded" *figure*. Thus, while Jeff's scale-tune may look and sound the same as a formal structure, he "thinks the same thing in a different way, by means of different mental operations."

To help Jeff become more familiar with the low-to-high series, I encouraged him to practice building his scale-tune during the next weeks. And as he did so we talked about "higher-than" and "lower-than," or about how "the tune is getting higher now" or "that's a lower bell." And when the tune-scale was completed, Jeff played "up and then down" on his bells. Interestingly, going *up* was easy—that was how Jeff built the tune each time; but at first he had to think hard in order to reverse his path and go *down*. With time and practice Jeff learned to "build a scale," which he described as, "It goes lower and then higher, higher, higher." High and low had gained specific meaning, and Jeff's description of the ordering also captured the relational properties that are specific to its structure.

But to order the bells in this way did not immediately include the capacity to coordinate *this* well-ordered structure with the different but

---

* I find the term "concept" somewhat troublesome here, since it brings with it a lot of baggage that is not really appropriate. However, the general gist of Vygotsky's remarks still seems relevant to Jeff's situation.

Figure 11–5

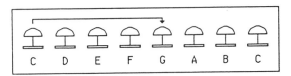

I jumped across to the G-bell

equally well-ordered structure of a tune. This became quite clear when I asked Jeff one day if he could play Twinkle *on* the low-to-high ordered bells *without moving them*. I showed him what I meant by starting off the tune for him. Starting as usual with the first bell (C), I played it twice (for "Twin-kle") and then jumped across to the G-bell and played it twice (making the next "twin-kle"; Figure 11–5). Watching my performance carefully, Jeff looked puzzled and even rather upset. For him it was clearly uncomfortable, even disorienting, to see the tune *looking* so different—how could two events that were *next* to each other in the tune, and that had always before been next to each other in table-space, be so far apart, requiring a big leap to get from one to the next? Jeff's response to my demonstration was a surprise, but in retrospect it should not have been. Instead of simply imitating what I had done, Jeff once again remained true to his own believable strategies: hesitating for just a moment, he picked up the C and G bells, hugged them to his chest almost possessively, and then put them down on the table *next to each other* (Figure 11–6).

But Jeff didn't stop there. He quickly took apart the rest of the low-to-high ordered collection, rebuilt his transitional bell-path (Figure 11–7), and played Twinkle on it in his by-now familiar way—all in one rush

Figure 11–6

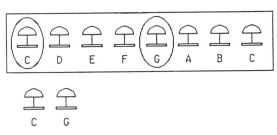

put them down on the table next to each other

Figure 11-7

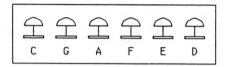

his transitional bell-path

Figure 11-8

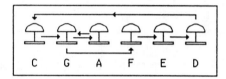

played Twinkle in his by-now familiar way

of uninterrupted moves (Figure 11–8). Jeff could focus his attention on ordering the bells from low to high when the task was "to build a scale," and he could focus his attention on constructing Twinkle. But when he was asked to map one sort of tune onto the other, the two structures remained disjunct from each other. The two tasks, building a scale and building Twinkle, simply called up two separate and distinct *tunes* for Jeff, and each needed to be instantiated by its own ordered set of bells.

COORDINATING SCALE-TUNE AND TWINKLE-TUNE

By March, five months after we had begun our work together, Jeff settled into what was to become his final, formal phase. Constructing the scale-tune became easy. And as it became more familiar, I helped Jeff to think of the scale-ordered series not just as another tune, but as an *instrument to play on*—an instrument with a particular, stable geography (Figure 11–9). With practice, he learned to keep the bells steady while he

Figure 11-9

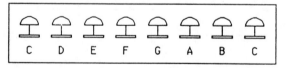

an instrument with a stable geography

Figure 11–10

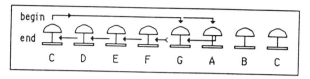

playing Twinkle on his new instrument

searched within this fixed, ordered series for the particular sequence of pitch-events that would play his chosen tune. This meant, of course, that in order to play Twinkle on this new instrument, he had to move about *on* the fixed, scale-ordered bells—forward, backward, skipping (Figure 11–10). Although Jeff eventually succeeded in doing so, still, to find and play Twinkle within the unmovable, fixed series of bells was a risky business. Some of the new strategies he needed to develop were partially prepared by his work during his transitional phase, but others necessarily required upsetting fundamental aspects of his organized mental settings for constructing and playing tunes—aspects that had previously given meaning and coherence to the tune and to his work. For example, even in building the tune, he needs to coordinate two structures that he had previously built and thought of as quite separate from each other. That is, keeping the sequence of tune-events in mind, he must *coordinate* this sequence with the prearranged ordering of the bells in space—an order that is different from and independent of the tune itself.

How does he do that? As before, Jeff must move around in a search-space to test bells for next-in-tune. But this new search-space is of a quite different kind from those he had used before: while previous search-spaces had always been occupied by an arbitrarily mixed array of bells, the bells in this search-space are already ordered, and the order is fixed in its spatial configuration. And the relation between search-space and work-space has changed as well: there are no longer two separate spaces; the fixed and preordered search-space must also function as work-space. That is, in the previous construction tasks, the unordered bell collection in the search-space was transformed into a tune-ordered collection in the work-space; now the two spaces are one and the same. Consider the process: Jeff begins his construction by searching for next-in-tune within the fixed search-space, starting from the beginning of the tune each time as before. But now, upon finding a bell for next-in-tune, instead of *removing* it and adding it cumulatively to an emerging bell-path in a *separate* work-space, Jeff must leave the bell where it is! As a result, Jeff's search-and-find process leaves no trace behind—no new arrangement of objects in space that embodies the temporal sequence of events in Twinkle.

The difference is a critical one. Before, as Jeff removed bells from the search-space to the work-space, the trace left behind made the results of his moves manifest; the cumulating bell-path was not only an embodiment of the tune, it was a concrete, palpable structure that he could see and play on, and with which he could keep track of how far he had gotten toward completing the tune. And it is exactly in this sense that the cumulating bell-path was a *reference entity:* it held still in space the results of Jeff's search—a line-up of bells arranged *in terms of the tune,* to which Jeff could refer as he continued on with his construction; and when he was finished, the results of his work were still there, standing still in table-space. But with the fixed and preordered series as search-space now one with Jeff's work-space, all that remains of his construction process is a *configuration of moves,* although each move is targeted to a particular position within the fixed terrain of bells. So with Jeff's previous construction strategies, his actions and decisions left behind a tune-ordered configuration of objects in space with the consecutive position of each bell marking the consecutive *position of events in the tune.* In contrast, his new construction strategy leaves behind a configuration of moves unfolding in time; and while each move is anchored by bells that play the sequence of tune-events, the bells themselves hold their fixed positions as *members of the scale-ordered series.* Thus, the sequence of search-and-find moves must be one of continuously coordinating the two different, well-formed structures—the unfolding structure of the tune with the unmovable structure of the low-to-high ordered bells.

As I intimated earlier, some of these new strategies were prepared by Jeff's work in his transitional phase. Among these new developments were the possibility for holding single bells/pitches invariant despite their changing position and function in the route followed by tune-events, and with this the breaking apart of the rigid correspondence between bell-path, action-path, and tune-path, each with its somewhat differing trajectory in space/time. Both of these can be seen as developments that prepared the possibility for keeping the entire preordered bell-path invariant while moving on it to find the sequence of tune-events. Indeed, this coming-apart was particularly important, for in that process Jeff was also developing an ability to differentiate among various possible dimensions of the tune and the task, and at the same time learning to coordinate these dimensions so that while one remained fixed another could move on.

But even though these newly liberated possibilities were important developments with respect to Jeff's previous figural strategies, they differ in kind and in degree of restructuring when compared with the strategies involved in Jeff's learning to construct Twinkle on the fixed and preordered bells. Most important, the changes Jeff made in moving from his figural to his transitional bell-path can be seen as *modifications* of familiar turf, *exceptions* in a structure that otherwise remained the same as in his previous figural phase. For example, transitional moves such as the switch-backs and the skip-a-bell could be seen *in terms of old moves:* a switch-back could be thought of as, "Instead of going on to the next bell for the last event in the first phrase, go back and play the previous bell again" (Figure 11–11). Or, "Instead of *going on* to the next bell on the words 'how I,' *skip a bell* and then continue on to 'how I'" (Figure 11–12). Although these new moves were certainly disruptive changes at the time, still the basic terrain remained the same—the bells were in principle lined up in order of occurrence in the tune, and in principle they "held" the chronology of tune-events. Any moves that did not conform to these principles were deviations from the norm, but not a whole new ground plan, a whole new design. In short, if we look back at these transitional moves now, they can be seen as an *elaborated version* of the old familiar world.

Figure 11–11

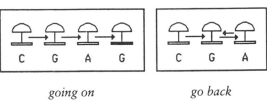

going on   go back

Figure 11–12

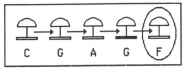

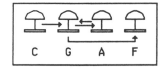

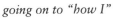

going on to "how I"   *skip a bell and continue on to "how I"*

Figure 11–13

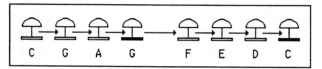

Jeff's figural action-path

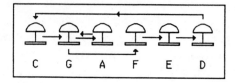

A "bent" version

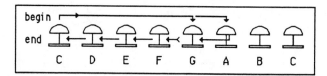

The new action-path for Twinkle

But when I asked Jeff to play the tune on the scale-path, familiar ground was literally pulled out from under him. The low-to-high, preordered sequence of bells had its own design, its own internal structure, which on its surface was unrelated to the previous spatial layout as well as to the temporal chronology of Twinkle. There was no way, for instance, that Jeff could look at his new action-path for Twinkle as a "bent" version of his figural action-path (Figure 11–13). In retrospect, then, we can see Jeff's transitional constructions as moves *away from* what he already knew; but at the same time they resulted in transformations of his current mental setting that brought with them the liberation of "possibles" that could be exploited as *moves toward* a distinctly different way of representing Twinkle to himself.

Thus, my proposal to build the low-to-high ordered series was initially an imposition, a disruption in the course of Jeff's work. But Jeff met it in his own way, as he did each of my interventions, making his own sense of it and eventually using it on his own terms. Indeed, from a practical point of view, and one that is probably closer to Jeff's own, learning to play Twinkle on the scale-path was probably more a process of practicing and gradually internalizing the appropriate configuration of targeted moves on his new instrument. That is, what was initially a step-by-step search-and-find construction process became with practice a single *chain* of moves, with each action calling up the next—a *felt path*.

What, then, was Jeff learning, once he was willing to suspend his initial disbelief in order to construct and to practice playing Twinkle on the scale-path? What know-how was being internalized along with this felt path? Answers did not come until later, for the significance of this work really only emerges explicitly in Jeff's invention of his own notation.

DESIGNING A NOTATION FOR PLAYING TWINKLE ON THE FIXED BELL-PATH

How was Jeff to make instructions for playing Twinkle that would coordinate on paper two clearly distinct but equally well-ordered structures: the unique internal structure of the tune, on one hand, and the scale-ordered internal structure of the instrument, on the other? His solution was quite remarkable. And yet his new notation, like his construction strategy, is in some ways a continuation of his evolving instructions for playing the tune on his transitional bell-path. Jeff's instrument, the low-to-high ordered bells, and his instructions for playing Twinkle on it are shown in Figure 11–14. To understand how the notation works, it is important to keep in mind just how I put the task to Jeff here as well as earlier: "Can you make some instructions so someone else could play Twinkle on the bells as you have them set up?" The task was a practical one. The notations are a set of *directions* to the performer—they show someone else how to move on the bells so as to make the bells play the tune. Jeff's notation process, then, is always closely allied with the construction process: the notation depends on how the bells have already been arranged and also on the underlying mental settings that have vari-

Figure 11–14

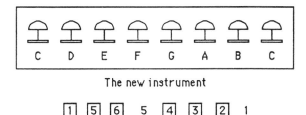

The new instrument

and Jeff's instructions for playing Twinkle on it

ously guided that construction process. So it is not surprising that in producing the new notation on paper, Jeff reenacted the coordination process he had used in constructing Twinkle.

I will use Jeff's procedure for making the second symbol in the notation path, the 5 with a box around it, as an illustration. Starting from the beginning of the tune, he played the first bell twice for "Twin-kle," then searched along the scale for the bell-pitch that matched the second "twin-kle." Having found it, Jeff counted up along the scale-path from the lowest bell (1) to this found bell (5) and wrote down "5." He then put his bell-box around the number to show that Bell 5 should be hit twice. Repeating this procedure for each tune-event in turn, being careful to leave a number unboxed for the single hits at the ends of phrases, Jeff built up the whole notation step by step. The result is a notation-path in which the left-to-right sequence of symbols on the page shows the player the chronological sequence of events in the tune, and the numbers tell the player *where to find each tune-event on the instrument*—that is, where to go on the instrument to find the correct bell. In turn, the system of box or no box tells the player whether to hit the designated bell twice or only once.

Following Jeff's instructions, then, the first boxed number in the notation path stands for the first tune-event; the "1" inside the box tells the player to play Bell 1 in the scale-path, and the box tells the player to play that bell twice. The second and third boxed numbers stand for the second and third tune-events, telling the player to play the fifth and sixth bells in the bell-path and to play them each twice. The fourth symbol in the notation-path is for the fourth tune-event; but now the *unboxed* "5" tells the player that he must go backward on the scale-path from the previous event on Bell 6 ("lit-tle") to play Bell 5 ("star") and play that bell once (Figure 11–15).

Figure 11–15

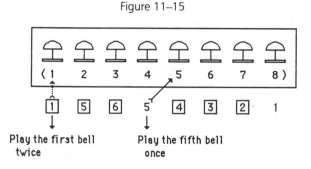

Play the first bell
twice

Play the fifth bell
once

Figure 11–16

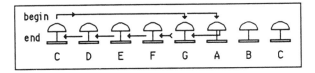

could have used his arrow notation

Figure 11–17

Transitional Notation 3

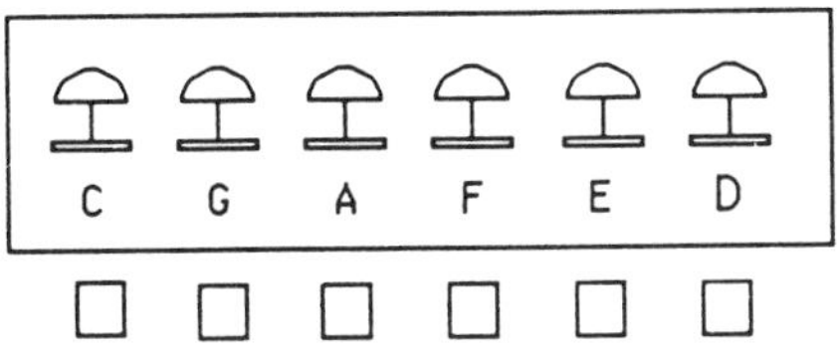

the boxes, by themselves, showed the normal "walk through the tune"

Of course, Jeff could have used his arrow notation to capture the procedure for playing Twinkle, much as I did in my diagram of Jeff's felt path for playing the tune (Figure 11–16). The fact that he did not is an important clue to the shift in his focus of attention and to elaborations of his inner representation as well. Recall, for instance, that in making his transitional bell-path Jeff still added bells in order of occurrence, and when he made his successful notation path, the row of boxes became synchronous with the row of bells. As such, they were sufficient *by themselves* to show the "normal" left-to-right action-path, together with the bells that were to be hit twice (Figure 11–17). Jeff added the arrows as *directional action signals* only to show the *deviations* from the figural straight-ahead action-path—that is, the contrary right-to-left directional moves, the skip-a-bell, and, with the added "1's" at their points, the bells to be hit only once (Figure 11–18).

But now, with the preordered bells holding pitch direction and distance stable, and with the straight-ahead action path for playing tunes no longer a norm, Jeff shifts his focus away from graphically describing direct actions on a bell-path, and with this, he gives up his use of the arrows as direction signals as well. Indeed, the fact that Jeff gives up his arrows in making his new notation is strong evidence that significant cognitive work has gone on during this final phase, and that as a result

Figure 11–18

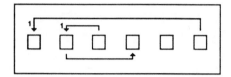

the arrows as directional signals to show the deviations

the fixed, ordered bells have assumed an entirely different function from his earlier bell-paths. Beginning by building the scale as simply a new tune different from the Twinkle-tune, Jeff comes to think of it as "it starts lower and then goes higher, higher, higher," and he also plays on it "going up" and "going down." Then learning to hold the series steady while he finds the sequence of tune-events within it (perhaps as a more elaborate version of "I had it already"), Jeff uses the low-to-high series as a fixed terrain on which to plot and internalize a path of targeted moves. In that process, the preordered series gains existence as an invariant structure, separate from the tune but still one that the sequence of tune events can be mapped onto, coordinated with. Through this evolution it seems quite natural that Jeff comes to see the potential for using the low-to-high bell series as a stable *reference structure* in making his notation. And this means that Jeff recognizes in this stable structure the possibility for using it to describe the unique structure of the tune in terms of structural relations that remain invariant and outside of any particular tune. This is an important contrast to Jeff's graphic arrow notation, which was still dependent on, and was made in terms of, the particular internal structure of Twinkle.

But Jeff's success in using the prearranged bells as a fixed reference structure depends on a critical first step, namely, using the bells as things to count on. In doing so, Jeff makes a one-to-one correspondence between a sequence of symbols, the sequence of number-names going from "lowest to highest," and the sequence of bells ordered from lowest to highest. The serial position of each number-name then corresponds with the serial position of each bell in instrument-space.* In this way, the scale-path as implicitly numbered becomes a kind of "look-up table" for making the notation (Figure 11–19). Counting up on the bells as he

---

* It should be emphasized that Jeff never explicitly wrote out the entire ordered sequence of numbers, 1–8; the match between the low-to-high ordered bells and the sequence of numbers was implicit in the process itself.

Figure 11–19

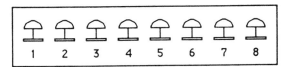

a kind of look-up table

makes his notation, Jeff "looks up" the serial position of each tune-event and "transports" the found *number* to the paper. This process represents an important contrast to directly transporting a *pictured image* of the found *bell* to the paper, as Jeff had done in his earlier notations. Moreover, in contrast to Jeff's figural notation, numbers maintain a singular reference in spite of changing positions and functions of the bells within the tune. Iterations of this process result in a row of numbers that designate, *point to*, a sequence of bell positions which in turn corresponds to the sequence of pitch-events in the tune. In short, by using the bells as reference *structure* (in contrast to his earlier reference *entities*) and as "look-up" table, Jeff creates a code; its fixed referents serve as the means for *denoting* (rather than graphically picturing) the sequence of tune-events, while at the same time they effectively direct the player's actions to the correct targets for playing Twinkle on the new instrument (Figure 11–20).

In sum, Jeff's new notation reflects his continuing development away from his earlier direct *correspondence* strategy to a much more complex *coordination* strategy. Notice that there are three distinct and separate kinds of paths in his new notation, each with its own meaning and its own trajectory: a notation-path in paper-space, a bell-path in instrument-space, and an action-path in time-space. Left-to-right in paper-

Figure 11–20

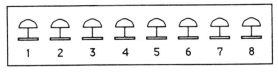

"Look-up table"

A code denoting the sequence of events

Figure 11–21

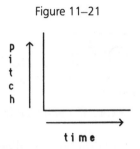

Jeff has invented a coordinate space

space shows the temporal sequence of tune-events; this is separate from and nonsynchronous with left-to-right in instrument-space, which embodies the low-to-high ordered series; and each of these, in turn, is different in trajectory from the forward and backward movements of the action-path in playing the tune. And with the possibilities Jeff finds for coordinating these divergent spaces and trajectories, his new notation also succeeds in coordinating meanings in two symbolic paper-spaces. Indeed, Jeff has invented the *coordinate space* that Met had envisioned early on (Figure 11–21).

Moreover, with position in the fixed reference coupled with the box/ unboxed contrast, Jeff at least hints at another feature in his notation: he is on the verge of inventing a kind of *proportional duration notation,* albeit one that applies particularly to the features of Twinkle. If we consider that all the single-hit events in Twinkle are twice as long as all double-hit events (or putting it the other way, two double hits are equal in time to one single hit), then boxed events have a 2:1 durational relation to unboxed events. And with this hint at proportional duration notation, Jeff's notational symbol—boxed and unboxed numbers—comes very close to the symbol used in standard music notation, namely, the "note." Like Jeff's symbol, the single "note" symbol includes both the position of an event on an instrument (or more generally, its pitch) and also the duration of a tune-event. The position of a note on the lines of the "staff," like Jeff's numbers, shows its position in the fixed reference structure—for example, the low-to-high ordered piano keys. Duration is shown conventionally, for example, by notes that are joined together by a "beam" (♫), these events being twice as fast as events notated as standing alone (♩). Just so, by joining together with "cross beams" the lines that initially stood for separate hits on a single bell, Jeff made boxes, and there as in the new notation, boxed events go twice as fast as events

Figure 11–22

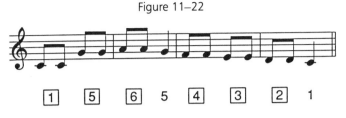

standard music notation along with Jeff's formal notation

shown by numbers standing alone. The potential similarity becomes quite clear if we look at standard music notation for Twinkle along with Jeff's formal notation (Figure 11–22). Of course, it seems unlikely that Jeff actually represented these proportional duration relations to himself as such, and equally unlikely that he recognized these implications in his notation. Nonetheless, it seems worth observing that, given the simple proportional rhythmic relations in Twinkle, Jeff's notation at least holds immanent in it the possibility for capturing these relations.

TRACING THE COURSE OF JEFF'S NOTATIONS

The evolving course of these rather dramatic transformations in Jeff's notational strategies is perhaps best illustrated by his changing use of counting and the counting numbers. Jeff liked to count; it was something he knew how to do; indeed, counting seemed to function for him as a prototype for *making order.* But when he applied this know-how to making his new notation, both counting and the referents for the number series took on quite new meaning. Jeff had used the number series before in his figural notation, although only after I had suggested "putting in some numbers that would help." But there, with the figural arrangement of bells as instrument to play on in one-to-one correspondence with the chronology of the tune, the numbers referred *through the pictures of the bells* to the chronology of tune-events. But once the scale-tune was constructed, with its own separate internal structure, it became impossible to represent the tune as copies of the bells, because to "transport" the bells as pictures in paper-space would only produce pictures of the scale-ordered bells again. And numbering these pictured copies of the bells would show the position of each bell in the low-to-high series (Figure 11–23), but it would not serve as either instructions for or a description of the *tune.*

However, taking this step was an important precondition for Jeff in

Figure 11–23

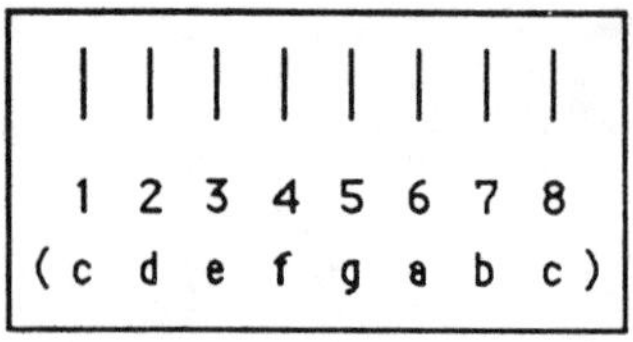

```
| | | | | | | |
1  2  3  4  5  6  7  8
( c  d  e  f  g  a  b  c )
```

the position of each bell in the low-to-high series

making his new notation. That is, in counting up on the bells in order to make his new notation, he tacitly labeled them, so that the bells themselves remained as place holders within the fixed structure. In turn, Jeff "peeled" these invisible labels off the objects, carrying the *labels* over one by one into paper-space. And in this process, the number-names could gain an independent existence: they could be "picked up" while still maintaining their connection with the object from which they had been removed. Moreover, each time Jeff peeled off and carried over a number-name, the process left a trace; the cumulating row of numbers also gained a separate existence as a "notation" that *referred to* rather than *imitating* the sequence of objects that would play the tune. And this is the essence of what we mean by "reference."

Indeed, Jeff's final notation can be called "formal" precisely because it depends on his invention of a rule system through which he can show the intersection between two structures, each with its independently ordered sets of relations: one, the bell series, which remains fixed in its order; the other, the sequence of tune-events, which is mobile depending on the tune involved, but with the second always described in terms of the first. The rule is easily expressed graphically by a two-way matrix, as shown in Figure 11–24. The vertical series of numbers shows the fixed ordinal positions of the bells in the low-to-high ordered series; the horizontal series of numbers shows the ordinal position of events in the tune (excluding repeated hits on the same bell).

If we compare this graphic representation with Jeff's own, it is interesting to note that it is unnecessary for Jeff to label explicitly the ordinal position of tune-events (Figure 11–25). Using the convention that time goes from left to right in paper-space, Jeff assumes that in following the boxed and unboxed signs, the reader/player will simply "take them as they come." In contrast, the number-names that label the ordinal position of bells in the low-to-high series can be "taken out of order." Like names that refer to all longs or shorts, all Tuesdays or all orange things,

Figure 11–24

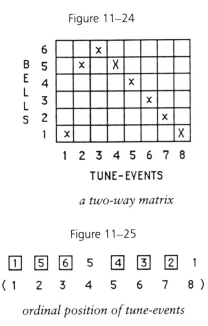

TUNE-EVENTS

a two-way matrix

Figure 11–25

boxed: 1   5   6   5   4   3   2   1
(1   2   3   4   5   6   7   8)

ordinal position of tune-events

the sequential order in which the names occur has no influence on the *meaning* of the objects or the properties to which they refer. No matter in what *order* they occur, the referent for the number-names always remains the same—the number-names always refer to the object that holds that ordinal position in the bell series.

Indeed, the sequence of numbers that can be left unstated in Jeff's formal notation, the series showing the ordinal position of tune-events, was the *only* sequence of numbers in Jeff's figural notation. The numbers 1 through 8 in the figural notation show the ordinal position of the eight tune-events (exclusive of repeated hits on the same bell) and also show the ordinal position of a bell in the *bell structure*—that is, the sequence of bells lined up on the table as shown by the pictures of them. Thus, with bell structure and tune structure in one-to-one correspondence, both in order of occurrence in the tune, a single row of numbers was sufficient to mark both the sequence of bells on the table and the sequence of tune-events (Figure 11–26).

This comparison between Jeff's figural and formal notations captures most vividly the transformations that have occurred in his mental representations of melodic structure—from an initial, undifferentiated meld, where features of the tune all belong to a single representational space, to the liberation of the many possible aspects of that space along with

Figure 11–26

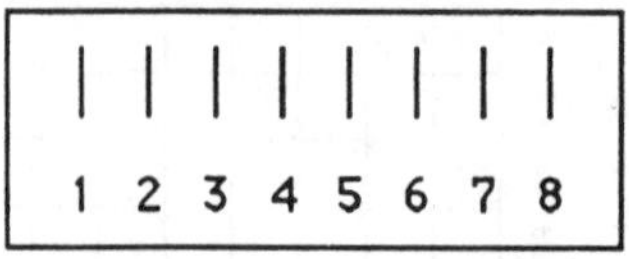

| | | | | | | |
| 1 | 2 | 3 | 4 | 5 | 6 | 7 | 8 |

the sequence of bells and *the sequence of tune-events*

systematic means for coordinating them. And yet Jeff's formal notation strategy, despite its important differences, resembles his figural notation strategy in an interesting way: in making his figural notation, Jeff's search, find, remove, and cumulatively add process also left a trace, but it was the cumulating row of *bells* in table-space that did so. The process, then, resulted in an embodied description, a *reference entity*. Similarly, Jeff's formal construction and notation process involved search, find, remove, and cumulatively add. But with the bells now a reference *structure*, *labels* rather than bells could be removed and added. This cumulating row of labels resulted in a *symbolic description* precisely because the number-names systematically *refer to* rather than *being* the bells.* But interestingly, Jeff assumes a common convention in both descriptions: in following their different meanings, the player always goes straight ahead, left to right, on both kinds of traces.

We can now answer the question, what did Jeff internalize along with his new felt path? The first thing was the sense of a fixed terrain with a particular internal structure; the second was a feel for the pattern of moves in traversing this fixed terrain that would produce Twinkle. The two together, then, generated the rule for making the intersection between the two structures. Using the rule as initially embodied in action, Jeff made it explicit in the invention of his notation strategy.

Finally, it is important to note that, as with the formal rhythm drawings, neither Jeff's formal notation nor standard music notation explicitly shows *the grouping of events into figures* or the changing *function* of events within these figures. Only Jeff's figural bell-path explicitly showed the grouping of events into figures, with the boundaries marked by the spatial gap. And only Jeff's figural notation, in parallel with the pictured

---

* For more on the distinction between reference entities and a reference structure, see Bamberger and Schön 1991. There are also interesting relations between the developing mental construction and use of a fixed reference pitch structure as seen in Jeff's work, and Piaget's analysis of the developing mental construction and use of fixed reference spatial structures (Piaget 1967, pp. 44–79).

bell-path, suggested the changing function of events; for instance, with the presence of two C-bells, each of them was labeled differently—the C-bell at the beginning was labeled "1" while the C-bell at the end was labeled "8." In contrast, in Jeff's scale-path where there is only one token of each bell type, Jeff's number-names label all tune-events that share the same bell as the same—the labels implicitly *classifying* each event according to its position in the low-to-high ordered series. Jeff's figural notation is, then, a true narrative—the story line continues ever-onward, with bells and actions moving along together; the story ends far away from where it began. But the player following Jeff's formal notation ends the tune in the same place where he began. And that is a kind of Alice in Wonderland story—even though you are going ever-onward in time and in paper-space, you end up just where you started on this general-purpose instrument. Each of Jeff's notations tells a different story of the same tune.

CHAPTER 12

Met and Mot's Reflections on Jeff's Story

JEANNE: So that's the end of Jeff's story. What do you think of him now?

MET: I was pleased to see that my hunches about what would get him to a formal notation actually worked out.

MOT: Yes, but Jeanne was certainly right that there was a lot of work ahead for Jeff.

MET: True, but it was worth it. For instance, I was fascinated to see the way the bells changed their function—or I guess I should say the way Jeff changed the use he made of the bells. In a way, the bells became a kind of transformation machine.

MOT: A *what?*

MET: A transformation machine. You see, in the beginning Jeff used the bells just to build up the tune—it was as if he made a one-to-one swap between the tune in his head and the bells on the table. He used the bells as a way of almost literally grabbing Twinkle.

MOT: Or at least grabbing each of the events in Twinkle.

MET: That's what I mean—picking out each bell like finding a handleable object that he could take and line up on the table. And when he was finished, there it was; the once-invisible tune-in-his-head standing there in 3-D space.

MOT: Is that what you mean by a transformation machine?

MET: Actually, no. The bells were more of an *instantiation* machine in that situation.

248

MOT: Pretty clever, Met. So what did you mean?

MET: The bells really only became a transformation machine when Jeff made his final notation. Of course, first he had to suspend his disbelief, as Jeanne put it, and agree to build the Twinkle-tune on the scale-tune. Once he got used to doing that, then the scale-tune became a machine that transformed the Twinkle-tune.

MOT: I begin to get it. But it doesn't seem right to call that line-up of bells a scale-*tune* anymore. A scale maybe, but not a tune.

MET: I agree, and that's just the point I'm trying to make about the bells as a transformation machine. It's as if Jeff puts Twinkle through this specially structured machine—the bell arrangement now instantiating a consistently ordered set of pitch property relations—and because of that structure, out of the other end of the machine comes a transformed Twinkle.

MOT: And that's the new notation.

MET: Exactly.

MOT: So the bells when ordered from low to high embody a principle for devising the transformation rule that Jeff uses in making his notation. He feeds the sequence of tune-events in one end, and the inner structural workings of the machine turn that sequence into a new structure. Twinkle comes out of the other end looking very different.

MET: You got it. Maybe it's just a more animated version of Jeanne's fixed reference structure, but it appeals to me.

JEANNE: I rather like it too, Met. And the machine works, of course, for any tune that uses this collection of pitches—or in fact any major scale collection.

MOT: Weren't you anticipating that in your analysis of Twinkle, Jeanne? I mean, you couldn't have made it without first assuming that fixed reference and then using it as a transformation machine.

JEANNE: Absolutely right, Mot, and thank you for reminding me of that. Remember, I also said that giving names to bells or to pitches, as in my analysis, implicitly assumes the construction of a fixed reference structure in terms of which these names can gain meaning. And by way of anticipation I said that the construction of such a framework plays a critical role in the course of an individual's musical development and also in the transformations implicit in moving between figural and formal tune-building strategies, maybe even between figural and formal hearings of melodies as well.

MET: I didn't quite get that at the time, but looking back, that sort of sums up the story of Jeff's work.

JEANNE: Perhaps. But remember, too, that as I started out with the story, I worried about giving readers the names of the bells right from the outset. As I said, bells don't come with names already on them. With that fixed reference framework already implicit in the conventions for naming, I risked the possibility that readers would read that framework back onto Jeff's work and wouldn't recognize and appreciate what was involved in Jeff's decisions, his invention of strategies, and his devising of all those notation systems.

MOT: Maybe it was a danger, but I, for one, had no trouble appreciating Jeff's work and the learning going on, especially in his struggles during what you called his transitional phase. But I still have a couple of questions.

MET: Yes. So do I.

JEANNE: I'm not surprised. Ask away.

MOT: My question is about something you promised you would tell us about, but then you never did.

JEANNE: What was that?

MOT: You said that Jeff moved into his formal phase without "wiping out" the earlier representations. But then you didn't say any more about that. Are you going to tell us what you meant?

JEANNE: You're right, Mot, I did forget about that. There's a nice story about Jeff and his friend Robbie that I think will show you what I mean. One day toward the end of the school year (it was actually in May), I suggested that Jeff invite his friend Robbie to visit the Lab. I thought it would be interesting for Jeff, and I was also curious to see how Jeff would tell Robbie what we had been doing. Robbie, who was 10, was having even more trouble than Jeff in school subjects, so I thought it would also be interesting to hear how Jeff would explain things to him.

MOT: It was sort of another version of asking Jeff to make instructions so that someone else could play Twinkle on his bells. Except now the instructions would be "personalized" for Robbie; the generalized "someone else" was a specific person.

MET: Sounds like show-and-tell to me.

JEANNE: Right, Met, and the "showing" part makes things much easier than just "telling," as we shall see.

MET: Of course. *Demonstrating* saves lots of words, to say nothing of numbers, line-ups, symbolic space, and all that.

JEANNE: Indeed. Anyhow, before Robbie came, Jeff and I agreed that he would show Robbie "all the different ways of building Twinkle." And

Figure 12–1

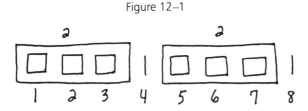

Jeff's new version for playing Twinkle on his figural bell-path

that is exactly what he did. Robbie came along a few days later, look-ing eager but a little confused about what this was all about. After introductions, but very little by way of explanation, Jeff started right in. He built his figural bell-path and told Robbie you could play Twinkle on it.

MOT: I guess that's the first sign that Jeff hadn't wiped out his earlier ways of doing things. I mean, he still remembered how to build the tune his old way.

JEANNE: That's true. Then, with the figural bell-path on the table, Jeff made "instructions" on paper for Robbie, but without actually play-ing the tune for him first.

MET: I assume his instructions were also his old figural ones, in which case we have another example of not wiping out the past.

JEANNE: Yes and no. This was his new version (see Figure 12–1).

MOT: That's pretty interesting. The old lines that were stick-figure pic-tures of the bells have turned into boxes.

MET: Yes, Jeff's boxes seem to have become a real notational convention for him. Born out of the troubles with his lines-as-hits in his *transi-tional* notation, they show up here in his *figural* notation.

MOT: And the single-hit bells are drawn differently from the double-hit bells—again, like the way they were in his transitional notation.

MET: In fact, Jeff is using a kind of classification scheme here. The big boxes that enclose the three smaller boxes group bells together ac-cording to their "hit properties": all the double-hit bells are grouped together and separated from the single-hit bells. He's really being very explicit in this new notation. I mean, even though *he* knows that the boxes mean to hit a bell twice, for Robbie he's not taking anything for granted; he puts in the 2's as well.

MOT: I guess he must have remembered that from your bothering him about it in his transitional notation, Jeanne. It's really funny—like reading history back on itself. This notation is for his first, *figural* bell-

path, and you can see there's still a one-to-one correspondence between bells and graphics; but the graphics themselves, the boxes,
come from a *later* notation made for the transitional bell-path.

MET: That's right; and I guess that's a pretty clear example of mapping—at least mapping one notation onto another.

JEANNE: It's a little like transcribing the early notation for medieval
chant into modern music notation. In the process we read onto the
chant itself the kinds of entities that are implicit in our modern notation, but those entities weren't necessarily present at the time. For
instance, I've even seen bar lines in modern chant notation, and the
music itself was certainly not metric. Similarly, in making his new notation with its implicit classification by "hit-properties," Jeff reads
back onto his old figural strategy entities that probably weren't present at the time—I mean when he was thinking of the tune purely
figurally. It reminds me of something I read the other day in a different
context: "We seem always to parse the past in the present tense."

MOT: If you mean by "parsing" the way you group or "chunk" something, like the parts of a sentence, then Jeff is certainly parsing his past
notation in *his* "present tense." What did Robbie make of the notation?

JEANNE: Jeff explained how the "instructions" worked, using a good
deal of pointing , along with a few words. According to my notes, just
about all Jeff said was, "You play this one and this one two times
[pointing to the first two white bells], and you play these once [point-
ing to the brown bells]."

MOT: So even there, he told Robbie only about the single and double
hits. Was that enough for Robbie to play the tune?

JEANNE: Yes, it worked just fine.

MET: But I assume that Robbie knew Twinkle. I don't think it would
have been so easy otherwise.

JEANNE: You're right, Met. Again, it's like earlier music notations; the
squiggles that made up these notations only worked because the
monks who used them knew the tunes already. The notation was
more of a mnemonic device—it just helped to recall the tune.

MOT: It's really interesting how Jeff's story keeps bringing up other his-
tories. But what happened next in our *present* story?

JEANNE: When Robbie had finished with the figural version, Jeff moved
right on. He took away the matching brown bells and built the tune
using just the white bells.

MOT: You mean his "transitional bell-path"?

JEANNE: Yes. And it was interesting that Jeff had trouble again around the first switch-back.

MET: I could imagine that he was just as glad to forget that version. After all, it was such an "in-between" thing, and besides you really forced Jeff into it.

MOT: Oh, come on, Met, I don't think it was as bad as you make it sound. It's true that Jeanne forced the *issues* and the confusions that followed. But I thought it was pretty amazing how Jeff worked his way through it and came out the other end with some really new ideas.

JEANNE: And he worked himself out of his troubles this time too, in short order. Once he had the bells arranged, Jeff made his same transitional notation—remember, with the boxes and the arrows?

MOT: How did Jeff explain the arrows and the switch-backs?

JEANNE: Pretty much the same way as he had explained the figural notation. He showed Robbie how the first arrow worked, and that seemed to do it. He said, "When you're on this one [pointing to the A-bell], then you go back to this one [pointing along the arrow to the G-bell]" (see Figure 12–2).

MOT: And could Robbie follow that arrow notation?

JEANNE: It took a little time, and a bit of fumbling around, but with Jeff's help, he got it.

MET: Jeff is checking out his instructions this way, too. They seem to work pretty well for Robbie. But then, I guess that's not so surprising; after all, these early notations of his are really graphic. As Jeanne said, this one is like a trail map or maybe like a treasure-hunt map. But I wonder what Robbie will do with Jeff's formal notation?

JEANNE: We'll see in a minute. But first something else happened that was really interesting. I put the brown bells back in the bell-path, and asked Robbie to play the tune again. That was no problem. When he

Figure 12–2

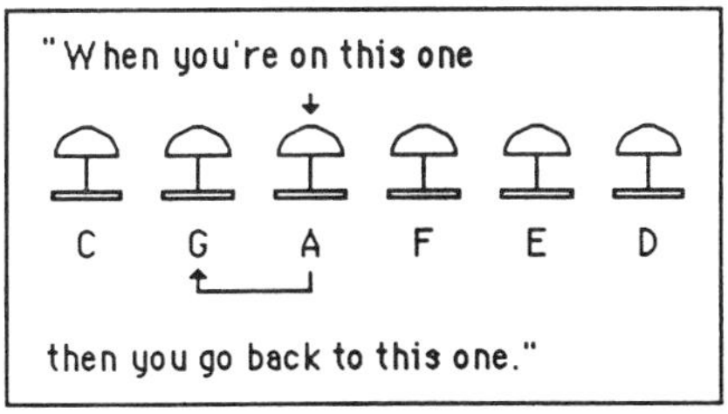

Figure 12–3

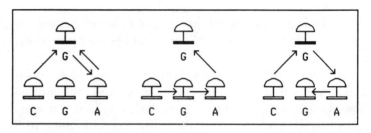

different ways you could use the bells to play the beginning of Twinkle

finished, I couldn't help probing a little. I asked Robbie, "How come it works either way?" Robbie said, "I don't know." But then he played around with the bells for a while and in the process, quite on his own, he *discovered the brown and white matches.*

MOT: That's neat. It's like watching Jeff's process in reverse.

JEANNE: I hadn't thought of it that way, but why not? Anyhow, Robbie's discovery led to a new game that both boys played together. The game was to find all the different ways you could use both the white G-bell and the matching brown G-bell to play the beginning of Twinkle (see Figure 12–3).

MET: What a great invention! And what a good way to pull apart the action-path from the sequence of tune-events. It even pulls apart function in the tune from pitch-property. I mean, in those examples the brown G-bell functions as a middle *and* as an end, or *only* as an end, or *only* as a middle. And the white G-bell does almost the same— they're totally interchangeable.

MOT: In fact, it's almost like Jeff's big switcheroo. Only in this game, instead of moving the bells—switching *them* around—the kids switched their *moves* around. It reminds me of other games kids play—like seeing how many different paths you can make, jumping from one rock to another, but still keeping some part of the order the same. In this game, one G-bell or the other always has to come in between the other two bells.

MET: Yes, it's like permutations of the same path. If you called the G-bells 2 and 4, then either one of those has to alternate with 1 and 3, which have to stay put (see Figure 12–4). Then you can go 1-2-3-4; or 1-4-3-2; or 1-2-3-2; or 1-4-3-4. I think those are all the possible permutations if you follow those rules.

Figure 12–4

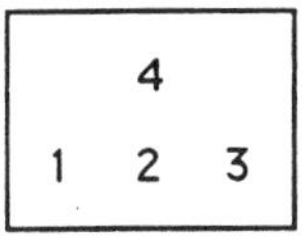

	4	
1	2	3

call the G-bells 2 and 4 and alternate them with 1 and 3

MOT: *Permutations?* But what has that got to do with Twinkle, or even music, for that matter?

MET: I don't know, exactly. Maybe it's a way of *abstracting* the pattern of pitch-relations from the tune—you keep the pitch-sequence the same, but fool around with the sequence of moves on the bells themselves. It seems to me that a lot of Jeff's evolving depends on switching his focus and making changes in what's moving and what's standing still. As Mot said, sometimes he's moving the bells around and sometimes he keeps the bells the same but moves himself around. I think that's important, somehow.

JEANNE: It seemed so to me, too, at the time, Met. We'll have to think about it some more. Anyhow, the boys had a good time with it. But we had better move on. So far Jeff had built his figural bell-path and his transitional bell-path, and made instructions for both. I must say I was really pleased to see that he had hung on to those different representations of the tune.

MOT: I guess that's multiple representations, all right.

JEANNE: But the next thing that happened really amazed me. At the end of their game, when it was time to build the scale-path, the bells somehow ended up in their pure figural form. Well, Jeff proceeded to turn that figural bell-path into the scale-path in one quick move.

MET: I don't get it.

JEANNE: Neither did I, at first, even though I watched him do it. He just grabbed the last six bells in one bunch and turned them around on their axis (see Figure 12–5).

MET: That is truly amazing. It never occurred to me that Twinkle had the scale right in it, only backwards! I mean, if we accept the convention that "forward" means that low to high goes left to right. But you know, in order to see the scale at all, you really have to cut right across the boundary of the two figures.

MOT: Wait a minute. I'm totally confused. You mean if you ignore the

Figure 12–5

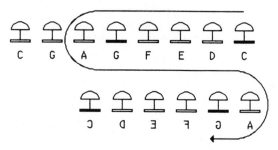

grabbed the last six bells and turned them around on their axis

Figure 12–6

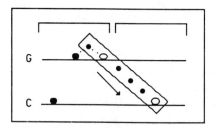

you start in the middle of the first figure, then the pitches go straight down

way we've been grouping the tune into *figures* all along . . . Oh, I get it. In fact, if you start in the middle of the first figure, on the A, then the pitches go straight down from there.

JEANNE: Exactly. Maybe you can see it better if you look at my old diagram of the tune (see Figure 12–6).

MOT: But that's a whole different way of thinking and seeing the tune. How did Jeff know that that would work?

JEANNE: I can only make a hunch. I suppose that in working with this tune, with the bells and with notations, in so many different ways, he really knew it inside out—if you'll pardon the pun. I suppose that's really just another way of saying that he had multiple mental representations of the tune.

MET: But that makes it sound so intellectual. It seems to me that these "mental representations" you're talking about are very closely tied in to Jeff's actually *handling* the bells—moving *them* around, moving *himself* around on them—and doing that in real time and real space. After all, the flip that made the figural bell-path into the scale-path is also an *action,* a move. He has multiple ways of *seeing;* or maybe multiple ways of seeing *possibilities.*

MOT: I see what you mean, Met. In fact, a lot of Jeff's transformations are new ways of ordering or grouping the bells—new boundary-making. For instance, the scale-path is another way of ordering or lining up the bells; and this last flip involved regrouping the bells—literally seeing them in a new way.

JEANNE: Yes, but seeing in a new way doesn't just happen; it has to involve new ways of *thinking,* too. The two are really happening together. As Ben Shahn said in talking about the evolution of a painting: "It is an intimately communicative affair between the painter and the painting, a conversation back and forth, the painting telling the painter even as it receives its shape and form."

MOT: But still, this whole story of Jeff and Robbie convinces me, anyway, that Jeff certainly had not wiped out his earlier representations—or "ways of seeing," if you insist, Met. It's clear that Jeff can make and use any one of his multiple "possibilities," that he can choose among them as he needs to, and furthermore, that he can map one onto another. Maybe you would be satisfied, Met, if we just said he "had them all in hand."

MET: I'll rest my case with that one, Mot.

MOT: But what about Jeff's notation? How did he explain his formal notation to Robbie, and what did Robbie make of it?

JEANNE: Actually, that's very much to the point. Jeff made his formal notation, just as it had been before. What Robbie made of it is clear from what he said, even before Jeff could say anything. Robbie looked at the notation and said, "Oh, I see; you hit this one once [pointing to the first bell] and this one five times [pointing to the second bell]" (see Figure 12–7).

MOT: Oh dear. It looks like Robbie has a fix on numbers as hits.

Figure 12–7

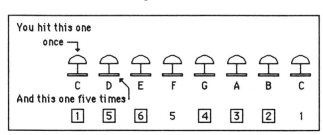

MET: And why not? That's what numbers meant before. We call that "learning."

MOT: But it makes you realize the complexity of Jeff's notation. The two line-ups—bells and bell-boxes—are both going along left-to-right, but they don't go along together; they don't simply match up anymore.

MET: Yes, that's my whole thing about the transformation machine. Robbie's confusion makes it clear that there is a transformation going on in Jeff's notation, and Robbie doesn't understand it.

MOT: So what did Jeff do?

JEANNE: I'm afraid he resorted to showing instead of telling. He just played Twinkle on the scale for Robbie. After one or two tries, Robbie was able simply to imitate what he saw Jeff do.

MOT: So Jeff never did try to explain how the notation worked?

JEANNE: That's right.

MET: Do you think he couldn't explain it? Or was it just too much trouble? After all, given what Jeff probably knew about Robbie and his troubles with numbers, it would have to be a pretty long story.

JEANNE: I suspect it was the latter; and I think I may have evidence for that. But I'll have to tell you another story. In April, I had written to Jeff's mother (Mrs. G.) telling her what we had been doing and asking her to come visit the Lab. A few days after Robbie had been in, Jeff's mother came. Jeff seemed really eager to *explain* things to her. He showed her a lot of the computer stuff first, and then when we got to the bells, he jumped right into the formal version of Twinkle. He built the scale, showed his mother the notation for it, and asked her to play the tune. Mrs. G. didn't get it at all. And now Jeff *did* explain. Apparently now it was worth the trouble—maybe because he figured his mother ought to be able to get it. Jeff explained: "The 5 here means you play the fifth one, see?" And he showed her how to count up, 1-2-3-4-5, on the bells. But Mrs. G. was still quite confused. Jeff went over it again, asking his mother to try it but without actually showing her. Mrs. G. never did quite get it. So Jeff finally showed her—played Twinkle on the scale-path—and it was clear that Mrs. G. was very impressed. So was Jeff; he looked really pleased. I guess it gave Jeff a real kick, knowing how to do something that his mother *didn't* know how to do.

MOT: That's a really nice story. It must have convinced Jeff that he had done something pretty far-out and complicated in his formal notation. And, considering that he wasn't all that great in school, this must have been a real turn-on for him.

MET: Well, I suppose I have to admit that Jeff probably knows Twinkle better and in more different ways than anyone else in the world. But I still have a question. It may sound sort of unkind, but I don't mean it that way. I really want to hear what you have to say, Jeanne.

JEANNE: Please, go ahead.

MET: It's this: How come you didn't just teach Jeff to play Twinkle on the piano? Wouldn't that have saved a lot of time and trouble? After all, his "general-purpose instrument" is basically a piano keyboard, isn't it?

JEANNE: I'm glad you asked, and I don't think it's an unkind question at all. In fact, it's not only quite appropriate but it gives me a chance to say some things I really care about. Let me begin by suggesting to you that this whole long process began with Jeff *coming to know what he knew already.* Do you understand what I mean by that?

MET: I remember we talked about how Jeff's notations, for instance, helped *you* to know what Jeff knew already. And that was true about his particular confusions, too. But I don't quite see how that helped *Jeff* to know what he knew already. Doesn't that require a kind of ability to look *at,* to reflect *on,* what you're doing and to make what you find very explicit?

JEANNE: Not necessarily, Met. I don't mean to suggest that Jeff's "knowing" what he knew was of the same sort as mine or yours and Mot's, for that matter. Remember Jeff's first tune constructions and notations for HOT and Twinkle? I would suggest that he came to know what he knew only as he built those bell-paths and made those notations. And even those didn't emerge full-blown—he *practiced* them, experimented, worked them out over and over again. And in doing that work, making those *external* actions that he could see and feel, he was also coming to know what he knew.

MOT: So "reflection" doesn't need to be in words.

JEANNE: That's right. Reflection can be quite silent—maybe it most often is. It is embedded in actions and responsive to actions, as well. Each bell construction out there on the table, and each of Jeff's descriptions on paper, became "things to think with." The bells were objects to be played *with* and also to be played *on.* And as palpable, external manifestations of his inner thinking, they also *held still;* they reflected *back* to him. The process of arranging and rearranging and of listening back to the results was a process of *reciprocal reflection,* and that "conversation back and forth" helped Jeff to crystallize and to internalize a particular way, his way, of representing the tunes.

MOT: But wasn't it that same kind of process that led Jeff to restructure his representations at moments when you disturbed them? As Met said before, it was in actually handling the bells, moving *them* around, moving *himself* around on them, improvising in the midst of confusion, that the potential for new ways of seeing emerged. Each one of his constructions and descriptions turned into a particular way of shaping his experience. And what fascinates me in all of this is the way each *present* moment, each new modification, always contained *past* experiences in it, too.

MET: So what you're saying is that each new transformation has Jeff's personal history of this tune embedded in it.

MOT: Exactly that, Met. And we just saw an example of it in Jeff's revisiting his own history in the Robbie story.

MET: You mean the transitional bell-box becoming a convention that crept back into his figural notation, for instance?

MOT: Right.

MET: And I see more clearly now what you meant, Jeanne, when you said that reflection isn't necessarily in words; it isn't even necessarily a stop-and-think. Reflection happens. And it probably helps to account for those otherwise mysterious moments when you say, "Oh, I get it!" and for Jeff's on-the-spot inventions, too.

JEANNE: Does what you're both saying help to answer your question, Met?

MET: Well, partially. I suppose, for one thing, if you had just given Jeff a ready-made instrument and an off-the-shelf notation, neither of them would have had any history in his own experience.

MOT: And considering all the work that went into the evolution of his quasi-standard notation, I wonder what the real thing—the standard notation—could have meant to Jeff if you had given it to him right at the beginning? Without that history it surely would have meant something else, or maybe not much at all. From what we've seen of Jeff and his ways of staying true to *his* understandings, he probably would have just turned off.

MET: I see what you're saying. And I suppose that even if he had given it a try, he would have been stuck with only those kinds of features, just those entities, that are captured in standard notation.

MOT: Exactly! It would be the *only* way, and sort of laid on—a *fait accompli.* All that work Jeff did and all those confusions gave a very special meaning to his formal notation when he eventually got to it. It was a *possible* view, one among many—for instance, and most especially, it leaves out a view that pays attention to figures and to the functions of events within them. And furthermore, as we just saw, Jeff wasn't even stuck with his last, formal representation—he could access all his representations; he could find one in the other, map one onto the other. And I suppose in doing that, he was also shifting his focus from one aspect of the tune to another.

MET: Yes. Whatever Jeff has learned is, in a way, his own invention, the result of his working experiments; it has evolved from the *inside out.* If you had just given Jeff the standard stuff at the beginning, it would have been a construct imposed from the *outside in.*

MOT: And like other laid-on constructs, it probably wouldn't ever have become his own. In fact, maybe the most important thing in all this is Jeff's new sense of himself as someone who can learn. That must have been especially important considering his other experiences in school.

MET: But it's a particular way of learning. It reminds me of myself sometimes. It's a kind of learning where you recognize in a new situation a version of some previous one that's already familiar. It's like when I find in some problem-set a problem that I've never seen before; the first thing I do is to say, "Hey, what have I seen before that's sort of like this?" I may be wrong on the first hunch, but then I try another. Learning how to do that turns out to be a pretty powerful tool for learning anything. I suppose that's a kind of reflection, too—the past *reflecting forward* into the present. And in the process the new problem makes sense, but the old situation, the one that's serving as a prototype, takes on new meaning too. It's as if the prototype has grown and changed by finding a new version of itself.

MOT: I could imagine something like that happening if Jeanne took Jeff to the piano *now.* For instance, he might see the keyboard as a version of his familiar scale-ordered bells. And if he did, he could probably find the pitches for Twinkle and play it right off. If she gave him standard notation now, he might see that as a version of his last notation. Even if he didn't get it right off, I should think it would be a lot easier to explain to him how it works—after all, the basic idea of the notation is something he already invented.

MET: But at the same time, he wouldn't be locked into just that one notation; his own experience tells him that formal notations are only one story of a tune. For instance, I would imagine that it would be easier for Jeff to hear that middle C on the piano, which is always in the same place on the keyboard and in the score, doesn't always *sound* the same. His history provides him with the potential for multiple views—multiple representations, as Jeanne has been calling them all along.

JEANNE: It looks as if you've answered your own question, Met.

MET: But you had a lot to do with it too, just as you did with what and how Jeff learned. Do you think, for instance, that he would ever have left his figural approach without your probing and questioning?

JEANNE: I guess we'll never know. But I can tell you this: in traditional ways of teaching kids to play the piano, the focus in the beginning is usually on what's in the score. So there's a lot of emphasis on learning to count and to play "in time," naming pitches, and getting them off the score onto the keyboard. But then we despair as beginning students play rigidly, almost doggedly—with every beat marked, every downbeat doubly marked. At this point we tell the student that he or she needs to play "more musically," to "put in the phrasing," or even to "play with feeling." Then much later, in advanced music theory classes, we have to work at helping students to deal with structural functions. After they've learned to measure intervals and recognize them as the same *in spite of context,* they often find it very confusing to consider and to hear the changing meaning of a pitch or a figure as it's embedded in new contexts. It's the same with rhythm: we have to teach students to pay attention to *figural groupings,* to "phrasing," in contrast to the metric units that so visibly dominate the printed score.

So what we're doing is asking students to learn to do what they probably knew how to do already, long before—to hear figures and figural functions when they were probably intuitively hearing just those kinds of entities and relations. If we recognize these intuitions at all, we tend to think of them as belonging to a different world: the features captured by formal notation are public, available for scrutiny, and thus teachable; figural hearing is private, a matter of "personal expression," difficult to communicate, even a matter of "innate talent"—either you've got it or you haven't. Sometimes I think that if children manage to develop their figural/functional hearing and to learn how it intersects with the pitch-property universe, it's more in spite of our teaching than because of it.

MET: There's one other thing that I've been meaning to say for a long time. Maybe I've sort of said it before, but it's this: Not only the way Jeff learned, but all this business of what is an entity, a "thing," constructing and reconstructing boundaries depending on what kinds of features you're paying attention to and at what level of detail, and the nesting of entities within one another—all of that seems to me so much like the way we do math and science. I mean, I never expected, when we started these conversations, that learning about learning about music would show me, an MIT computer science student, something about *how* I learn and about *what* I'm learning, too. That's a very unexpected result of all this.

MOT: I have something to say about that, too, only maybe it's the opposite. As a humanities major, I started out thinking that learning music, and maybe music itself, was mostly an intuitive thing—either you get it or you don't. It wasn't something you *think* about; in fact I kind of resented the idea of thinking about it. But now I feel as if things have been turned on their head. There is certainly thinking going on, and furthermore, it seems to be a kind of thinking that I thought I wasn't good at. It makes me see that "being analytical" doesn't have to mean being cold and dry or leaving yourself—your feelings and your senses—aside. Quite the contrary—now I have a whole new way of approaching subjects that didn't especially interest me; like Jeff, I'm learning to go from the inside out. Instead of just sitting there and staring at a problem, I'm beginning to play with possibilities, to improvise, and to pay attention to what happens.

JEANNE: What I seem to hear each of you saying is that puzzling over Jeff's story and the children's rhythm drawings has liberated aspects of your own learning that until now have remained hidden in that great meld of experience we call "going to school." If so, I think that these new insights are due not only to what you have seen in the children's work, but also to the differences between the two of you—your attraction to the humanities, Mot, and yours to computer science, Met—and most of all to your willingness to confront and grapple with your respective views. I'm talking especially about your willingness to look for and to reassess those learned and internalized assumptions that have so strongly influenced your individual ways of constructing coherence in the world around you. Learning how to do *that* helped us to see implications in the children's work that go beyond what a single view such as mine could have achieved. And finally, I have to say that I had hoped our conversations might result in just that kind of reflection on your own learning; what you've both said just now reassures me that perhaps this hidden part of my agenda has been successfully played out, too.

SUMMING UP: COMMENTS AND SPECULATIONS

Stepping back from these cumulating stories and conversations, it would seem useful now to ask: what does Jeff's story tell us about the more general course of developing musical intelligence? Looking back at the processes that characterized Jeff's evolution from his initially figural strategies of construction and his embodied descriptions of tunes, through his transitional phase, to his formal construction and his symbolic description, we observed the following critical moves:

- His growing capacity to pull apart the initially singular representational space, to differentiate the multiple aspects of the tune, and to hold them steady in spite of change in position or context.
- His growing capacity to build new coordinating structures which not only include but give new meaning to the multiple aspects that have gained independence from one another.
- His growing capacity to distance himself from a dependence on objects and actions on them as the singular means for representing the tune and its structure.
- Finally, his capacity to invent a rulelike system which could be expressed symbolically rather than iconically, to show the intersection between two separate and independent ordered series.

Generalizing from these observations of Jeff's work, it would seem that a crucial part of that process through which change in inner strategies for constructing musical relations occurs is one of *progressive articulation:* a gradual coming apart of the possible features and relations of musical structures that are initially taken as unitary wholes and that are rigid particularly in their sequential ordering. As a result of this rigidity, the constituents of musical structures—for example, pitch, duration, tune-events, their embodiment in the bells, and the sequence of actions on them—can at first only be given meaning in the *fixed order in which they occur,* next-next-next.

The dependence on the chronological or serially ordered nature of representations in the early stages of development is reflected in F. C. Bartlett's general comments on the construction of "schemata" through which we represent, remember, and act upon past experiences:

> Whenever there is any order or regularity of behavior, a particular response is possible only because it is related to other similar responses *which have been serially organized,* yet which operate, not simply as individual members coming one after the other, but as a *unitary mass* . . . Every incoming change

contributes its part to the total "schema" of the moment *in the order in which it occurs*. That is to say, when we have movements a,b,c,d, in this order, our "plastic postural model" of ourselves at the moment d is made depends, not merely upon the direction, extent and intensity of a,b,c,d, but also upon the *chronological order* in which they have occurred . . . So in order to maintain the "schema" as it is . . . a,b,c,d must continue to be done, and must continue to be done *in the same order*. (Bartlett 1932, p. 203; emphasis mine)

And in anticipation of the conditions that might liberate mental representation (or "schemata") from their dependence on the fixed order of occurrence, Bartlett says, almost poignantly: "If only the organism could find some way in which it can break up this chronological order and rove more or less at will in any order over the events which have built up its present momentary 'schemata' " (p. 203).

We might compare this dependence on the fixed spatial and temporal ordering of objects and actions during the initial stages of musical development with a dependence on just such spatially ordered objects during the initial phases in the development of an understanding of arithmetic relations. Consider, for example, the use of fingers for counting or the abacus for doing calculations. In both cases, the properties of numbers are locked into the fixed order of the objects that embody these properties, and operations on them depend on an ordered series of actions on these objects. As Richard Feynman puts it in describing the work of a man who was a real virtuoso in the use of the abacus: "I realized something: he doesn't *know* numbers. With the abacus . . . all you have to do is learn how to push the little beads up and down . . . you just know that when you add 9, you push a ten's bead up and pull a one's bead down. So we're slower at basic arithmetic, but we know numbers. Furthermore, the whole idea of an approximate method was beyond him . . . So I never could teach him how I did cube roots" (Feynman 1985, p. 178).

Through a process of growing mobility and deconstruction of these unitary wholes, the various features of a tune which at first remained unnoticed become liberated from the meld, and this process needs to occur over and over again in different ways: at each stage new entities, new features are made to come into existence, requiring in turn the mental construction of new relations and new coordinating schemata. And as features and relations become accessible for manipulation and scrutiny and are coordinated in new ways, the coordinations form the basis for the construction of stable *general structures* in terms of which particular, unique instances can be described, compared, and understood.

Over longer periods of time, through the continuing process of construction and reconstruction, other *possible* relations will emerge leading to an evolving network of intersecting relations which can be perceived or sometimes only imagined at all levels of structure and among all dimensions. As Piaget puts it: "Equilibrium is reached when all previous schemata are embedded in present ones and intelligence can equally well reconstruct past schemata by means of present ones and vice versa" (Piaget 1960, p. 146).

Indeed, given what we have observed in Jeff's work so far, we can imagine the direction these processes might take. For instance, as long as pitch and time remain "qualities" that are locked into the objects and actions/events that are currently present (and this is still the case at the end of Jeff's work), the potential for constructing relations and for constructing new meaning remains limited by the given *spatial or temporal chronology of these objects*. A later stage might include the capacity to mentally disengage pitch relations from the objects and actions that embody them. In doing so, these relations, which have been associated only with positions in the given ordering of these objects, can become "thought-relations" and "thought-actions," mentally freed from any fixed positions in space and limited only by imagination and thought. For instance, in giving number-names to the bells as arranged in the linear, low-to-high ordered series, these number-names for Jeff referred most explicitly only to the *positions* of the bells in this fixed series. In turn, all tune-events that are matched in pitch with a particular position in the series are named the same. While this was a critical move in Jeff's development, this systematic notation failed to capture the changing *structural functions* of these events—an aspect of a tune that had played such a prominent role in Jeff's figural constructions and notations. But when, in the course of later development, pitch properties can be disengaged from the objects that embody them and from their position in a particular linear ordering, these numbers as referring to pitch properties within a tune can regain some of the functional meanings that Jeff's notation lost. Moreover, in thinking and hearing in terms of pitch relations themselves rather than in terms of the positions of objects that embody them, the structure of one tune can be compared with that of another. And in the course of making such comparisons, certain common structural "plans" emerge—those which I have earlier called "structural simples."

But still, an essential reciprocity must remain between an immediate momentary perception and its not yet articulated formal implications.

Indeed, it was just such reciprocities between an unexpected discovery, on one hand, and its implications for liberating new and different kinds of features and relations, on the other, that we saw so often in Jeff's work—for instance, the still-to-be-realized implications in Jeff's discovery of the bell that he "had already." To elaborate on this, consider an experience, not unusual among musicians, where one has a vague, momentary apprehension of some kind of *similarity relation,* but now between two musical passages rather than just two melodic events that are separated from each other in time. Hearing this similarity depends, first, upon the two distanced passages being somehow (often quite spontaneously) juxtaposed in thought. The apprehension of similarity depends upon mentally going backward or forward in time, free of the fixed chronology of the piece, or, as in Jeff's case, the fixed chronology of actions on an instrument in playing it. However, at the moment when the apprehension of similarity occurs, the particular features that generate this perceived similarity may still be hidden in the apprehension itself. But upon puzzling over and *mentally practicing* the apprehended relation, the subtle bases for the "hearing" will often emerge. As Kuhn puts it in talking about scientific discovery, one sees (or hears) a similarity without being able to say with respect to what (Kuhn 1977). Probing for the bases of this spontaneously apprehended similarity suggests a puzzle which, in turn, charts a course for work to be done. The outcome of the probes (which may be carried out over long periods) leads to the articulation of the similarity relations; features and relations of both passages are "liberated" which, in their given chronology, remained unrecognized. The new features and relations that emerge in carrying out this investigation may lead, just as they did for Jeff, not only to a mental restructuring, perhaps a new formal understanding, but to actually coming to "see" the phenomenon itself in new ways. It is through just such processes, then, that the vast network of *possible* musical relations for "making meaning" is continuously emerging and intersecting as one learns to hear these relations in the unfolding of large complex works.

This, then, is what I mean by multiple hearings and the multiple mental organizing strategies which we may presume are shaping them. I include here the apprehensions that are dependent on the direct chronology of events/actions and on their immediate, local contextual meanings, as well as those that are distanced in time and thus dependent on "thought relations" through which we invent and give meaning to structures that have not yet happened or recognize new implications in those that have. This includes the unique meaning which we find (or make) in individual works, together with the general structures that underlie their particular coherence—the two together generating the complexity, the artistry, that we associate with "great works."

The goal of the continuing course of musical learning and development, then, is to be able to choose selectively and at will among these multiple mental organizing strategies and the multiple foci of attention that they guide. In this way, listeners and performers (and performers must, after all, be the most active listeners) are able to move freely among the multiple intersecting dimensions of a work, shifting their attention at will so as to develop multiple hearings, finally choosing the one or the combination of several that seems best to reflect the critical intersection of detail and larger design that generates the unique coherence of the work.

CHAPTER 13

Conclusion:
Educational Implications

I BEGAN this book with the observation that the questions I have found compelling most often emerged in the natural course of everyday events as I worked with students in the classroom. And I added that events attracted my attention when they were surprising or unexpected because they implicitly challenged some deeply held tacit assumption. By way of accountability, I would now like to revisit some of the stories I have told in order to ask not only where did my questions come from, but also where do the answers go? In particular, I would like to consider what we can learn from these studies that can be applied not only to music but to teaching and learning in other domains as well— that is, to children in their everyday work in classrooms. For instance, could the rhythm studies and the observations of Jeff's work help us to account for those moments when the understanding between teachers and students breaks down? And could such an accounting help, in turn, to guide teachers' next moves at those frustrating moments when their students seem unable to learn? In what follows I will revisit events that most clearly illustrate issues that suggest starting points for answering these questions.

I begin with a finding that continued to gain importance throughout the studies, namely the power of descriptions to both *reveal and conceal.* While this is not often recognized in school settings, the studies showed that common descriptive conventions such as those we teach as normal fare in schooling can subtly constrain the *kinds* of things we choose or are even able to describe. Putting it more strongly, the studies showed that conventional symbol systems, such as music notation, numbers, or the signs that refer to functions in arithmetic, select for attention certain aspects of the material to which they refer, and in doing so, the symbols carry implicit assumptions concerning the kinds of objects and relations we take to exist in a domain. Moreover, once these conventions for describing have been internalized through learning and practice, they become a transparent lens through which we seem to see and hear spontaneously. Thus, as we look through it but rarely at it, the lens *conceals* its power to shape and to organize our perceptions—to aggregate, bound, and determine what we see or hear as the same and as different.

For example, take the common expression $7 + 7 = 14$, and consider what is implicit in the symbols + and = . Do we mean by that expression that 7 *and* 7 *is the same* as 14? And what could have gone wrong when Jeff told me on the first day we met that "7 and 7 is 77"? Jeff was obviously seeing the symbols + and = differently from the way he was expected to, and he was also giving a different meaning to the term "and" as well as the term "is." But interestingly, the meanings he is giving to these terms are also embedded in our conventional use of them. For instance, the meanings Jeff assumes for "is" as well as "and" are quite appropriate in answer to a common school question such as, "What is I and T?"; a quite acceptable answer might be, "I *and* T *is* IT." This is an example of what I meant when I observed that the everyday events I marked for attention were those that were surprising because they created conflict or tension with respect to my until-then tacit assumptions. But if conventions and their implicit assumptions can become transparent to the uses we put them to, how do we ever bring them to the surface to be looked *at?*

The image of internalized descriptive conventions as a lens suggests another image, that of a windshield. A windshield is also a glass, and you can do three different kinds of things with a windshield: you can look *through* it in order to focus your attention on the road ahead as you drive; you can look *at* it if, for instance, something on the glass is obstructing your view and you want to see what it is (but that shift in focus might endanger your view of events ahead and also your safety); and the glass can also *reflect back* to you: you can see yourself in it, but that is best done when the car is standing still—a kind of stop-and-think. Descriptions can be put to all these uses, too. As in driving a car, we mostly look *through* a description, the marks on paper becoming transparent to their meaning, or to what they tell us to do next. But when there is something obstructing that transparent view, something you don't understand, something in an expression that interferes with going ahead, you might look *at* the word or expression to see just what it is that's making the trouble. And finally, descriptions can also *reflect back*. As Met said about his own descriptions, "When I put something down on paper, then everything that was sort of floating around in my head holds still; I can look at it, talk to it, have a conversation with it." And as in using a windshield to reflect back, using a description to reflect back is most often associated with a pause in moving on with your work—a kind of stop-and-think.

How does this imagery help us to understand how and what a child is learning in school, and how that learning may be going astray? This is where the power of descriptions to reveal comes in. For looking *at* a child's invented description can help to reveal what he intends us to see in looking *through* it. For instance, in looking at the children's drawings of rhythms, I found that they could reveal the kinds of features their makers were paying attention to and how these might differ from the features we implicitly see in looking through the conventions of music notation. But at the same time these invented descriptions revealed the meanings their makers were giving to the descriptive conventions they had learned. For instance, as in most line-ups of symbols on paper, moving left-to-right across the paper was used to mean going onward in time, and making bigger spaces between lines or circles was used to mean that there was more time between the events (claps) that these marks stood for. But an invented description can only reveal if we take it seriously, and as I showed through the conversations with Met and Mot, that is not always easy to do even in the best of circumstances.

In school settings it becomes even more difficult. Seeing a child's anomalous description in the midst of the pressures and demands of the classroom, it is easier to mark the child's answer as simply wrong, and tempting just to "turn it aside and call it an exception, an aberration, a contaminant," as McClintock said of "so many good clues." To notice the invention as interesting or useful requires looking *at* it, letting it reflect back to you; and just as in looking at the windshield, this means interrupting or even endangering the going ahead. To look at a puzzling description, and most of all to look at rather than through the lens that is shaping the materials, most likely means a stop-and-think on the part of both teacher and student.

But there is another kind of reflecting as well, which Don Schön and I have called *reflection-in-action* (Bamberger and Schön 1979, 1991; Schön 1983). Instances of reflection-in-action are quite common in teaching, but they are uncommonly difficult to notice. And this is precisely because the reflecting is embedded in the teacher's and the student's continuing actions rather than in a stop-and-think. For instance, upon hearing a child's puzzling response to a question, a teacher will notice some clue in it, and grabbing the clue "on the wing," she will respond with a probing remark. Then, continuing to pursue the child's response, she may follow the first probe with another. As in my work with Jeff, these conversations back and forth, with each participant's response reflecting off that of the other, are often critically revealing in two ways: first, they may help the child to recognize *his* way of seeing the materials, and at the same time to recognize the mismatch between his view and the teacher's; second, the probe, as an on-the-spot experiment, will often help the teacher to test a hunch, albeit one that is probably unarticulated. That is, the probe is initially motivated by what teachers will describe after the fact as an "intuitive" hunch concerning how the child is thinking about the materials at hand; and by observing the child's response to the probe, the teacher can confirm or disconfirm the validity of her hunch.

The problem is that once such interchanges happen, the moment seems to disappear, absorbed into the ongoing work of the class; thus the process becomes transparent to its effective result. These are important moments for learning, but exactly because they are most often looked *through,* the power of reflection-in-action as a critical means of teaching and learning also tends to disappear from view. And with the disappearance of the moment, the teacher's sensitivity and insight that generate these probes also disappear from *her* view. For instance, when I have asked teachers to recall such moments, they are hard put to come up with examples; indeed, it is usually only after I have been able to catch one actually happening that others will recognize instances of these improvised moments of reflection-in-action in their own work. These are, of course, just the kinds of moments I was referring to when I talked about the important convergence of teaching, learning, and research in effective schooling. But it is also the ephemeral nature of these powerful moments that makes it so difficult to account for and to describe what it is that those whom we think of as artist-teachers do so well.

Improvised experiments such as those I have seen in classrooms were a primary research tool in both the rhythm studies and later in my work with Jeff. I used the conversations with Met and Mot as a vehicle for playing out some of these moments; the dialogues showed what is involved in *recognizing* an improvised experiment and also suggested how one learns to *capture the results* before they disappear into the continuing flow of events. An essential part of that process was helping Met and Mot to confront and make explicit their differences with each other, while at the same time holding onto the possibility that each of them was making sense. Having learned to do that helped them later on to make sense of the children's anomalous drawings of rhythms and of puzzling moments in Jeff's work, too—what we called "giving a child reason." I am proposing now that, using Met and Mot's learning as an example, teachers can make better use of their on-the-spot experiments if they see these moments as an occasion for looking at their own ways of making sense of the materials at hand. At the same time, this will help them recognize the potential for differences between their understanding and the ways students are making sense of the "same" materials. To help in this regard, I will recall some of the on-the-spot experiments that I discussed with Met and Mot, pointing particularly to how their results revealed common conflicts between assumptions hidden in what we rather loosely call "the curriculum" and those that children may be holding.

One such assumption was that counting is simply a neutral and "objective" act. When Met, Mot, and I were looking for the sense the children *could* be making as they "put in numbers that seemed to fit" in their rhythm drawings, we were led, for example, to question just what was an object to be counted and also when to start counting over again with "1" in counting up. We found that while standard rhythm notation implicitly assumes that measured time units (beats and beat groups) are objects to be counted, for the children each action, each clapped event, was a thing to count. As for counting up, the drawings revealed that actions in clapping generate trajectories toward goals; in turn, arrivals at goals, which are not shown at all in standard notation, were particularly memorable because they formed the boundaries of *figures,* and these were also the boundaries within which to make a count-up. Given these bases for counting on and counting up, the children's numberings were clearly different from conventional counting of rhythms, and as such they were also solid clues to potential mismatches between "the curriculum" and the student.

Looking more closely at these count-ups, we found that they were clues to differing strategies for boundary-making as well. And once that was seen, the boundaries that were described by the count-ups also provided clues to the differences in kinds of features that children were at-

Figure 13–1

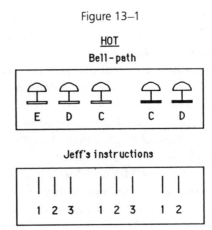

tending to. Thus, by probing for the sense that we were prepared to assume was hidden in the "objective" act of counting, we found that minds behind musical ears were constructing objects and marking features for attention that were specifically different from those that some of us, in internalizing standard rhythm notation, have come to take for granted as "simply there."

Later, in puzzling over Jeff's instructions for playing HOT on the bells, Met, Mot, and I discovered that he was also counting up within the boundaries of figures (Figure 13–1). While we thought at first that Jeff was giving names to the bells, our "thought experiments" through which we considered alternative possibilities demonstrated that the numbers were actually showing the *place* of both a bell and a tune-event inside of each melodic figure. But this only became clear when, in adding two more lines for bells that played the next figure, Jeff started over again with "1" to mark the beginning and ending of that new figure.

We found another use of numbers as well, but only as a result of my on-the-spot experiment during that same session. Asking Jeff to clap the rhythm of HA, then watching as he drew his claps on paper and added numbers, I saw that a count-up could also be packaged to show the number of *hits* on each bell. But with the two kinds of numbers representing two different kinds of things, they had to be kept neatly separate from each other—either one kind or the other (Figure 13–2).

These issues of counting, including the different uses and meanings given to numbers, illustrate the kinds of confusions that children may be facing, but they are issues that often remain unrecognized in school settings. Buried within tasks we give to children, the conflicts and confu-

Figure 13–2

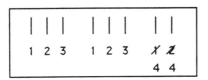

two kinds of numbers

sions between what a child takes to be a thing to count or the meaning he gives to the numbers he sees are often equally buried in what may at first appear to be simply "wrong answers." Learning to look *at* these confusions and reflecting on her own reflections-in-action, one teacher said: "[These confusions] . . . are critical in understanding where a kid is at. Because you're teaching this, and the kid is giving these weird answers. But if you can go over where the kid is looking from, and you look out from there, *that's exactly what he ought to be seeing*. And then what the kid was saying makes perfect sense" (quoted in Bamberger 1990).

An on-the-spot experiment in Jeff's very first tune-building session, reconstructing HOT with tuneblocks, illustrated another potential basis for conflict between teacher and student—a mismatch with respect to the *level of detail* at which teacher and student are focusing their attention. In an effort to probe Jeff's understanding of the referents for the tuneblocks HO and HA, I asked Jeff to shift from one medium to another—that is, I asked him to shift his attention from the virtual world of the computer as a medium for making music to the much more intimate medium of his own singing. The result was both surprising and revealing: responding to my request that he sing the tuneblock HO, Jeff sang not one HO but two. Puzzling over this unexpected result led to a discovery: the structural entities described and labeled by my computer procedures were different from those that Jeff was hearing. What Jeff had heard as one thing, |HO HO|, I had broken up into two. Here was a clear example of multiple possible hearings that were in conflict, the teacher making one, the student making another. As Met put it, "You were at a *finer level of structural detail* than Jeff was, and the result of that was to create boundary conflicts between his hearing and yours." And Mot added, pointing to more general implications of that moment: "Yes, you really put Jeff in a kind of bind—caught between his hearing and yours. I'll bet these kinds of problems come up a lot in schools; for instance, the teacher and the student *using the same words but meaning different*

Figure 13–3

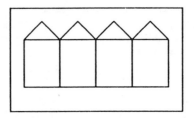

"how many things?"

things. In fact, I'll bet it happened a lot to Jeff in school." And I responded to Mot's comment with, "The trouble is, as you're discovering yourselves, it's not so easy to find out that *that* is the problem."

These issues of counting, together with conflicts raised by level of detail, recall an incident that took place while I was working with a teacher and her nine-year-old students in a rather special classroom setting.* After the children had reconstructed several tunes using the computer and tuneblocks, the teacher drew a picture on the chalk board and asked the children to "find how many things there are in the picture" (Figure 13–3). Their count-ups differed markedly from one another, but what was most revealing were the differences in the kinds of entities they took as things to count. Like my college students in describing their hearings of the Beethoven sonata movement, two of the children, Steve and Simon, agreed that there were three things in the picture, but the three things they counted were almost entirely different (Figure 13–4).

Steve was an adept computer person like Met, and that was reflected in his selection of "three things." For example, he completely ignored the obvious figures, the enclosed shapes that formed recognizable "things"; he also ignored the differing functions of his chosen elements within the context of these figures—top or bottom, inside or outside boundaries. Taking the picture apart at a fine-grained level of detail, he focused his attention on decontextualized lines, counting up the minimum number of line segments that were the same with respect to the property of

---

* The special classroom was the Laboratory for Making Things at the Graham and Parks Alternative School in Cambridge, Massachusetts. The Lab, which I developed together with teachers in the school, was motivated by ideas resulting in part from these studies. It is an environment in which teachers and children are learning and probing their own understandings by building structures that work, making descriptions of them in various media, and watching, talking, and reflecting on their varied ways of seeing and making sense of one another's work. For more on the Lab, see Bamberger 1990.

Figure 13–4

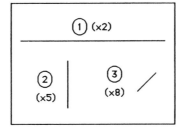

Steve's 3 things

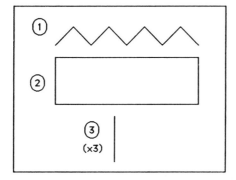

Simon's 3 things

length. Then, explaining that the computer could simply reverse the slanting line symmetrically, he counted up the number of times each line segment was repeated ($\times 2$, $\times 5$, $\times 8$). Steve's drawing led to a discussion among the children about how many "things" there really were. Using Steve's criterion for what was a thing, there were three *kinds* of things, but there were also multiple *instances* of each kind, making 15 things in all. Steve's strategy was, in fact, a more fine-grained version of mine in making the tuneblocks for HOT: using the criterion of identical properties as Steve did (but pitches and durations rather than same length), I selected just two *kinds* of things (HO and HA) from the whole tune, and, ignoring their position and function in the tune, I counted up within each kind—there were $\times 3$ of HO and 1 of HA, making 4 things in all.

In contrast, Simon's focus was at a more aggregated level of detail, and most important, his focus was primarily on *figures,* albeit not the most obvious ones. But because he kept his chosen figures intact, their functions within the larger picture were still visible as well—the squiggle that ran across the top of the picture to form the roofs, the rectangle that formed the center, and only then the repeated line segments (×3) that functioned to divide up the rectangle. Interestingly, although both boys' count-ups included a shared entity (the line segment that formed the inner boundaries of Simon's rectangle), even here the count-up, the number of repetitions of that segment, differed. This was, then, a striking example of selective differences in focus of attention with respect both to kinds of things to count and also level of detail. But these differences only became available for scrutiny because they were expressed in descriptions that everyone could look at. As a result, instead of generating confusion or conflict (as might have been the case if this had been a quiz with a particular answer as the right one), the differences the children saw among their drawings launched them into a discussion about just how each of them was seeing the picture differently. Through the discussion each of them came to see and appreciate the "same" drawing in new ways; and as "possibles" were liberated, all the children invented other alternatives as well. Steve, for instance, perhaps learning from Simon's picture, ended up making the most parsimonious and also the most clearly figural selection (Figure 13–5). This is one small example of what I mean by helping children to develop strategies for making multiple representations of the "same" material, here in a medium quite different from music. It is also an example of how inherently conflicting ways of seeing, when made accessible for scrutiny, can be the source of new ideas.

But it was the potential for *tensions between figural and formal strategies of representing phenomena* (which are also reflected in Steve's and Simon's respective views of the picture) that accounted for Jeff's most intense confusions and (with my help) also his most significant insights. I will argue now that conflicts between figural and formal modes of representing phenomena may be the most general factor underlying the

Figure 13–5

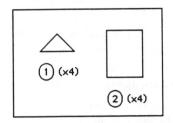

the most parsimonious selection

common breakdowns in understanding between teachers and students. But as with Jeff, these conflicts, when they are recognized, also hold the greatest potential for triggering new insight.

To make this argument more convincing, it will be helpful to distinguish between the data from the rhythm studies and the data from Jeff's work. The drawings of rhythms were momentary snapshots of separate individuals at different ages and stages of development, and with differing musical backgrounds. Thus, with the data from the rhythm experiments, I could differentiate among subjects' hearings but could only speculate on the learning processes that might contribute to these differences. The typology of rhythm drawings and even the college students' accounts of the Beethoven sonata movement can be useful, then, in helping a teacher recognize where a student might be in the developmental course of events, but with only that information available, the teacher has little with which to continue from there.

In contrast, because I was able to trace the course of Jeff's work, I was also able to observe *changes* in his strategies for constructing and describing the tune. And from these observations I could also infer changes in the kinds of elements and relations to which he had access or to which he was giving preference in organizing the materials at hand—what I call his *network of organizing constraints*. Thus, with Jeff's story I could ask further questions that bear more directly on learning: What are the characteristics of organizing constraints at *various moments within the work of a single individual*? How can these constraints be perturbed so as to bring them into conflict with one another? What is the effect of these interventions, and what are the evolutionary processes through which specific constraints are loosened and cumulatively elaborated? Thus, while I could mark differences in organizing constraints at separate moments in individual lives in making the typology of rhythm drawings, it was possible through the close observations of Jeff's work to observe organizing constraints actually changing—in short, to see learning going on.

The questions I have just proposed can be used as a kind of ground plan in actually helping children to learn. For example, if teachers who are working with children in their classrooms can at least generally identify a child's network of organizing constraints—that is, what aspects of the materials at hand he or she is attending to in making sense of them—the teacher can then go on to look for moments when the child's current organizing constraints are changing. This means to take special notice of, to grab "on the wing," moments of disequilibrium that might be signaled by the child's construction (awareness) of new kinds of features, even new kinds of objects; and also to watch for the emergence of conflict among them as a potentially generative source for new insight. It is just such moments that hold the greatest potential for helping children not to fail but rather to learn by developing multiple possible ways of seeing and hearing.

The most telling clues to recognizing hidden conflicts between networks of organizing constraints are often a child's surprising judgments concerning which events are the same and which are different. As an example, recall once again Jeff's first session in reconstructing HOT using the computer and tuneblocks. The initial clue to Jeff's confusion was his impasse in completing the tune; and the basis of this confusion emerged when he met with surprise and disbelief my demonstration that the single block named HO, which he had described as "the first one" and which functioned as a beginning, could also be used as an ending. Here, two structural entities which were the same for me and to which I thus gave the same name were not the same for Jeff. I focused on their *identity* with respect to *properties* (pitches and durations) that were simply givens for me; but Jeff was focusing on the figural *differences* between the two blocks—they occurred in different places in the tune, within different contexts, and with different structural *functions*. When we came to this moment in my conversations with Met and Mot, Met's formal persuasions made it difficult for him to understand what Jeff's problem could be. It was simply obvious to him: "The HO at the beginning and the HO at the end are exactly the same!" But Mot, who was more understanding of Jeff's figural organizing constraints, took issue with Met: "Being into properties, of course you wouldn't have any trouble recognizing those 'invariant properties' to which you give the name HO, whenever or wherever they happen . . . but they sure aren't the same if you're listening to *function.*"

In pointing out the potential educational implications of what seemed obvious to Met, I argued that his view is important because it is typical of those assumptions made in school settings that lead people, even those with the best of intentions, to think that a child like Jeff (and there are many like him) is a "slow learner," has "attention problems," or is "unmotivated." Moreover, assumptions that give priority to representations that focus on "objective properties" are, like those concerning counting, often left unrecognized; but they are also just those that we too easily equate with "knowledge" in a domain. Indeed, it is just this common-sense view of knowledge that is expressed in the conversation with which

I began the Prologue: the person who agrees, when asked, that she can clap simple rhythms, recognize tunes she has heard before, even sing or whistle at least some of them, but who hastens to add: "But of course, I don't *know* anything about music."

In this regard, my interventions in working with Jeff on the bell tasks point to another strategy that is important for teachers: the interventions were partly aimed at shaking up and rethinking those common views of knowledge in a domain. This was particularly the case with interventions directed toward *unpacking my own tacit organizing constraints*. As I suggested earlier, this is often a necessary first step toward finding out the kinds of organizing constraints that are guiding what a child knows how to do already. For it is only when we have looked at (rather than through) our own organizing constraints (which may sometimes be different from those assumed in the curriculum) that other ways of making sense of the materials can become clearer. Once these ways are recognized, teachers can then go on to design interventions that are specifically meant to help a child *confront and make explicit* for himself the features of the materials that are inherently in conflict between teacher and student. In working with Jeff, for example, it was by first recognizing the nature of the mismatch between the formal organizing constraints implicit in standard music notation and Jeff's figural organizing constraints that we were eventually able to find a resolution to those conflicts. And through the resolution, Jeff was later able to elaborate (rather than discard) his earlier figural constraints; this, in turn, led him eventually to the construction of an independent and *generalizable* structure, in terms of which he could describe the formal as well as the *unique* structure of a particular melody.

As I watched Jeff at work inventing graphics and symbols that eventually could *refer to* rather than being *copies of* objects and actions on them, another aspect of that process became quite clear: to invent a symbol system that consistently refers to particular aspects of the materials at hand, it is necessary first to construct mentally (to find and hold steady) the relevant and invariant properties and relations to which these symbols are to refer. This can be seen clearly if we recognize that a necessary precondition to Jeff's invention of his final symbol system was doing the work, including the periods of cognitive disequilibrium, involved in mentally constructing properties that were at first hidden in the materials, properties that could stay put "in spite of the route traveled." He was then able to build a framing structure that could include those properties and in terms of which the symbols were subsequently to refer.

In this case, the particular and generalizable relations of Jeff's framing structure were those he described as, "it goes lower and then higher, higher, higher," or what is more formally described as a structure in which each pitch-making element in the series is both higher than the one to its left and lower than the one to its right. For it is only with respect to these structural relations inherent in Jeff's built-form, the low-to-high ordered bell series, that he could use the analogous number series to give unchanging names to the bells. The names, in turn, gained invariant referents and invariant meaning only in terms of the relations built into Jeff's fixed reference structure.

In school settings similar issues arise. For instance, in order to understand the conventional names that are given to objects, a child must first differentiate, sometimes even construct, and then pull out from the multiple *possible* features of objects, the particular property that is the relevant one—the one that the name names. And as I have shown, the particular property to which a name refers may not yet be an aspect of the materials to which a child has access. Indeed, helping children do the work of differentiating among the possible features to which they might attend, and then going on to find the particular features to which conventional names refer, may well be a critical part of helping children to succeed in school.

There is an interesting reciprocity to be found here that harks back to my earlier point about the capacity of descriptions to both reveal and conceal. It is the reciprocity between the meaning a child intends in making an invented notation, on one hand, and a child's inability to understand the conventions she is expected to learn in school, on the other. For in both situations, if the reader of the symbols (teacher/researcher or child) has failed to do the work of constructing the elements, properties, and relations inherent in the framework through which these symbols gain meaning, neither a teacher/researcher reading a child's invented symbol system nor a child reading the privileged symbol systems taught in school can ever make of the phenomena described by the symbols the particular sense the symbol-makers intend.

This point was dramatically illustrated in the story of Robbie's visit and later the visit of Jeff's mother. Without doing the work that Jeff had done in constructing the kinds of objects and structural relations that he subsequently built into his reference structure, neither Robbie nor Jeff's mother could make sense of Jeff's symbol system or follow his final instructions for playing Twinkle. But the story of Robbie's visit was important for another reason as well: with it, we saw convincing evidence that in the course of liberating new formal features and relations, Jeff had not wiped out or replaced those associated with his earlier figural constraints. Rather, he could hold in mind multiple mental representations of Twinkle, together with their multiple organizing constraints. This was most clearly evidenced in Jeff's ability to make multiple descriptions of the tune—the various embodied descriptions as seen in his constructions and performances, and on paper his changing uses of numbers and graphics, with the numbers taking on different meanings and referring to different kinds of objects and relations in each new pencil-and-paper transformation. Moreover, in Jeff's last remarkable switch where, by a seeming sleight of hand, he turned the figural bell-path into the low-to-high ordered series, he also demonstrated his ability to find in a figural embodied description the makings of his formal fixed reference structure, with its quite different sequence of objects, events, and meanings.

Finally, throughout my work with Jeff, it is the reciprocity between teaching, learning, and research that emerges as a particularly important aspect of schooling. Their convergence is most evident in the interaction between, on one hand, Jeff's integrity as he held firmly to his convictions concerning what made sense to him, and, on the other, my pursuit of the sense that he was making. This continuing tension shaped the thinking of both of us, reciprocally suggesting what our next moves might be. In my case, these were on-the-spot experiments that tested hunches, often by perturbing what I believed to be the mental organizing constraints currently guiding Jeff's construction or notation strategies, and by inference, his ways of constructing coherence. For Jeff, this reciprocity meant a willingness to take risks, to suspend disbelief, and in doing so, sometimes to find himself faced with disorientation and confusion, but never despair.

My hope is that, like Jeff, teachers will maintain their integrity and at the same time be willing to take risks, to query their own beliefs, to become more intimate with what they know how to do well; and that through looking *at* the window that shapes their view of a child's world instead of always looking *through* it, they will come to know better what their students know already. For building on this mutual knowledge may be the critical turning point in helping children to succeed rather than fail in school.

References

Bamberger, J. 1978. Intuitive and formal musical knowing. In *The arts cognition and basic skills*, ed. S. Madeja. St. Louis: CEMREL.

———. 1981. Revisiting children's descriptions of simple rhythms: A function for reflection-in-action. In *U-shaped behavioral growth,* ed. S. Strauss. New York: Academic Press.

———. 1986. Cognitive issues in the development of musically gifted children. In *New conceptions of giftedness,* ed. R. J. Sternberg and J. E. Davidson. Cambridge: Cambridge University Press.

———. 1990. The laboratory for making things: Developing multiple representations of knowledge. In *The reflective turn,* ed. D. A. Schön. New York: Teachers College Press.

Bamberger, J., and H. Brofsky. 1988. *The art of listening: Developing musical perception.* New York: Harper and Row.

Bamberger, J., and D. A. Schön. 1979. The figural/formal transaction. Cambridge, Mass.: DSRE Working Paper no. 1.

———. 1991. Learning as reflective conversation with materials. In *Research and reflexivity,* ed. F. Steier. London: Sage Publications.

Bamberger, J., and D. Watt. 1979. *Making music count.* Newton, Mass.: Education Development Center.

Bartlett, F. C. 1932. *Remembering.* Cambridge: Cambridge University Press.

Carroll, Lewis. 1960. *The annotated Alice,* ed. Martin Gardner. New York: Clarkson N. Potter.

Cooper, G., and L. B. Meyer. 1960. *The rhythmic structure of music.* Chicago: University of Chicago Press.

Feldman, D. H. 1980. *Beyond universals.* Norwood, N.J.: Ablex.

Feynman, Richard P. 1985. *"Surely you must be joking, Mr. Feynman!"* New York: Bantam Books.

Gardner, H. 1973. *The arts and human development*. New York: John Wiley & Sons.

Gjerdingen, R. O. 1988. *A classic turn of phrase: Music and the psychology of convention*. Philadelphia: University of Pennsylvania Press.

Gruber, H. E. 1981. *Darwin on man*. Chicago: University of Chicago Press.

Hildebrandt, C., and J. Bamberger. 1979. "Claps and gaps." Unpublished ms.

James, W. 1956. *The will to believe*. New York: Dover.

Keller, E. F. 1983. *A feeling for the organism*. New York: W. H. Freeman.

Kuhn, Thomas S. 1977. *The essential tension*. Chicago: University of Chicago Press.

Lashley, K. S. 1951. The problem of serial order in behavior. In *Cerebral mechanisms in behavior: The Hixon symposium*, ed. L. P. Jeffress. New York: John Wiley.

Lerdahl, F., and R. Jackendoff. 1983. *A generative theory of tonal music*. Cambridge, Mass.: MIT Press.

Lewin, D. 1986. Music theory, phenomenology, and modes of perception. *Music Perception* 3 (no. 4):327–392.

Lynch, K. 1960. *The image of the city*. Cambridge, Mass.: MIT Press.

Meyer, L. B. 1973. *Explaining music: Essays and explorations*. Berkeley: University of California Press.

Narmour, E. 1977. *Beyond Schenkerism*. Chicago: University of Chicago Press.

Papert, S. 1980. *Mind storms: Children, computers, powerful ideas*. New York: Basic Books.

Peattie, L. 1987. *Planning: Rethinking Ciudad Guayana*. Ann Arbor: University of Michigan Press.

Piaget, J. 1967. *The child's conception of space*. New York: W. W. Norton.

———. 1960. *The psychology of intelligence*. Totowa, N.J.: Littlefield, Adams.

Plato. 1956. "Meno." In *Protagoras and Meno*. Harmondsworth, Middlesex: Penguin Books.

Rosenfield, I. 1988. *The invention of memory*. New York: Basic Books.

Shahn, B. 1957. *The shape of content*. Cambridge, Mass.: Harvard University Press.

Sinclair, H. 1990. Learning: The interactive re-creation of knowledge. In *Transforming children's mathematics education*, ed. L. P. Steffe and T. Wood. Hillsdale, N.J.: Lawrence Erlbaum.

Schön, D. A. 1983. *The reflective practitioner: How professionals think in action*. New York: Basic Books.

———. 1987. *Educating the reflective practitioner*. San Francisco: Jossey-Bass.

Treitler, Leo. 1989. The beginnings of music-writing in the west: Historical and semiotic aspects. *Language and Communication* 9 (no. 2/3):193–211.

Vygotsky, L. S. 1962. *Thought and language*. Cambridge, Mass.: MIT Press.

Wittgenstein, L. 1953. *Philosophical investigations*, trans. G. E. M. Anscombe. New York: Macmillan.

INDEX

Abstraction, 165

Accent: metric, 61; change of function, 84–85; delineates groupings, 86. *See also* Beginning/ending

Action-path, 185–186, 241; definition, 131; separated from bell-, tune-paths, 202, 207, 210, 234. *See also* Felt path

Alice (*Alice in Wonderland*), 56, 112, 173. *See also* White Queen, Red Queen, and Alice

Antecedent-consequent, 181

Artificial Intelligence Laboratory, MIT, 104n

Bartlett, F. C., 167, 264

Beat: background, 59; definition, 60; at several levels, 60; generation of, 61

Beginning/ending, 86, 147; bowing, fingering, breathing, 39, 86

Bell-path, 133, 168, 234, 241; definition, 131; switched ("Hot"), 171–172; switched ("Twinkle"), 199–202; figural, 184–187, 255–256, 283; separated from action-, tune-paths, 202, 207, 210, 234; transitional ("Twinkle"), 208

Bell-pitch, 131

Boundary, 35, 273; differing perceptions, 19–20; change of pace, 38, 43; generation, 43, 65; by numbering, 78, 274; conflicts, 82, 111, 275; context for naming, 161

Cambridge Alternative Public School, 101

Carroll, Lewis, 56, 75

Children's rhythm. *See* Class Piece

Class Piece: rhythm (children's), 20, 23; Hindemith *Kleine Kammermusik* (op. 24, no. 6) as model, 21–23; metric hier-

archy, 61–62; hierarchical structure, 121–122

Clustering of shapes, 25–26. *See also* Grouping

Coherent mental universe, 167

Conventions, 48, 89; influence when internalized, 49–50, 57, 90–91; efficacy, 89; paradox between limits and freedom, 90; vehicle of insight to new hearings, 93; bending liberates new meanings, 94; as windshield, 270–271

Conversation (with material), 29, 48, 52, 87, 259–260; definition, 10n; importance with puzzling behavior, 66; facilitated by drawing or writing, 113; not intuition, 223

Counting: up, 53, 57, 240, 274, 276; on, 53, 57, 240; not objective, 58, 273–274; Met's and Mot's different methods, 58, 60; used to express musical meaning, 92; up vs. on in "Twinkle" notation, 191

Dialogues, 4, 29; modeled on Galileo, 5–6

Dot drawings. *See* Drawings of rhythms

Drawings of rhythms, 21, 23; two types, 3, 24; conflict in explicit feature focus, 29; types by age of drawer, 46, 51–52; scribbles, 48–49; dot drawings, 49; referring to vs. resulting from actions, 49, 52, 54; hand drawings, 50; reflection and distancing from immediate experience, 52, 53–54, 55; typologically errant, 68; hybrids of the two types, 81; as imitations, 125. *See also* Metric (drawing type)

Emerson, Ralph Waldo, 80

Entity, reference. *See* Reference entity